DATE		

DISCARDED

THE NYPD TAPES

THE NYPD TAPES

A SHOCKING STORY OF COPS, COVER-UPS, AND COURAGE

★

Graham A. Rayman

palgrave
macmillan

THE NYPD TAPES
Copyright © Graham A. Rayman, 2013.

All rights reserved.

First published in 2013
by PALGRAVE MACMILLAN®
in the United States— a division of St. Martin's Press LLC,
175 Fifth Avenue, New York, NY 10010.

Where this book is distributed in the UK, Europe, and the rest of the world,
this is by Palgrave Macmillan, a division of Macmillan Publishers Limited,
registered in England, company number 785998, of Houndmills,
Basingstoke, Hampshire RG21 6XS.

Palgrave Macmillan is the global academic imprint of the above companies
and has companies and representatives throughout the world.

Palgrave® and Macmillan® are registered trademarks in the United States,
the United Kingdom, Europe, and other countries.

ISBN 978–0–230–34227–9

Library of Congress Cataloging-in-Publication Data

Rayman, Graham A.
    The NYPD tapes / by Graham A. Rayman.
      pages cm
        1. Schoolcraft, Adrian. 2. Police corruption—New York (State)—New York—
Case studies. 3. Police—New York (State)—New York—Case studies. I. Title.

HV8148.N5R39 2013
363.209747'1—dc23   2013009901

A catalogue record of the book is available from the British Library.

Design by Newgen KnowledgeWorks

First edition: August 2013

10 9 8 7 6 5 4 3 2 1

Printed in the United States of America.

For my boys, William and Nicholas

CONTENTS

ACKNOWLEDGMENTS

In telling the complex story of Adrian Schoolcraft and the NYPD, relationships built up over many years were a constant blessing, and so many people need to be thanked for the realization of this project.

In particular, I am indebted to the brilliant, always competitive, but also close-knit fraternity of law enforcement reporters here in New York City. Leonard Levitt and Sean Gardiner, among them, have been great friends and counselors. Tom Robbins, columnist and author, was always right there with sterling advice and wry commentary. Brooklyn College professor Paul Moses, my former editor at *Newsday*, gave me a great gift in making a key recommendation that started the ball rolling. I owe special thanks to Abby Wasserman, who took a fine-tooth comb to the manuscript, and my agent, Jason Allen Ashlock, whose sheer perseverance and steady faith got the project off the ground. Thanks to the roof-climbing photographer C. S. Muncy, and my patient, understanding editor, Laura Lancaster, and everyone at Palgrave. I also want to thank folks at the *Village Voice*, former and current, who supported an intricate story that evolved over three years. Finally, I cannot name some sources for obvious reasons, but I want to send thanks to them as well, including my friend from Staten Island, the boss, the country gentleman, the retired sergeant, and others in the great NYPD diaspora, and the lawyers from all sides who found themselves caught up in this fascinating case.

KEY CHARACTER LIST

Police Officer Adrian Schoolcraft, from Texas, who joined the NYPD in 2002

Larry Schoolcraft, his father, a former Texas police officer from upstate New York

POLICE OFFICIALS
(IN ORDER OF SENIORITY)

Raymond Kelly, Commissioner, New York City Police Department

Paul Browne, Deputy Commissioner for Public Information, senior aide to Kelly

Charles Campisi, Chief, Internal Affairs Bureau

Chief Gerald Nelson, Commanding Officer, Patrol Borough Brooklyn North

Deputy Chief Michael Marino, Second in Command, Patrol Borough Brooklyn North

Deputy Inspector Steven Mauriello, Commander, 81st Precinct, Brooklyn

Capt. Theodore Lauterborn, Executive Officer, 81st Precinct, Brooklyn

Adhyl Polanco, Police Officer, 41st Precinct, Hunts Point, the Bronx

Harold Hernandez, Detective 1st Grade, 33rd Precinct, Upper Manhattan

ELECTED OFFICIALS

Michael Bloomberg, Mayor, City of New York

Christine Quinn, Speaker, City Council, New York

Albert Vann, Member, City Council, New York, representing Bedford-Stuyvesant

Peter Vallone, Jr., Chair, Public Safety Committee, City Council, New York

The lobby of the 81st Precinct Stationhouse. (CS Muncy)

Bed-Stuy resident Alston Story claimed he was injured by overly aggressive police during a 2006 arrest. (CS Muncy)

Bed-Stuy resident Rhonda Scott claimed police broke her wrists when they accosted her for not having an ID card. (CS Muncy)

81st Precinct commander Steven Mauriello (in uniform), in the audience at a precinct community council meeting. (CS Muncy)

PROLOGUE

HALLOWEEN 2009: "WHAT IS THIS, RUSSIA?"

The right of the people to be secure in their persons, houses, papers, and effects, against unreasonable searches and seizures, shall not be violated, and no Warrants shall issue, but upon probable cause, supported by Oath or affirmation, and particularly describing the place to be searched, and the persons or things to be seized.

—U.S. Constitution, Fourth Amendment

Adrian Schoolcraft's babysitter, a lieutenant, leered at him and said, "I bet you wish now you had come back to the 8-1 like you were told."

Schoolcraft ignored the remark. He sighed and slumped backward on his gurney in the hallway outside the emergency room in Jamaica Hospital, Queens, New York. He stared at the incessantly humming fluorescent lights, at the concrete block walls slapped with some vague sort of beige paint, at the sign over the nurses' station that read, "We are here to help you."

He sniffed at air that smelled of floors cleaned too many times with heavy chemicals. He pulled halfheartedly at the handcuff on his right wrist and listened to the metallic clink and rasp along the steel railing. He self-consciously tugged at the backless hospital gown the sergeants had made him don in the broom closet. He listened to a woman force herself to vomit again, to a guy who smelled like feces mumbling to himself in the corner. He wondered whether it was day or night. It still felt dark outside.

He reflected on the events of the past month: How his bosses at the 81st Precinct in Bed-Stuy put the black spot on him and stuck him with desk duty. The calls from Internal Affairs. The messages they left for him in the station house. The looks and sideways comments. The journey into Brooklyn to sit with the investigators for three hours. All his documents painstakingly assembled. Their earnest promises that his identity would stay a secret.

And then, that morning, all those hours ago—a whole career ago, it seemed—the lieutenant snatching his memo book and doing god knows what with it in the records room for two hours. His dad telling him to get out of there, him going home on a flimsy excuse; the dreamless nap, and hours later, looking out his window, the street lit up like Christmas Eve with NYPD rovers, red and blue flickering off the trees, the lamp posts, the houses, hearing them on the stairs, an army of white shirts crowding into his apartment, the key turning in the lock, the chief on his bed, arguing with him. Schoolcraft asking, "What is this, Russia?" Being thrown to the ground and rear-cuffed like any skell caught holding a deck while someone stood on his legs, and the chief stuck a boot on his head. The cops finding one of his digital recorders and saying something like, "He's playing some kind of game."

And then the dark ride down the Van Wyck to the ER where the nurses looked at him like he was Hannibal Lecter.

Lying there on his gurney, he looked fruitlessly for a clock. He needed to use the phone to check in with his dad, who had been calling investigative agencies to try to get some attention for his son. Later Adrian said he expected that at any moment someone would come through the door and order his immediate release. He felt watchful, expectant, his mind keeping him awake. His back and neck ached from his "arrest."

Noting then that the sergeant had dozed off in his chair, Schoolcraft extended one bare leg to the floor and quietly, carefully, pushed the gurney along the linoleum toward a pay phone on one wall close to the nurses' station.

The distance was only about 20 feet, but Schoolcraft felt that at any moment someone would come along and grab the gurney and pull it back to where it had been parked for the night. He made it to the phone, though, and dialed his father collect.

A few minutes into the conversation, he noticed that the nurses were suddenly giving him more attention than he thought necessary. He told his dad they needed to hurry. Basically, there was no news. No one was interested in the bizarre events of the evening, not Internal Affairs, not the FBI, not the local prosecutor's office. Worse yet, neither the NYPD nor the hospital were telling him anything about where this thing was headed.

At that point, his minder appeared next to him with another sergeant who had evidently come in to relieve him. Soon, Adrian was tussling over the phone with them, and then he was being pushed back to the spot in the hallway, the phone growing smaller, the handset swinging by its cord.

"What—I can't use the phone?" he yelled. "Have you arrested me? I have rights."

"Just shut the fuck up," one of the sergeants said and tightened the cuffs.

It must have been after 8 a.m. that Sunday, about 10 hours in, when a doctor wandered by. She sounded Eastern European and spoke with a thick accent. She asked him some questions. He made it clear to her that he was upset about his treatment, that he had been beaten up and dragged to the hospital, but he was most definitely not a danger to himself or others, and thus there was no reason to hold him.

"Do you feel they are coming after you?" the doctor asked.

"Well, they did," Schoolcraft replied. "They came and got me."

A couple of hours later, the new sergeant, James, arrived, and the nurses asked her within earshot, "His dad keeps calling. What are we supposed to tell him? What are we doing with this guy?"

"Tell him to call the 8-1," James replied.

She made a phone call and then walked around a corner, outside of Schoolcraft's field of vision. She was gone for about 30 minutes.

When she returned, there followed whispered conversations between the cops and the doctors, nodding of heads and making of notes, and then they told him he was going to be admitted to the psychiatric emergency room.

"For what?" Schoolcraft had asked. "For what?"

No explanation followed. He was simply, wordlessly wheeled into the psych ER and deposited on a chair in a corner, near the television. He sat there, dozed a bit, found some paper, and made notes of the sequence of events. He watched the television. It was stuck on the Fox News channel, and at one point, the police commissioner's son came on and did a segment about beating a parking ticket. Sunday stretched into Monday before they came to him again.

Another doctor with a heavy accent came by to question him. And Schoolcraft asked the same question that had been bouncing around his head the whole time.

"Why am I still here?"

"We're just trying to make sure you're not going to hurt anyone."

"Well, I'm not going to hurt myself or others," he replied.

"Okay," the doctor said. "But sitting there, and taking notes, it makes you look manicky."

"Is that a diagnosis?" Schoolcraft asked. He didn't get an explanation, but he could see that the machine was moving in only one direction.

He knew he hadn't acted out, hadn't done anything crazy. So why was he there? What did the cops tell the doctors? Could they have lied? This was the New York City Police Department, after all. The NYPD wouldn't lie. Especially about a member of its own *thin blue line*, right?

And what about his apartment? Were they there, searching it? Did they know his secret? Had they discovered the digital recordings that he had so carefully made?

Schoolcraft's ordeal had just begun. He spent days in the psychiatric ward without any real explanation for it. His dad made calls to everyone he could think of, but no one would listen.

A week later, he was on the phone with an attorney, Stuart London. Adrian asked, "What about my rights? What about the Constitution?"

"They don't really go by the Constitution," replied London. "They go by the Patrol Guide."

CHAPTER 1

"I WILL FAITHFULLY DISCHARGE THE DUTIES"

In New York City, heroes are a dime a dozen. So are miracles. A white tourist with a crushed skull in Central Park is worth ten times a bullet-riddled black teenager in Bed-Stuy. Facts are fungible. Opinion is not. You tell a lie long enough, it becomes the truth. Speak the truth, and nobody believes you. It's a lot easier to leave than it is to come back.

In summer, bodies fall in the heat stricken with bullets, or knives, or fists. In spring, puffed-out corpses float to the surface, the leavings of weekend benders. In autumn, there is peace of a kind. And in winter, folks caught out freeze solid as hardwood.

Potter's Field beckons. August, not April, is the cruelest month. November, not June, is the kindest. If you have nothing better to do, you can always drink, no matter the season.

The mayor talks in a blue room. Television guests wait in a green room. The Empire State Building changes colors. At night, through windows, flat screens flicker like fire pits whether you live in Hunts Point or Carnegie Mews. A newspaper can print a column on the sanctity of marriage next to a blowup of a salacious babe in a leopard-print bikini and still pretend to occupy the moral high ground.

Villains make better heroes. The best guy in the world is your worst enemy. The worst guy in the world makes miracles. The Bowery used to be interesting. The front page is called The Wood. Highway therapy is real. If you don't go along with the program, they will dump you in a precinct as far from home as possible. And you need a rabbi to rise in the ranks, even if you aren't Jewish.

But Schoolcraft, he never had a rabbi, and that was a problem.

It all started well enough, seven years before that night in Jamaica Hospital when it all finally, utterly, went to hell. The day happened to be in July, the year was 2002, and Adrian Schoolcraft was standing in the ranks of that year's police recruit class in the gym of the old academy on East 21st Street in Manhattan, an ugly stone and steel and glass and gray building designed specifically to look boring. He wore the beige and gray tunic and dark pants and had a gym bag at his feet, just like the rest of them. The night before his dad—that's Larry Schoolcraft—had given him some advice. His dad, a man for whom a sentence easily became a paragraph, which easily became a Shakespearean oration, and then an epic speech that mentioned the mayor, the commissioner, the FB-fucking-I, pudding, hand grenades, the mob, steroids, corrupt state senators, the Patrol Guide, and Frank Serpico.

But this time, the story goes, the elder Schoolcraft was mercifully brief. Bring two things, he said. Bring a watch. Bring a pen. The watch, so you'll always know what time it is, and the pen, to make a note of it. Sure enough, that was the first question out of the instructor's mouth. He checked the ranks for those two things. The guys who didn't have them got written up. This man had another rule: black ink only. No blue ink in this department.

Schoolcraft was 27 then, beefy around the middle, about six feet, 240 pounds, balding slightly. In his first NYPD picture, he pulled his head back, leaving a slight jowl visible under his chin. He stared grimly straight ahead. His file listed him as of average build, with straight brown hair, a receding hairline, and of part American Indian descent. His face carried some acne scarring. He had a large cranium, an effect magnified by his short haircut. He looked like a guy who could, if he wanted to, walk through a brick wall. He did not have the personality to fit his size. He was soft-spoken, a bit shy, somewhat cerebral, quiet. He didn't drink alcohol or smoke. He found bars boring and didn't make friends easily. There was something about him that suggested he was looking at what was immediately in front of him and either judging the subject before him or considering the alternatives.

Schoolcraft stood in those ranks with that group of men and women, white and black, Hispanic and Asian. Most were in their twenties, and most had either come from one of the boroughs, one of those places where the chicken bones roasted on the asphalt in summer, or an old-country ethnic enclave like Bay Ridge or Gerritsen Beach, or some suburban paradise-in-quotes on Long Island, Staten Island, or Rockland, with single-family houses on cul-de-sacs and above-ground pools in the backyard. Schoolcraft wasn't even a New Yorker, in fact. He was from suburban Texas and was a registered Republican. He knew absolutely nothing about the big city. Depending on how you looked at it, in the end, that quality was either fatal in the NYPD or it allowed him to do what he did.

His full name was Adrian P. Schoolcraft. He used his middle initial in his signature. Growing up in Arlington, Texas, the thought of becoming a cop hardly crossed his mind. The family already had one police officer—his dad, Larry. His mom, Suzanne, worked her whole career in a bank.

Larry Schoolcraft and Suzanne Wait had met in high school in Johnstown, New York, a most anonymous of anonymous rust belt towns first settled in 1758, about 40 miles northwest of Albany, just under the gaze of the looming Catskills. The few highlights of Johnstown's history include one of the last battles of the Revolutionary War; Congressman Silas Talbot, who oversaw the building of the USS *Constitution* (Old Ironsides) in 1797; and Elizabeth Cady Stanton, who helped organize the first women's rights convention, which eventually led to women gaining the right to vote. Though it was once the site of dozens of tanneries and factories that specialized in leather gloves, the industrial core of the town had slowly dwindled over the decades. In 1975, a plant that made gelatin, founded in 1890 by one of Johnstown's other famous residents, Charles Knox, shut down after the company was sold to Lipton.

Larry was adopted and grew up in relative comfort in a nice colonial on a 14-acre spread. His father, who spent his career at General Electric, believed the family's most famous ancestor was Henry Rowe Schoolcraft, who was born in 1793 about 30 miles southeast of Johnstown in Guilderland, New York. This ancestor was a geologist and ethnographer, but he also founded a newspaper and a magazine, taught himself French, German, and Hebrew, and wrote poetry, all as a teenager. He worked in glass factories and then left New York for Missouri. He worked as an Indian agent in Michigan and recorded the lives of the Ojibwa Indians, and these writings won him a prestigious literary award. He opened schools to educate young Ojibwa and became a University of Michigan board member. His biggest contribution to literature was that Henry Wadsworth Longfellow relied heavily on his ethnography in the writing of the famous poem, "The Song of Hiawatha." He is remembered in Michigan today by Schoolcraft College in Livonia and Schoolcraft County.

A month after they graduated from high school in June 1974, Larry and Suzanne married in the First Methodist Church in Johnson and had their reception at the VFW Hall. Just 18, Suzanne stitched her own wedding dress and all the gowns and hats for the bridesmaids. The couple desperately wanted to leave the oppressive confines of Johnstown, particularly Suzanne's immediate family, and begin a life together elsewhere. Suzanne had the grades and the smarts for college, but Larry hated school and had no interest in college. He joined the army that August and went to Fort Dix in New Jersey, then to Fort Gordon in Georgia for military police school. During that period, Suzanne periodically came to visit on the weekends, and that was, as Larry recalled, "when Adrian came along."

"She certainly wanted to get out of Dodge and so did I," Larry said. "She was very capable and probably should have gone to college. She ended up being the only bank officer who didn't have a college degree."

In January 1975, Larry landed at Fort Hood, the sprawling military post outside Killeen, Texas, and the headquarters of the 1st Cavalry Division. Suzanne moved to Texas to live on the base with Larry. On June 21, 1975, *Soyuz 19* returned to earth, the Beach Boys played Wembley Stadium, the movie *Jaws* opened, and Adrian was born. Thirteen months later, on August 12, 1976, Suzanne gave birth to a daughter, Mystica. Larry and Sue were just 20 and 19, respectively.

Once Larry's army stint ended, the couple opted to remain in Texas. The family moved to a small ranch-style house at 2811 Roberts Circle in the Dallas suburb of Arlington. Larry took a job in law enforcement, based on his military police training, and Suzanne found work in a well-known Dallas bank.

Over the next 25 years, Larry worked with the Austin Police Department, the University Park Dallas Police Department, and the Fort Worth Marshal's Office. Later Suzanne took a second job in the bookkeeping department for the Texas Rangers.

The Schoolcrafts moved to a townhouse on the north end of Arlington at 1301 Lovell, where Adrian spent much of his middle school years. At some point, the developers of the housing tract fell into a conflict with the homeowners. Litigation followed. It was a sour experience for Larry and Suzanne and caused some financial strain and tension in the household.

Salvation from the housing conflict came when family friends—a bank official and his wife—said they were moving to Maine and offered their home to the Schoolcrafts. Their third move was into that house, where they would remain until the kids graduated from high school.

In his youth, Adrian was fairly outgoing. He played sports—soccer and football—but they never became a passion like they did for most Texas kids.

In his freshman year, Adrian attended Lamar High School in Arlington. He played football, mainly to get into shape. As a sophomore, he transferred to Martin High School, with 5,000 students, one of the largest in the state. It was an easy place to disappear. He did not play sports for his final three years of high school.

That may be because he had found another interest—making money. At the age of 14, he started working at the local Food Lion supermarket. "He was a checker, a bagger, a stocker, he did everything," Larry said. "He always worked."

The atmosphere in the household was often tense, Larry recalled. Both parents worked constantly. Juggling jobs and children and bills caused friction between two people who had different ideas about a lot of things. (Larry recalled years later that in one election he voted for Ralph Nader, the ultra-liberal, and Suzanne voted for George W. Bush.) Suzanne also had trouble with her health.

"There was a lot of fighting," Larry said. "A lot of time, it was like a battle zone at home. The difference was that I would blow up and five minutes later, it was over. With her, once she got mad, she stayed mad."

The couple came close to divorce a number of times.

"Sometimes, the only reason I stayed was for the kids," he said. "My friends were saying different things. Stay for the kids or leave, it's better for the kids."

"But I loved her and she loved me. She was a good mother, honest, hard-working. Money did not motivate her. She was a good person. She was talented and smart. She just had a real problem with saying she was wrong."

Larry chuckled at that point, years later, wistfully. "The thing is, 98 percent of the time, she was right."

There were days when Larry would go stay at a friend's house just so he and Suzanne could have some time to cool off. "And then before long, I'm calling her or she's calling me and saying it's time to come home," Larry said. "She was always there for me."

Against this broad family backdrop, somewhere around puberty, Adrian's personality underwent a change. While his sister, Mystica, was outgoing (a "social butterfly"), Adrian drew inward. He spent a lot of time by himself.

"He was much more outgoing as a kid, but after puberty, he kept his own counsel," Larry said. "He wasn't that impressed with the people around him. You gotta understand that the kids in his neighborhood had money and nice cars. They ran pretty fast. He didn't drink or smoke. Didn't see the need for it. He just didn't fit the group."

"He worked and he went to school, that's what he did," Larry went on. "No social life. No serious girlfriends. If he wasn't working, I would drop him at the movies or at a mall. I would take him to work if I was working a special function. He liked movies and books, and he played video games a little bit. He always had money, and he liked to spend it. He outfitted his room with a nice stereo, television, high-end toy models. He would buy the models, and have a professional put them together and paint them so they looked really good."

Why Adrian underwent this personality change in his teenage years is something of a mystery. It could have had to do with the wages of puberty. It could have been a latent streak of independence and self-involvement that had not yet bloomed or solitary interests that presented themselves. It also could have been the family's money troubles and the arguments between his parents. It could have been the experience of dealing with his mom's health troubles. Or it could have been a stew of all of these things. But these were experiences that would inform the person he later became and provide a clue as to why he was able to do what he did.

Adrian graduated from Martin in 1993, a year that was very difficult for the family. On a single day, Larry was suspended indefinitely without pay from the Marshal's service, sparking litigation that went on for years, and Suzanne decided to quit her job. The banking industry was going through a series of collapses and mergers. Suzanne had worked for First City Bancorp for many years. Texas Commerce Bank swallowed the company and began laying people off and mistreating the old employees. Suzanne didn't like what she was seeing and couldn't stomach it anymore, Larry said. "We went from having decent jobs to having no jobs in one day," he recalled.

Larry's legal battles grew out of his union activism. Working for the University Park Police Department during the 1980s, he recalled, he ran afoul of the chief for ticketing an influential schools administrator. That led to an indefinite suspension in 1984, which led to a lawsuit and an eventual $80,000 settlement.

In 1987, he went to work for the Fort Worth Marshalls office, serving warrants. He also shut down strip clubs violating a law that women had to wear pasties over their breasts. Meanwhile, he and a fellow officer unionized the force—which, he says, got him labeled a troublemaker.

Eventually, as he tells it, he was suspended indefinitely without pay in 1993. Trying to gather evidence of retaliation, he secretly recorded a city official telling him the suspension was arbitrary, but he never ended up using the recording.

He sued the city in 1995 and worked as a limo and shuttle driver to support the family. His claim was finally rejected on appeal in 2001 by Texas's high court.

Ironically, many years later, his son would also be indefinitely suspended from a police department and would file a lawsuit that would take years to resolve, but for completely different reasons.

Whether what was happening at home factored in, or whether it seemed like a good idea at the time, in August 1993, a couple of months after graduating from high school, Schoolcraft joined the U.S. Navy while many of his future fellow police officers were still steaming down the Long Island Expressway, drinking at Jones Beach, or ogling the girls in Coney Island.

Never attracted to glamour, Schoolcraft decided to become a Navy corpsman, doing work similar to that of a paramedic. He graduated from a special school in Michigan and was then assigned to the USS *Blue Ridge*, the command ship for the U.S. Seventh Fleet, based in Japan. He labored on the ship treating the kinds of injuries that come with working long hours in a giant casing of thick steel and stress—shattered bones, broken backs, gouged eyes, concussions, wide-open gashes.

Schoolcraft spent four years in the Navy. He was honorably discharged in July 1997 and returned home with two medals: the National Defense Service Medal and the Good Conduct Medal. By then, his parents had moved back to Johnstown, New York. "Sue wasn't feeling well, and money was tight, she was looking for an escape and she thought she would find relief at home," Larry said. "I really didn't want to go back, but we were a team, and would be a team to the death."

Then 22 years old, Schoolcraft enrolled in Fulton-Montgomery Community College in Johnstown and, according to his father, actually did quite well, well enough to get accepted to the University of Texas (UT), the large state school in Austin. Larry had a hand in this move, enlisting a friend who was in the UT law school to help Adrian through the application process.

Adrian started at the school in January 1999 and took a part-time job at Walmart. He had a car, a decent apartment, and a mountain bike he used to get to class. Larry was still consumed with his lawsuit against the city of Fort Worth and at the time was flying back and forth between Johnston and Austin every three months or so. He would stay with Adrian and work for an air conditioner repair company.

The University of Texas was a pretty good school, and Adrian had worked hard to get there. Strangely, despite the opportunity, despite his academic ability, he dropped out after just one semester.

"He was miserable I guess," Larry said, still dismayed at the result years later. "I don't know what happened. I thought it was absurd to have an opportunity like that and piss it away. I have no idea why that did not work."

These may be the words of a father, but it is an interesting observation: On the threshold of something better, Schoolcraft decided to walk away.

After leaving UT, Adrian took a full-time job at Walmart in the electronics department, which sold digital recorders, among other things, and then left after a while to work at Motorola.

There, working for the technology giant, he assembled microprocessors in a secure, sanitized room. He worked 12-hour shifts, dressed in a white jumpsuit and mask in order to prevent contaminating particles from entering the microchips. The work seemed to suit his solitary nature, and he remained there for about two years.

"It was a good job, good money, benefits, but not a very friendly working environment," Larry said. He added, with another chuckle, "No interaction. I'm sure that's why he did it well."

In 2001, Adrian left Motorola during a round of cutbacks and returned once again to Johnstown. His mother's health had worsened. She was diagnosed with breast cancer and underwent new rounds of chemotherapy, radiation, and surgery. She also had to undergo kidney dialysis on a regular basis. Adrian and his parents lived together in the house where Larry had grown up. Larry's parents had long retired and were living in Florida, and the house needed upkeep and caretaking. So did Suzanne. Adrian and Larry drove her to her appointments with specialists in Albany and elsewhere over and over again.

"It was 24 hours a day, 7 days a week," Larry said. "Her family wasn't helping, and my parents were in Florida most of the time."

Then, on September 11, 2001, two jet airliners crashed into the World Trade Center, killing 2,753 people. Twenty-three of those killed were New York City police officers. At some point in those first months, when the media was thick with images of smoldering fires and cops and firefighters pulling 12-hour shifts in the rubble looking for body parts, Suzanne saw a television ad for the NYPD—recruiters were going to visit the state university at Albany. She had an idea. She thought Adrian should become a New York City police officer. He would make a decent candidate. He had the navy experience, the medical corpsman training, and nearly two years of college.

At first Adrian declined on the spot. He didn't really want to go to New York City—too big, too loud. He had no interest in becoming a police officer. He was still trying to figure out who he wanted to be. His mother persisted.

"Adrian didn't seek out this thing at all; the NYPD might as well have been Mars," Larry said. "She could see some resistance, so she says, let's go to Albany, we'll go to Cinnabon, we'll go to Chili's, we'll go to a movie, and you'll take the police academy test. We'll make a day of it. For Adrian, it had nothing to do with 9/11 either. It was really about a son going along with or placating his sick mother's wishes."

Adrian P. Schoolcraft finally relented, spent the day with his mother, and took the academy test. A few weeks later, the results came back. Suzanne called the recruiter, and he told her to read the number on the envelope. "He scored in the very top of the class; he'll be hired," the recruiter told her.

Several months later on July 1, 2002, Schoolcraft signed the NYPD oath, which said in part, "I will faithfully discharge the duties of the office of police officer... according to the best of my ability." There he was, standing in those ranks in the academy gym. He would enter a police department that, in the previous ten years, had gone through revolutionary changes that altered the city's entire underlying law enforcement strategy, and eventually the law enforcement strategy of many police departments around the country.

CHAPTER 2

"THE PROFIT
I WANTED TO
DELIVER"

In the vast lore of the NYPD, the story goes, CompStat began in crayon.

In 1990, when Adrian Schoolcraft started high school in Texas, the number of New Yorkers annually shot, stabbed, bludgeoned, and otherwise dispatched with bad intent in a single year climbed above 2,000. Crime was up in every category, and few people thought it could be brought down. A pudgy transit police lieutenant named Jack Maple, frustrated with the spiraling crime rate, came up with an idea far enough outside the box to be considered, by police standards, radical.

On the walls of his modest apartment, Maple—who affected a homburg, a bow tie, and Allen Edmonds Spectator shoes and spent his evenings in high-toned places like Elaine's and the Oak Room at the Plaza—taped up a 55-foot-long diagram of every station in the city's sprawling subway system. Using crayons of various colors, he placed a dot representing each solved and unsolved major crime at the station where it took place.

"I called them the Charts of the Future," Maple told interviewer Raymond Dussault in 1999. "The beauty of the mapping is that it poses the question, 'Why?' What are the underlying causes of why there is a certain cluster of crime in a particular place? By looking at this, you can figure out where you need to be and when."

In that initial phase, with his rudimentary map, Maple was able to spot, for example, the stations with the highest number of assaults. He could then review the actual complaints and look for trends or commonalities in those cases. Were there a lot of homeless people in the station? If so, that required more homeless outreach officers. Did the assaults take place after school? Then the city needed more cops in those stations during the after-school hours. Were folks drinking in the station? That should lead to more summonses for open containers. Rather than waiting for crime to happen, cops would now come up with ways to stop it from happening in the first place. The truly big idea here was that it moved commanders from reacting to crime to being "proactive."

Maple's Charts of the Future showed immediate results. Back then, the NYPD and the Transit Police were two separate agencies. Maple's boss, Transit Police Commissioner William Bratton, recognized the value of those charts.

Meanwhile, with the city's murder rate soaring, the mayor at the time, David Dinkins, and his police commissioners—first, Lee Brown, and later, Raymond Kelly—were employing their own strategy, known as "community policing."

Under this strategy, specially trained police officers were put on foot patrol in troubled neighborhoods, the idea being that it was easier to interact with the community on foot than in patrol cars. Residents, the theory went, would then be more willing to talk to police about trouble in the neighborhood. The strategy required money, and for that Dinkins, Brown, and Kelly went to President Clinton and secured hundreds of millions of dollars from the federal government to hire thousands more police officers. Eventually, the money would swell the NYPD's ranks to more than 40,000 officers, but a lot of it wouldn't arrive in time to benefit Dinkins.

Even though crime began to drop in the last year of Dinkins's term, he could not overcome the tabloid hammering over the crime rate. "Dave, Do Something," one famous headline demanded. In a vastly Democratic city, he lost his re-election bid to a Republican, former federal prosecutor Rudolph Giuliani, in a rematch of the 1989 mayoral race. Giuliani beat Dinkins in that racially polarized race by almost the same narrow margin that he lost to Dinkins in that earlier election. The crime rate, it seemed, had cost Dinkins his job, and Giuliani would do everything in his power to make the public forget his predecessor's accomplishments.

Schoolcraft was most of the way through his senior year in an Arlington high school when Giuliani snubbed Dinkins's commissioner, Ray Kelly, and selected Maple's old boss, William Bratton, who had left the transit police to run the police department in Boston, as his first NYPD commissioner.

Bratton elevated Maple to the status of deputy commissioner. By then, Maple had adapted his crayon-on-paper method of tracking crimes to computer spreadsheets and electronic maps. And he developed a four-part theory of crime fighting: "accurate, timely information, effective tactics for specific problems, rapid deployment of police to those areas, and relentless follow-up to make sure the problem was solved." Bratton ordered the NYPD to adopt the strategy.

In other words, this computer "pin mapping" would quickly identify hot spots. Commanders would flood those hot spots with police officers ordered to address the specific problem and make sure the problem didn't return.

At around the same time, an obscure 1982 essay published in the *Atlantic Monthly* by two social scientists, George Kelling and James Q. Wilson, had grabbed the attention of Giuliani, Bratton, and Maple. The essay was called "Broken Windows: The Police and Neighborhood Safety."

The operative quote was this: "If a window in a building is broken and is left unrepaired, all the rest of the windows will soon be broken. This is as true in nice neighborhoods as in rundown ones. Window-breaking does not necessarily occur on a large scale because some areas are inhabited by determined window-breakers whereas others are populated by window-lovers; rather, one unrepaired broken window is a signal that no one cares, and so breaking more windows costs nothing. (It has always been fun.)"

By this, Kelling and Wilson meant that unless one repairs the broken window, the house will soon suffer other indignities. The other windows will be shattered. Pests and water will get inside. The pipes will freeze. The timbers will rot. Folks will steal the fixtures. Eventually, the house will collapse.

They cited a fascinating 1969 study by Stanford University psychologist Philip Zimbardo. Zimbardo left one car each in the Bronx and in a higher income section of Palo Alto, California. Neither car had license plates, and both were parked with their hoods up. Within ten minutes, the car in the Bronx was targeted, amazingly, by a father, mother, and young child who stole the radiator and battery. In less than a day, the car in the Bronx had been stripped of everything of value. In subsequent days, Kelling and Wilson wrote, the "windows were smashed, parts torn off, upholstery ripped." Most of the vandals, the authors noted, were white.

Meanwhile, for a whole week no one damaged the Palo Alto car. But after Zimbardo himself smashed the windshield with a sledgehammer, people started attacking that car, too. "Within a few hours, the car had been turned upside down and utterly destroyed," they wrote.

As it relates to crime fighting, the Kelling/Wilson concept suggested to the new leaders of the NYPD that if you leave minor crimes like panhandling, public urination, and public drinking unpunished, major crimes will follow because the failure to enforce law prohibiting the minor crimes creates an atmosphere of lawlessness that people will act on.

"The key is to identify neighborhoods at the tipping point—where the public order is deteriorating but not unreclaimable, where the streets are used frequently but by apprehensive people, where a window is likely to be broken at any time, and must quickly be fixed if all are not to be shattered," they wrote.

Indirectly presaging the Maple approach, they add that police departments should come up with a new way to assign officers. "To allocate patrol wisely, the department must look at the neighborhoods and decide, from first-hand evidence, where an additional officer will make the greatest difference in promoting a sense of safety," according to Kelling and Wilson.

Under Bratton, the "broken windows theory" became a mantra, leading to a strategy called "quality of life enforcement," which meant enforcing small violations of the law, like pot smoking, graffiti vandalism, and public drinking. Kelling and Wilson became icons. When Wilson died in March 2012, Ray Kelly, who had returned as police commissioner, called the article "a defining contribution to law enforcement philosophy."

A fact about this essay that would be forgotten in the Giuliani years was that it actually lauded the benefits of the old-fashioned strategy of police officers walking a beat and getting to know folks in the neighborhood—the very community policing model adopted by Dinkins and Kelly. Kelling and

Wilson spent many hours with police officers in Newark and learned that police foot patrols may not directly drive down the crime rate, but they made residents feel safer, and that led to safer neighborhoods. Giuliani and Bratton and his successors viewed foot patrols as ineffective and soft. One high-ranking NYPD official compared them to the plastic owls placed above the entrance to 1 Police Plaza that failed to scare away the pigeons pooping on the bricks.

As if he and his aides had reinvented the wheel, Bratton also brought to his administration something he called "accountability." In addition to cracking down on low-level crimes and tracking crime trends obsessively, police commanders would be held accountable for the crime rate in their precincts. That accountability would be examined in monthly meetings, in which top chiefs would grill precinct commanders on their numbers and their strategies.

When these elements—computer crime tracking and mapping, the broken windows theory, quality of life enforcement, and accountability—were put together, the strategy came to be known as CompStat, shorthand for "Compare Stats," according to criminologist Eli Silverman, author of *NYPD Battles Crime*.

With the implementation of computers, the strategy born in crayon became far more sophisticated. Using spreadsheet programs, clerks entered names, locations, times, victim information, suspect information, and a dozen other items into a giant database. At first it was just the major crimes and shooting incidents, but lesser crimes followed: marijuana busts, petit larcenies, trespassing cases, vandalism.

The lesser cases were crucial because of the underlying lesson of the broken windows theory. An intersection prone to minor drug dealing and public drunkenness was likely to generate a shooting or a homicide. The smaller cases amounted to red flags that serious crimes would follow. Commanders could then rapidly target their resources to a specific problem, rather than vaguely reacting to crime. Tracking of crimes over time allowed commanders to assess the success or failure of their tactics and allowed their bosses to assess the commanders' competence.

How did Bratton and Maple get their commanders to go along with the strategy? In the interview with Dussault, Maple repeated a maxim written by the Chinese leader Sun Tzu: "Sun Tzu says forward march. His troops giggle at him. So he beheads the squad leaders and puts new ones in charge. When he says 'forward march,' again, they do it."

Every four weeks, precinct commanders donned their best white shirts, picked up their clipboards, and made the miserable journey to 1 Police Plaza, where they were excoriated over the crime numbers in their districts by Maple, Chief of Department Louis Anemone, once dubbed the department's "dark prince," and other bosses at 7.a.m. *What are you doing about those push-in robberies? Why hasn't this homicide been solved? What about these shootings?* The stories filtered out slowly. Some careers bloomed in those meetings. Others rotted. In one infamous exchange, Anemone caricatured one of the chiefs as Pinocchio.

In his 1999 book *NYPD Battles Crime*, Silverman recounts one CompStat meeting from July 1995, chaired by a bellowing Anemone. "Is anyone going to take ownership of this case?" he asked loudly, referring to a string of robberies.

"We are getting on top of it," replied the precinct commander, whose name Silverman mercifully leaves out of his book.

Then, Maple asked, "What is the plan to go after this?"

The commander said his robbery unit was looking into it.

"Let's hear from RIP," Anemone said.

Now it was the robbery unit sergeant's turn on the griddle. "We are aware of this, chief," he said.

"Then why are we down in narc arrests in those areas?" Maple asked. "And who provides information to narcotics?"

Back to Anemone: "Where is the anti-crime unit? There's slippage between robbery squads and precinct teams. We all have ownership of good and bad things. We go to a lot of trouble tracking crime. I want you all to get together and have a plan by tomorrow."

For context, before Bratton came along, it would have been unthinkable for a top chief like Anemone in the largest police department in the country to question a precinct commander about one little robbery pattern, but that kind of thing became standard under the CompStat model. And though these ideas might seem fairly obvious management tools, they were foreign to the NYPD. When Bratton was appointed, he was shocked to learn that there was a three- to six-month lag in the reporting of crime statistics, and up-to-date reports were next to impossible to produce, Silverman wrote.

In 1995, the year of Silverman's CompStat meeting, the number of murders dropped 50 percent, to 1,181, compared to 2,262 in 1990. The six other major crime categories dropped significantly as well, and they continued to drop with each passing year. The press was full of laudatory accounts of the effectiveness of the strategy. Bratton, in a trench coat, graced the cover of *Time* magazine. In the limelight now, he wrote an entire book about himself, with CompStat as the second most important character. Maple's strategy made Bratton into a figure of national importance.

"We began to run the NYPD as a private, profit-oriented business," Bratton wrote in his book *Turnaround.* "What was the profit I wanted? Crime reduction. I wanted to beat my competitors—the criminals—who were out there seven days a week, 24 hours a day. I wanted to serve my customers, the public, better, and the profit I wanted to deliver to them was reduced crime."

In hindsight, Bratton's view of CompStat as a business foreshadowed the future focus on gimmicks and an inflated bottom line that would distort precinct reporting. It was like the auto industry in Detroit—bound to ultimately go bust because the cars they produced weren't really what the public wanted. The role of a police officer, after all, involves human interaction in a broad spectrum of community affairs, not the mindless building of widgets on an assembly line.

And quietly, there were senior bosses who thought CompStat was nothing new. Chiefs had been holding their subordinates accountable and focusing on trouble spots for decades.

But at the time, no one was publicly questioning the effectiveness of the program. In 1996, three years into New York's CompStat experiment, the Harvard Kennedy School of Government selected the program for a coveted innovation award.

By then Bratton was gone. Angry that his police commissioner had become too famous, Giuliani first gutted the press office at 1 Police Plaza, then forced Bratton out. Howard Safir, the prickly former U.S. Marshal who had overseen the Witness Protection Program, followed, and became known as the man who turned over control of the police department to the mayor.

He was more or less at war with the rapacious crowd of full-time tabloid police reporters for most of his three-year tenure.

Following Safir as police commissioner was the gregarious, charming, and corrupt Bernard Kerik, a former Giuliani driver who saw his career die in scandal and ultimately landed in federal prison. Riding on his post-9/11 popularity, Rudy tried to convince the city council to let him run for a third term, but that effort failed, mostly because folks in New York had tired of his domineering ways.

Through it all, though, CompStat thrived, and the crime rate continued to plunge. By 2001, Giuliani's final year in office, it was still the signature strategy of the previous decade in law enforcement. An entire generation of police commanders rose in the so-called CompStat era: men and a few women who bought into the drumbeat from 1 Police Plaza that said getting the right numbers was the key to promotion in the NYPD.

"Broken Windows" author George Kelling wrote that CompStat was "perhaps the single most important organizational/administrative innovation in policing during the latter half of the 20th century."

After eight years of Giuliani, the conventional wisdom said the city would be ready for a Democrat. Mark Green, a former environmental lawyer and the city's public advocate, was the front-runner. Bloomberg, another Republican, however, outwitted and outspent Green and squeaked into office.

In January 2002, billionaire Michael Bloomberg was sworn in as New York City's new mayor. Promising a new era of openness and transparency in the NYPD, Bloomberg appointed none other than Raymond Kelly as his police commissioner. It was the first time in the history of the police department that the same man served twice in the post.

For Kelly, his appointment was a satisfying outcome. Ever since Giuliani had snubbed him, Kelly had been serving a kind of high-profile exile. He had done a stint overseeing a multinational police force in Haiti. He had gone the route of many ex-cops by taking a high-end job with Bear Stearns. He had worked in the Department of the Treasury. He had been commissioner of the U.S. Customs Service. Sure, these were big jobs, but they weren't the NYPD, the place that had nurtured Kelly from patrolman, up through the ranks, through the Crown Heights riots, and the first World Trade Center terrorist attack. Kelly wanted that job, the only cop job there was. He wanted to sit again at Teddy Roosevelt's desk on the fourteenth floor of 1 Police Plaza.

Kelly's face had the look of a pit bull, or of "Popeye," in less flattering assessments on the cop bulletin boards. But he dressed like a CEO, with Charvet ties, gold watches, and tailored suits. For Kelly, the key to management was being involved, and so he acquired for himself the reputation of a micromanager. Eventually, no one got transferred unless Kelly himself signed off on it.

Over the next eight years, Kelly would vastly expand the NYPD intelligence division and anti-terror units and hire an ex-CIA official to run them. He would send detectives overseas to man offices in foreign cities—even though they had no jurisdiction outside the city. He would order heavily armed squads of cops to patrol high-profile areas, like Times Square and lower Manhattan. He would send out lines of patrol cars, lights flashing, to remind the public of his fight against terrorism. He would create a high-tech crime and terrorism command center complete with big-screen televisions and rows of shiny new computers.

He ordered the surveillance of dozens of peaceful anti–Iraq War groups and instituted an overly harsh crackdown on protesters during the 2004 Republican Convention. He also closed off many of the routes that reporters had traditionally used to obtain public information.

Kelly could focus his attention on all of these things because crime continued to drop. Why mess with a good thing? In fact, Kelly expanded CompStat's philosophy of tracking crime figures to other areas, including what he called "activity reports." Spreadsheets can be used with any kind of numbers, and Kelly's people began tracking the numbers of arrests and summonses of each unit in the city and, later, each cop in the city. They broadened what they were tracking to include stop and frisks, vertical patrols, community visits, and all manner of arcana. Soon, borough commanders were becoming concerned when the activity of a single police officer was down. This obsession with tracking statistics fit nicely with Bloomberg's management philosophy. The mayor believed strongly in tracking "productivity" in his massive media and technology company, and he brought those principles to City Hall.

The murder rate—that all-important bellwether figure of a city's health—dropped below 700 per year and kept going down. And Kelly was on his way to becoming the longest-serving police commissioner in the city's history and probably the most recognized cop in the country—more well known, maybe, than the director of the FBI. It seemed that every chance they got, Bloomberg and Kelly reminded New Yorkers about the crime decline. As Giuliani did before them, they distorted FBI crime stats and claimed New York was the "safest large city in the country."

Meanwhile, the success of CompStat had spread across the country. Among other cities, Washington, D.C.; Austin, Texas; San Francisco; Dallas; Detroit; Vancouver; Minneapolis; and Camden, New Jersey all adopted the strategy, or at least elements of it. CompStat even spread to London and Australia. By 2004, a third of the nation's police departments with 100 or more officers had implemented CompStat, with another 25 percent planning to do so.

That success opened up career opportunities for many ranking NYPD officials. Maple formed a consulting company and demanded handsome fees for spreading the gospel in the New Orleans; Birmingham; Philadelphia; Newark; and Jackson, Mississippi police departments. Bratton moved to Los Angeles and brought CompStat there. Much of his "cabinet" also found jobs with other police departments: Chief John Timoney assumed the helm in Miami and Philadelphia; Wilbur Chapman took the reins in Bridgeport, Connecticut; Gary McCarthy was the Newark police chief before moving on to Chicago; Ed Norris ran the Baltimore Police Department. Even ex-mayor Giuliani got in on the CompStat gravy train, scoring a $4.5 million contract to bring the strategy to Mexico City after he left office in 2002.

Over more than a decade, then, Jack Maple's modest proposal—the CompStat strategy—had burnished the careers of four police commissioners, two mayors, and countless underlings. It had influenced police chiefs across the country. It had generated scholarly articles and appeared in books. However, along the way, it had developed flaws that were, outside the police department, understood by very few people.

Some observers questioned the claims that CompStat led to the reduction in crime in New York City. There were attempts to attribute the crime drop to other things: fewer "crack babies," more mandatory prison sentences, more cops on the streets. Economist Steven Levitt pointed out in 2004 that while the media credited new police strategies like CompStat, a better economy, and tougher prison sentences, he believes there were more important factors, like the aforementioned massive funding for new police officers. Moreover, he noted that the sharp decline in crime was experienced across the nation, not just in New York, and in cities that didn't follow the CompStat model—suggesting that there was more at play than just what was going on in one city. In what must have been viewed as sacrilege by the CompStat devotees, he argued that "innovative police strategy" had little or no effect on the crime decline.

In the beginning, crime was so out of control that once the NYPD committed to CompStat, it was easy to reduce the numbers, but as time went on, it got harder. At the same time, crime numbers became inextricably linked to career trajectory. Those two factors combined to provide an incentive to precinct commanders to fudge the numbers to look better in those CompStat meetings.

Perhaps the first public example—and there were more that did not filter out of the department—took place in 1995 when the *New York Daily News* obtained a memo written by the commander of the Bronx's 50th Precinct that offered instructions to officers on how to downgrade felonies to misdemeanors. In 1996, the press reported on two rapes, a murder, and a shooting of a car thief by a cop that were not reported by the department. In 1996, the Bronx's 41st Precinct commander was suspended for downgrading crime complaints and tossing—or "shitcanning"—other crime reports. Two years later, then-Commissioner Safir was forced to disclose that subway crime had been under-reported by 20 percent for years. That disclosure led to the forced retirement of the commanding officer of the transit unit.

In 1998, State Comptroller Carl McCall tried to audit NYPD crime statistics as part of a broader audit of all city agencies. The Giuliani administration fought the effort, sparking a nearly two-year court battle. McCall ultimately won in 1999, but the report he released in 2000 was tepidly done. It focused on a small number of complaints and found an "error rate" in reporting of less than 5 percent.

In 2002, once again in the Bronx's 50th Precinct, a rape was logged as a lower crime. In 2003, the department disclosed that 203 felonies had been downgraded to misdemeanors in Manhattan's 10th Precinct, and that in the 50th Precinct, again, in March 2003, police refused to take robbery complaints from restaurant delivery people.

By then, there were only these few episodes, which the NYPD quickly dismissed as both proof of the quality of its oversight and isolated cases by rogue commanders. But then, in March 2004, Leonard Levitt and Rocco Parascandola of *Newsday* reported on a series of questionable cases, including the punishment of an officer who refused to downgrade a felony to a misdemeanor, a former police official who had intervened to get detectives to take a report, a precinct commander who was discouraging robbery victims from reporting crimes, officers talking victims out of filing reports, and the reuse of crime complaint numbers. After the articles went to press, Patrick Lynch, president of the powerful Patrolmen's Benevolent Association (PBA), the largest of the city's police unions, and Ed Mullins, the head of the sergeants' union, held a press conference and called on Kelly to investigate crime complaint manipulation across the city.

"With 5,000 fewer police officers than we had five years ago, we can no longer hold the line on crime, forcing local commanders to artificially hold down the crime statistics," Lynch said in a written statement.

Mullins chimed in by pointing out that accurate information was one of the bedrock principles of CompStat. "Deployment of police resources is based on where and when crime is occurring so underreporting felony crime makes a neighborhood more dangerous for the community and the sergeants and police officers who patrol the area," he said.

A month prior to these statements, 400 PBA delegates had issued a vote of no confidence in Kelly and called for his immediate resignation. That vote was sparked by other issues, including Kelly's "draconian" disciplinary system and his handling of a police shooting of an unarmed civilian. Kelly's people defended the 50th Precinct commander, flatly rejected the allegation that crime was being suppressed, and suggested that the union simply had an agenda to embarrass the commissioner. They also insisted that the NYPD carefully monitors crime reporting, and any unreported crimes are simply errors that rarely take place.

The NYPD was worried about articles attacking the accuracy of the crime statistics, and rightly so. The city's entire reputation is underpinned by the accuracy of its crime stats. It is the most important bellwether of the city's health, and low crime meant more tourists, more economic development, more revenue. Any perception that crime was increasing, or that the numbers were inaccurate, could damage the city's growth.

Lynch's statements would prove to be the most powerful broadside over the crime stats, but they would go nowhere. Kelly rejected the call for an investigation, and no outside monitors stepped in to examine the crime numbers. Lynch never said another public word about manipulation of crime statistics. The City Council, which holds hearings at the drop of a hat, did nothing. The city and state comptrollers stayed out of it. The feds stayed out of it. The lone voice who did try at least to step up was Mark Pomerantz, then head of the Mayor's Commission to Combat Police Corruption, a body formed by Giuliani following the Mollen Commission of 1992, which investigated corruption in the NYPD. By 2004, the commission was a gutted shell of its former self, confining itself to issuing reports on relatively minor issues and cloaking its activities in repressive secrecy.

Pomerantz, a former federal prosecutor who had handled major cases, decided to take on Kelly and Bloomberg, and asked for NYPD records so the commission could examine whether crime was being downgraded to create the perception that things were better than they were. Kelly refused to cooperate, saying that Pomerantz was overreaching his authority, which of course he was not. Pomerantz complained to the Bloomberg administration, and he got the stiff-arm. Bloomberg turned his back on him, and Pomerantz, having been undercut, had to resign. After Pomerantz's departure, the mayor's commission became even less of what it was before. Some years, it released just one report, written in the most boring possible bureaucratic style as if its authors did not want anyone to read it.

Among the rank and file, the problems with CompStat were already fairly clear, but no one would really talk about it. In part, this was because keeping crime down made everyone look good, and just as there was an incentive at the top of city government for lower crime numbers, so was there an incentive at the bottom, among the line patrol officers, sergeants, and lieutenants, to go along with the agenda of the precinct commanders. As Robert Zink, the secretary for the PBA, wrote in a 2004 essay for the union's newsletter, "When you finally get a real handle on crime, you eventually hit a wall where you can't push it down any more. CompStat does not recognize that wall, so the commanders have to get creative to keep their numbers going down."

Well aware that their careers were on the line, commanders evolved a series of techniques to "fudge" the numbers and trained their line supervisors—the sergeants and lieutenants—on how to do it. Zink wrote, "How do you fake a crime decrease? Don't file reports, misclassify crimes from felonies to misdemeanors, under-value the property lost to crime, and report a series of crimes as a single event. A particularly insidious way to fudge the numbers is to make it difficult for people to report crimes—in other words, make the victims feel like criminals so they walk away just to spare themselves further pain and suffering."

The manipulation of crime statistics wasn't confined only to New York, and CompStat—and some of the very same methods noted by Zink—fueled downgrading scandals that took place in other cities. In 2001, a Philadelphia newspaper exposed how 1,700 rape cases were dumped into a vague classification that allowed the Philadelphia Police Department to not count them as offenses. The scandal caused an overhaul of how rape cases were investigated. In October 2003, five New Orleans police officers were fired and a sixth demoted for downgrading crime complaints. A 2004 audit of the Atlanta police showed that 22,000 police reports of 911 calls vanished in 2002. In 2008, Detroit Police Chief James Barnes was fired after the department and the city medical examiner's office were caught classifying homicides as "self-defense and suicide."

In 2009, the Florida Department of Law Enforcement blamed chronic under-reporting of crime in the Miami Police Department on the pressures of CompStat. In Dallas, police were caught classifying people beaten with lead pipes as simple assault rather than aggravated or felony assault. Baltimore police were caught classifying a multiple shooting as a single incident. In other words, if six people were shot, that would be counted as a single shooting, rather than six shootings. The Baltimore Police Department was also downgrading the value of stolen property to classify thefts as misdemeanors, rather than felonies. By April 2010, the Baltimore police commissioner, Fredrick Bealefeld, was canceling CompStat meetings while he weighed changes to the management strategy based on complaints that the method led to browbeating of commanders and manipulation of crime statistics.

The irony was that while these disclosures in other cities led to investigations, hearings, firings, suspensions, and reforms, the CompStat scandals in New York had little or no effect on the NYPD, Kelly, or Bloomberg. Logically, if it was happening elsewhere, it had to be happening in New York, too. Sure, a few commanders got transferred or retired, but there was never any searching investigation of the numbers, nor did any outside agencies ever have the courage or will to do any comprehensive examination of the numbers. And unlike the Serpico years and the Mollen Commission, the city's newspapers and television outlets largely stayed on the sidelines. There were articles here and there, but nothing powerful enough to embarrass the mayor into doing anything about it. The few canaries in the coal mine who did hop forward were suffocated by the NYPD's rhetorical stone wall. And Kelly became the city's longest-serving police commissioner, his power only continued to increase, and his job approval ratings remained routinely higher than those of Bloomberg.

In short, if Ray Kelly was at the top of the NYPD, sitting behind his Teddy Roosevelt desk, running the war against terror, Adrian Schoolcraft was close to the bottom, making his anonymous rounds along forgotten streets, just another cop in the blue bag they call a uniform. Eventually, the journeys of the two men would collide.

CHAPTER 3

BED-STUY: DO OR DIE

By the end of his eight months at the Police Academy, Schoolcraft earned a fairly good rating of "competent" to "highly competent." He scored an average of 91 on academy exams, placing him high in the class. Not bad for a guy who didn't really want to become a cop in the first place.

Rookie police officers out of the academy are immediately sent to what is known as Operation Impact—one of Kelly's patrol initiatives. In the Safir era, there was the Street Crime Unit (SCU)—plainclothes cops patrolling high-crime neighborhoods—but it collapsed in 1999 when four officers approached a young immigrant from Guinea, Amadou Diallo, mistook his wallet for a gun, and fired 41 shots at him. Diallo was struck 19 times and died. The officers were later acquitted of murder charges, but the SCU was eventually disbanded by Kelly.

Kelly had Impact, which, from the lofty heights of the fourteenth floor at 1 Police Plaza, essentially looked like sending clouds of rookie cops into high-crime areas to bolster the ranks of veteran precinct patrol officers. The program got plaudits, but as Schoolcraft would soon learn, it also had its problems down at street level. His path into Impact took him to the 75th Precinct in the East New York section of Brooklyn, a place where they dumped bodies back in the mob days, a place that had been crippled by the crack wars of the 1980s and 1990s, and had 125 murders in one particular year. At any rate, on January 1, 2002, Schoolcraft reported for duty at the 75th Precinct. The NYPD was nothing if not obsessive about bureaucracy: His personnel card lists that he was issued shield number 12943, Patrol Guide 342563, handcuffs number 453802, and ID card 057143.

Michael Marino happened to be the precinct commander of the 75th Precinct at the time. If Schoolcraft looked like a guy who could walk through a brick wall if he wanted, Marino actually did and loved it. He was a hard-charging macho guy who liked lifting weights. His career burnished by the CompStat model, he would eventually rise to deputy chief, and he would become a hugely important character in the life of Adrian Schoolcraft seven years later, but at the time, the two men had no interaction. Schoolcraft was just another rookie, thrown into the streets of the 75th Precinct on foot without much supervision. He was told to just go out and write summonses—or tickets—for low-level offenses. Every so often, during the tour, a field sergeant would wander along and sign his memo book.

This was Schoolcraft's first indoctrination to the NYPD's unwritten quota system. He was supposed to write a certain number of summonses and make a certain number of arrests each month—and his "productivity" was closely tracked, even as the NYPD insisted up and down that there was no quota system. At that point, he went along with the program. He really had no choice—as a rookie fresh out of the academy, aka a "probationary" officer, he had no job protection. He could be fired for anything.

"Quotas have always been a part of the Police Department for as long as I can remember," Marquez Claxton, a retired detective and director of the Black Law Enforcement Alliance, told me. "When I started in the NYPD in 1985 in the 28th precinct, our quota was 20 parking summonses, 5 moving violations and two arrests."

Indeed, in the 1973 movie *Serpico*, during a roll call in one of the very first scenes, the tour commander said, "Now we want summonses, summonses, summonses."

That was 35 years ago. The difference in the Kelly era, Claxton said, is there were "quotas for everything." The CompStat model means numbers alone gauge the success of fighting crime. "It's like factory work. The difficulty is that you can't quantify prevention. There is no number which says I stopped seven burglaries today. People have made careers out of summonses and arrests, but that's not even the main component of police work.

"A lot of cops come on the job to have relationships with the community, to be public servants," he said. "But in today's PD, the officers are ostracized unless they have their numbers. You're punishing officers who say their job is not to be the hammer."

The other problem with quotas is that they take the discretion away from street cops. "Not everybody who violates a rule needs to be summonsed," Claxton said. "You can talk to them. You can give them a warning."

Schoolcraft was surprised at the relative lack of supervision of this group of rookie officers by the precinct bosses. Other police departments assigned a field training officer to each new recruit, who then learned on the job over a significant period of time, but not the NYPD. He had his quota. He was supposed to write tickets. He would get an occasional drive-by from a boss, and that was it. He got through it well enough, and the stint ended as quietly as it began. This was his first encounter with the contradiction between the mass public perception of how the NYPD operates, based on television and the movies, and the reality of how it really works. A patrol officer's work is usually incredibly mundane and bureaucratic. Standing on a corner. Working a traffic detail. Spending time in Times Square or another tourist-heavy area. Filling out paperwork triplicate. Filing carbon copies in the right inboxes. Cleaning the patrol car of garbage. Making sure you use the right color ink. Babysitting a drug addict or a homeless guy in the hospital. Getting upbraided because you don't have your required whistle holder on your belt.

Still, his work was rated "competent," and "highly competent" in two areas: police ethics/integrity and comprehension. "P.O. Schoolcraft is very respectful to supervisors and peers," Sergeant John McCarthy's evaluation read. "He responds to all jobs on his post in a timely manner."

After eight months in East New York, Schoolcraft had aged out of Impact and would now be sent to another command. He would have no choice in the decision. He got the message via Finest—an internal NYPD teletype system that announced personnel changes: who was being transferred, reassigned, charged, suspended, and promoted. The Finest system was the ultimate flat-toned arbiter of rising and failing careers in the NYPD. His new command would be the 81st Precinct in Bedford-Stuyvesant, Brooklyn. It was still unclear whether that was bad or good.

The piece of land in central Brooklyn known as Bedford-Stuyvesant began life as a forest of great oaks thence converted to pasture land hewn by Dutch farmers. The name derives from two of the early towns in the area, Bedford Village and Stuyvesant Heights, the latter of which was named for Peter Stuyvesant, a governor of the Dutch colony in New York known as New Netherlands.

The farms gave way to wood-framed houses for working- and middle-class immigrants from Europe, and as the population swelled, by 1890, the wood-framed houses gave way to brownstones.

As time passed, the neighborhood became largely African American, a cultural, economic, and religious hub for black families who had emigrated from the south and then left the overcrowding of Harlem for better, less expensive housing.

Things started to go bad, and the fortunes of the neighborhood suffered, most notably in a surge of gang violence beginning in the early 1960s. Bed-Stuy became a touchstone for many of the great racial and economic issues dividing the nation through the 1960s and 1970s, including the Ocean Hill–Brownsville school dispute, which pitted black parents against largely white and Jewish teachers.

In 1964, a riot that started in Harlem after a police officer shot and killed a black teen named James Powell spread to Bed-Stuy, causing the burning and looting of many white- and Jewish-owned shops. The tension between African Americans and the police was constant. Ironically, the 79th Precinct, which also covered a part of Bed-Stuy, was one of just three precincts that staffed some black patrol officers.

The social ills in the neighborhood were so problematic that after the 1964 election, Robert F. Kennedy, then a U.S. senator representing New York, ordered a study of Bed-Stuy because it received little federal funding despite being the city's largest black community. The findings inspired a new wave of community groups, and Kennedy's ideas were used in similarly afflicted neighborhoods across the country.

Bed-Stuy also became a voting rights battleground. In 1965, Andrew Cooper, an African American journalist, filed a lawsuit alleging racial gerrymandering. He alleged that five surrounding congressional districts had divided up the neighborhood to dilute the black vote so white politicians could remain in office in each district. He won the lawsuit, and the resulting Twelfth Congressional District votes selected Shirley Chisholm, the first black woman elected to Congress. Chisholm went on to a distinguished career on Capitol Hill.

A second round of race riots took place in 1967 and 1968, caused by high unemployment, poor housing, and civil rights issues. Yet another devastating riot took place during the 1977 blackout. Some 130 stores were either burned or looted or both, and some of the scars were visible for many years.

Bed-Stuy became a cultural touchstone, featured in *The French Connection*, *NYPD Blue*, *RFK*, and five Spike Lee films, including *Do the Right Thing* (1989), which portrayed the racial tension of the time. The comedian Chris Rock produced and starred in a sitcom about his life as a teen in Bed-Stuy from 1982 to 1987, and Dave Chappelle filmed *Block Party* there. Hip-hop and rap stars from the neighborhood include Jay-Z, Lil' Kim, The Notorious B.I.G., Mos Def, and Ol' Dirty Bastard, and for them, the neighborhood served as the metaphor for the tough urban milieu. "I rely on Bed-Stuy to shut it down if I die," B.I.G. raps on a Lil' Kim track. In a 2005 track, Young Jeezy raps, "I'm from even where the dead die, but try and do it big like the kid from Bed-Stuy."

The streets of Bedford-Stuyvesant have been angry, buildings have burned, drugs beset the corners, gunshots echoed in the night. But as the 1990s progressed, crime dropped in Bed-Stuy, as it did across the city, and this began to have profound effects in the neighborhood. As the new century began, as Adrian Schoolcraft moved closer toward his destiny, Bed-Stuy found itself in the beginnings of a new demographic movement—whites priced out of Manhattan and even the tonier areas of Brooklyn, like Prospect Park, began to migrate into the neighborhood, attracted by the brownstones and tree-lined streets. That gentrification had the effect of pushing out lower-income blacks, but it also resulted in the renovation of abandoned properties and a swell of new businesses, and it made the neighborhood more diverse ethnically and economically.

In July 2003, knowing little of the rich history of the neighborhood, Schoolcraft arrived at the 81st Precinct station house, a low-slung utilitarian fortress, with small windows all the better for defending and a walled parking lot on one end, along Ralph Avenue, a two-lane roadway set between the

C subway line along Fulton and the J and Z lines along Broadway. The station house sat across from a Baptist church and a school that had seen better days.

The architectural style of the building seemed to combine elements of 1970s school, 1980s penitentiary, and 1990s neighborhood fortress. Other than running water and electricity, the structure literally had no frills. It was just a block of concrete cubes that someone had tried to dress up with blue and white paint and vending machines, maybe to make it seem like a place where one would remotely want to be. Outside the lot, cops parked their civilian cars wherever they could. Often, they left them on the sidewalk. One window set into the steel front door was cracked, and there was probably a good story about how it happened. Ralph Avenue was a key artery for folks, high and low, through the area, but it had its share of boarded up storefronts, and the first flush of gentrification had only begun to sweep through the once majestic brownstones and walkups along the side streets.

The 81st Precinct is a 1.7-square-mile trapezoid, geographically one of the smallest precincts in the city, but it contains about 70,000 residents. At the time that Schoolcraft began his work there, it had an air of both rising fortunes and fallen aristocracy. The old touchstone buildings remained— the gothic heights of Boys and Girls High School, the curved turrets of the Renaissance and Alhambra apartment houses, the ranks of dignified brownstones, the peaked elegance of the John Wesley United Methodist Church— but crack violence had left its scars in urine-stained hallways of yellowing tenements, in the dented doors and grimy floors of the Brevoort Houses, in the suspicious bustle late at night on Ralph and Chauncey. In the meantime, the cost of living in Manhattan and wealthier Brooklyn neighborhoods like Prospect Heights was pushing pioneers into those rows of brownstones.

Among cops, the 81st Precinct had a certain reputation, accompanied by its own peculiar slang. The 81st Precinct was not a "hook house," like the 1st Precinct in Manhattan's financial district. To get assigned to the first, you needed a "hook," a connection, a rabbi, to get you in those doors. Nor was it a glamour precinct, like Midtown South or Central Park or the 19th Precinct on the Upper East Side. Nor was it an easy, low-crime precinct like the 122nd in Staten Island or the 111th Precinct in Bayside, Queens. And it didn't have any particular political juice, like the heavily orthodox Jewish neighborhood of Borough Park, Brooklyn's 66th Precinct.

The cops there labored in grim anonymity. The place had its share of horrific crimes, sure, but they rarely merited attention in the tabloids. Folks expected crime in Bed-Stuy. The robbery-assaults. The drug-fueled shootings. The odd slashing. These were poor folks killing poor folks, druggies killing druggies. It was an outpost, about as far as you can get from City Hall and still be within city limits, or that's how the cops viewed it.

If the precinct was known for anything, it was as a dumping ground for benighted cops, for cops with no rabbi, for cops in trouble with headquarters, for cops who ran afoul of a boss, for cops who had the black spot on them. Its most famous alum was Frank Serpico, the 1970s-era whistleblower, and even he was reviled before and after his information resulted in a huge corruption scandal that turned the department upside down.

Worse yet, there was a long history of tension between citizens of Bed-Stuy and the precinct, to the point where even after the turn of the new century, plenty of people viewed the police as an occupying force with no ties to the community. Think the Romans in Britain, or *Fort Apache, the Bronx,* without Paul Newman. Likewise, the police had their own views on the neighborhood, as a sergeant said in an unguarded moment during a precinct roll call: "You're not in midtown Manhattan where everyone is walking around smiling and being happy. You're in Bed-Stuy, where everyone probably has a warrant."

Schoolcraft, meanwhile, had no idea where he was. His very first 81st Precinct activity report from July 2003 indicated that he largely walked a foot post that month and wrote 30 parking tickets, made 18 radio runs, and did 8 patrols of public housing, known as vertical patrols. He took two complaints and did three stop and frisks.

He also wrote several "C" summonses, which are basically quality-of-life tickets, for infractions like loitering for gambling, disorderly conduct, and public drinking—the very heart of the now decade-old philosophy of making low-level arrests to deter bigger crimes. The practice had two major side effects: One, it created criminal records not only for criminals, but for people, many of them young black and Hispanic youth, who were just sitting on the stoop smoking a joint; and two, it also created a lot of dismissed arrests. Statistics show that something over half of C summonses were dismissed once they got to court, but arrestees had to show up, and that cost them work days and other inconveniences that built resentment of the NYPD. A lot of those arrests were generated in connection with stop and frisks, in which cops would stop people on vague grounds and find a sprinkling of pot in their pockets. Schoolcraft went along with the program at this point, not cognizant of the larger implications. And there was a certain energy in the specificity of his entries from this time, which suggests he was motivated to do the job.

His lieutenant of the period, Martin Zuniga, wrote in an evaluation that October that he "performs well with normal supervision. His motivation is steadfast. He performs above expectation."

Over the next six or so years, or the rest of his career, Schoolcraft would remain in the 81st Precinct, a fairly long period of time for any officer to stay in one command. He would make 71 arrests—17 for felonies, 42 for misdemeanors, and 12 for violations. Fifteen of those would be for resisting arrest. He would also earn two of the lesser NYPD medals—one for excellent policy duty and one for meritorious police duty. His personnel records listed his special skills as an "RMP operator," or someone who could drive a police car. It was a fairly light record, but one that was pretty common in the NYPD. He would also rack up his share of civilian complaints, nine in all, with several unnecessary force allegations. None of them would affect his career in any serious way.

As the year progressed, Schoolcraft listened to his father talk about Suzanne's health. She was ailing from cancer and getting sicker. Adrian took leave from August 28 to October 12 of 2003 to help Larry care for her in Johnstown, which meant repeatedly driving her to Albany and Schenectady for doctors' appointments. There was a point when the department began to resist his requests for time off. On one occasion, Schoolcraft wanted to take a few days to visit his mother, but his commanders refused and ordered him placed on forced overtime—an unofficial practice in which cops were basically required to work extra hours to fill in personnel holes.

"Adrian never forgave the NYPD for that," Larry said.

Forced overtime was a major issue for the line officers, but it was also a big incentive to work more. Rather than increasing the size of the police department, Kelly was essentially ordering a force that was 5,000 cops smaller than in the past to cover for the fact that the mayor didn't want to hire more police. Police officers became addicted to the extra overtime money but were constantly exhausted from having to work one or two extra shifts a week, often on special details outside the precinct. It was common to see cops from the "outer borough" precincts standing a post in Times Square or in Wall Street or walking some parade route.

At the end of October 2003, Schoolcraft received his second job rating. Sergeant Martin Zuniga rated him as competent: "This officer is well versed on precinct conditions. He works well with little or no supervision."

That December, he received another solid evaluation, which was particularly laudatory about an injury he suffered making an arrest on his own initiative: "He is motivated and maintains a high professional image. He performs above expectation."

The December reviewer was Lieutenant Timothy Caughey, who would become an antagonist five year later, but for now seemed to be in his corner.

On December 22, 2003, his mother Suzanne suffered a massive stroke while she was receiving dialysis treatment. She was rushed to St. Mary's Hospital and then to Ellis Hospital in Schenectady. Larry joined her there and called the 81st Precinct looking for Adrian. When his bosses finally located him, they planned to fly him to the hospital by helicopter, but there was too much fog. So they drove him, with lights and sirens, to Penn Station, where he took Amtrak and arrived in Albany at about midnight.

Suzanne survived for eight days, father and son held Christmas by her bedside, and then she died on December 30, 2003. She was 47 years old. For Adrian, his mother's death was devastating. She had been very important to him. He thought of her every time he put on his uniform and went to work. He took the first 19 days of January 2004 off of work. But he had to get back to the job.

At that point in his career, he was still enjoying the good graces of his bosses. He was the model CompStat officer, getting the numbers the bosses cared about. An activity report from June 2004 offered a glimpse of what Schoolcraft was doing on the job. In that month, he arrested a drunk driver, made a drug possession bust, and caught two people with active warrants. He wrote 14 C summonses and stopped 6 people. He did 26 radio runs and 16 vertical patrols in public housing.

He was improving, his boss wrote: "If he stays focused he will evolve into a well rounded, very active officer."

The boss added, "On occasion, he needs to be reminded to demonstrate courtesy when dealing with frustrated civilians, however, his overall demeanor is very respectful."

Perhaps in some way related to his mother's death, Schoolcraft racked up the most civilian complaints of his career: five in all, but he was found not guilty or the allegation was proved unsubstantiated in all of them. The cloak of protection was still around him.

But in November 2004, he was placed in what was known as "Level 1 force monitoring" for "negative performance/behavior" until November 2005. This designation had two significant elements: One, it meant that Schoolcraft would receive more attention from bosses about his work, and two, it also was a way for his bosses to control him. Like the Marine Corps drill instructors at Lejeune, the NYPD found ways to control its officers and insist on their "activity."

But it was all smoke and mirrors. Nothing really came of it, and that outcome would stand in contrast to what happened in 2009. At the end of 2004, his patrol sergeant, Michael Miller, gave him a rating of 3.5—or more than competent—saying he was "resourceful, never complacent, a well rounded officer capable of fulfilling any task given to him. He is an asset to the department."

This trend continued into 2005. Schoolcraft's March 2005 monthly evaluation written by Lieutenant De La Fuente read, "He is highly motivated and a hard worker. He maximizes the limited patrol duty he has."

In September 2005, he requested and received a two-month leave to care for his father, who was still depressed and seeing a psychologist after the death of Suzanne, and to winterize the Johnstown home. Adrian returned to duty in mid-November.

Adrian's personnel record for the year contained one other entry: that someone filed a complaint that he refused to take a crime report. This was ironic given what would take place years later.

At the end of 2005, his sergeant, William Meyer, once again gave Schoolcraft a 3.5 rating. He was again above standards, and he got a rare 5 for "police ethics/integrity."

"P.O. Schoolcraft's deportment and performance always reflects a high level of integrity," Meyer wrote. "He has proven himself to be a fine officer with great potential."

Meyer's lieutenant, Leighton Myrie, concurred. "P.O. Schoolcraft is a competent member of the 81st Precinct. His disposition is consistently courteous and we expect great things from P.O. Schoolcraft in the future."

By the end of 2005, crime in the 81st Precinct had dropped by 3.5 percent. Commissioner Kelly had sent Impact cops to the area for six months to patrol what was known as the Fulton-Nostrand Avenue business district and then ordered another six-month stint. Community activists started a campaign to change the neighborhood's unofficial motto from "Bed-Stuy Do or Die" to "Bed-Stuy and Proud Of It." The effort failed because the original slogan was so intertwined with the lore of the area.

In April 2006, Schoolcraft made his first formal foray into raising issues in the command, when he wrote a memo to Deputy Inspector Robert Brower about forced overtime. "This 49 is to notify you of a serious problem within the precinct, that I feel has now become a chronic safety issue. The problem that I'm reporting to you is forced overtime. Police officers are being forced to work double shifts and/or give up their regular days off, always at the last moment.

"Forced overtime is issued by department civilians who don't seem to be concerned about the safety of police officers and the public they serve. I'm also concerned that we could be violating department policy and/or state law by working so many days without a day off. I feel that this policy is leading to an increase in civilian complaints, sick days, accidents and injuries."

How the commander reacted to this memo is unclear from the record, but nothing changed. Schoolcraft was tilting at windmills.

Crime dropped in the precinct by 1.9 percent in 2006, and Schoolcraft's bosses gave him a rating of 3.5 on his performance evaluation again. The only black mark in his personnel record was that someone filed a complaint disputing a ticket that he wrote.

His father was impressed. "He was successful in the NYPD because he could deal in these weird, oppressive environments," Larry Schoolcraft said.

Though Schoolcraft was enjoying the good graces of his bosses for the moment, performance evaluations are strange documents. The reality was that much of a police officer's job involved interacting with citizens. Those interactions were difficult to quantify. How, for example, do you put a number to the fact that a cop picked up a child who had fallen off his bike, or helped an old lady cross the street, or diffused a brewing street fight with only words? How do you quantify an officer who resolved a situation by specifically not making an arrest? How do you quantify a decision *not* to take action?

On the other hand, it was fairly easy to quantify arrests, summonses, stop and frisks, sick days, and other indicators. The result was that a police officer's ability to generate numbers became more important than his or her ability to make good decisions. Performance evaluations are written to appear objective, based on statistics and hard facts, but, as Schoolcraft would learn, officers were actually extremely vulnerable to subjective views.

Another thing he noticed was the second-guessing that was taking place. If a patrol officer took a complaint, invariably there was a sergeant or lieutenant who would appear at the scene to essentially look over the shoulder of the cop. That boss would second-guess on the type of crime, on the circumstances of the crime, on how the incident should be classified. The patrol officer would be obligated to adhere to whatever he or she was told. Twenty years ago, patrol officers didn't have to deal with that kind of thing. They took a complaint and filed it and then moved on. Now, they were being forced to question what they had written. The reason was CompStat and the downward pressure on the numbers. Crime had dropped to a point where in order to come up with continued declines, commanders had to become very good at parsing complaints to look for opportunities to downgrade incidents or wipe them off the books entirely. In addition, the commander and supervisory bosses were calling crime victims and questioning them on details of their accounts of a crime for the purpose of reclassifying or downgrading a report to a lesser charge.

And then there was training. Roll calls, most days, were supposed to include an element of training, but often the "training" would mean just one sentence and then an order to "sign the training log." The officers were ordered to sign the training log as a hedge against lawsuits. If a cop shot someone or beat the shit out of someone "outside of guidelines," the NYPD could look at the training log and say, well, we trained the guy. But it was a fake log. Schoolcraft immediately recognized what was happening, and for the period, went along with it, but he was questioning it.

He did not really understand or appreciate the focus on numbers. He had not read about the Broken Windows theory first described by Kelling and Wilson, but he was being asked to embrace their model.

As he worked his tours in the 8-1, the Patrolmen's Benevolent Association, or PBA, was challenging the department's obsession with numbers in a case that showed striking parallels with what Schoolcraft would later experience. The case involved an officer named David Velez, who appealed his 2005 evaluation from the 75th Precinct, which he alleged was based on his failure to meet the summons quota.

In the lawsuit, Velez claimed that the commander of the 75th Precinct, Michael Marino, issued a quota of 10 summonses a month. If officers did not hit the quota, they would receive lower evaluations. Marino put this demand in a memo to his supervisors, who then passed it on to the cops in another memo written by an amusingly named sergeant called Lurch: "Failure to write the required amount of summonses and failure to make the required number of arrests will result in substandard performance ratings."

As he testified years later in an unrelated trial, Marino believed, when he started out as 75th Precinct commander, his officers weren't working hard enough. "They were doing five [summonses] a month, which was just not enough to address the problem," he testified. "It was almost malfeasance.... The level of activity they were performing was so low that it was a detriment to the community, in one of the most crime ridden precincts in the city."

So he spent weeks touring the precinct, making arrests, writing tickets, investigating. He concluded his cops could do a lot more. He set a standard of 10 tickets per month and one arrest per cop. "I set a standard that said do your job or suffer the consequences," Marino testified.

Now, Marino was not only Schoolcraft's former precinct commander, but also his future antagonist. The Velez dispute came to a head in January 2006, when a special arbitrator named Bonnie Weinstock ruled that, indeed, there was a traffic ticket quota in violation of state labor law.

"The memos could not have been clearer...I am completely persuaded that this is a quota," she wrote. The NYPD had violated state labor law. "The city," she added, "shall cease and desist from maintaining a vehicular ticket quota."

But in practice, nothing really changed. Marino continued to be promoted. And Schoolcraft was already aware of quotas. They were a constant in the NYPD, even if the bosses at 1 Police Plaza wouldn't publicly admit it. In fact, the pressure to produce arrests, summonses, and stop and frisks was hammered home in nearly every roll call.

In October 2006, a new executive officer arrived in the 81st Precinct. His name was Steven Mauriello. When Mauriello was promoted to precinct commander a year later, it would spell the beginning of the end of Schoolcraft's police career.

In June 2007, Adrian had a conflict with a Lieutenant Jones over whether he was properly authorized to leave work to help his wheelchair-ridden father get home from the hospital.

Schoolcraft was so irritated by the exchange that he wrote another notarized letter to the precinct's commanding officer. In the letter, Schoolcraft alleged that Jones threatened to punish the whole shift of officers for what Schoolcraft did.

"Every violation that I usually put in the minor violations I'm writing CD's for, so you can thank somebody for that," Jones said, according to the letter. "Schoolcraft, see me when you're finished."

"This is a formal complaint regarding the conduct of Lt. Jones," Schoolcraft wrote. "His retaliatory threats were intended to create a hostile work environment for myself and other officers."

By December 2007, perhaps because he had begun questioning things, Schoolcraft's rating dropped to a 3, which was still at standards, but teetering on the edge of unsatisfactory. The precinct's crime rate dropped 1 percent.

For the year, he had made 620 radio runs, done 71 vertical patrols, written 34 tickets, written 6 C summonses, and made 9 arrests. Those numbers were lower than his 2006 totals.

In the evaluation Sergeant William Meyer wrote: "He at times needs direction or prompting to resolve problems. He at times needs extra guidance to meet goals and deadlines. He does need extra motivation to perform his assignments and meet performance goals." This is the first time his evaluation sank to pedestrian margins.

CHAPTER 4

"PLAY THE GAME"

By the end of 2007 going into 2008, the precinct's executive officer, Steven Mauriello, was given command of the precinct and promoted to deputy inspector. Mauriello was born on Long Island, and he graduated from Valley Stream High School in 1985. As a high school kid, he worked as a stock boy, making $5 an hour at the local Foodtown supermarket. He attended college at St. John's University and graduated in 1989 with a bachelor's degree in criminal justice and a minor in psychology. His college transcript indicates that his grades were mostly Bs and Cs, but he did get an A in composition and rhetoric and a D+ in a criminal investigation class.

He joined the NYPD in 1989. In one of his very first evaluations, in February 1990, his supervisor wrote, "Officer Mauriello has excellent career potential. He is a reliable and dedicated police officer. He has good arrest and summons activity. He should have a good career with the department."

In other words, Mauriello learned the lesson fairly quickly: Good "activity" gets you places in the NYPD.

In December 1991, while Mauriello was assigned to the 34th Precinct in Manhattan, two men posing as Con Edison workers pushed their way into a Manhattan apartment occupied by a couple and their nine-year-old daughter. He and other officers blocked their escape and arrested them and then cared for the victims.

"The officers were aware of our horrible experience and treated us with care and understanding," the father wrote.

In 1993, a precinct resident wrote to Mauriello's boss, Joseph Esposito, who would become a top chief ten years later, "We feel he [Mauriello] deserves recognition for his deep concern in our dire need for help in this drug infested area.... We need more officers like Steven Mauriello."

Another 1993 letter thanked him for "his earnest attempt to make our life more bearable here."

By 1994, Mauriello had been promoted to sergeant and sent to work in the Brooklyn North warrants unit. He continued to garner good evaluations. "He can be counted on to get the job done," one read. Six years later, he was promoted to lieutenant, working in the 90th Precinct in Williamsburg and elsewhere.

As a lieutenant in 2001, assigned to the 88th Precinct, his captain rated him as high as he could on the form and wrote that he had great integrity, was a tireless worker, was an outstanding supervisor, and had excellent career potential.

Mauriello's Internal Affairs file remained clean, listing just four allegations, all of them unproven.

In October 2003, he was promoted to captain, working in anti-crime, where he was lauded for increasing arrest activity, and he started being recommended for a precinct command. When he arrived at the 81st Precinct, he initially worked as the executive officer before being promoted to commander.

The only official black mark in his file was a 2008 letter of reprimand. Evidently, Mauriello lost his temper with the Civilian Complaint Review Board and called investigators to question what they were doing and to attack the credibility of people who had filed complaints against his cops. "This conduct is inappropriate," wrote Chief of Internal Affairs Charles Campisi.

As commander, Mauriello adopted the hands-on, numbers- and productivity-focused approach that was favored by ambitious commanders in the era of CompStat. He was given to long grandiose speeches about the importance of getting numbers and being aggressive on the street.

As for Schoolcraft, in general, Mauriello said later that he viewed him as "unproductive" and felt that he didn't take instruction well. However, he did not believe Schoolcraft was a discipline problem.

Meanwhile, Schoolcraft didn't think much of Mauriello's obsession with numbers. Yet he soldiered on. The monthly performance reports that he was required to file, listing the number of radio runs he had, the number of arrests, and 21 other statistical categories, offer a roadmap to the shift life of a typical police officer.

For example, in January 2008, he responded to 23 radio runs, did 4 vertical patrols, took 5 complaints, responded to 2 accidents, and made out 5 domestic incident reports. He did not make an arrest. He wrote that month that he "performed directed patrol at high crime location, conducted vertical, responded to multiple radio runs, multiple domestic incidents."

That month, he also did ten shifts just working security at MetroTech, an office/housing complex in Brooklyn where the 911 dispatch system is located. That meant that he was away from his patrol duties a third of the month. This is a common but little-known problem in the NYPD. Police officers are constantly being removed from their regular duties to stand security or attend some detail. That practice often guts the number of patrol cops on a given shift. But precinct commanders are still expected to make their "numbers," even with a constant deficit in the number of officers they can field.

In February 2008, he spent four shifts at MetroTech, two shifts babysitting prisoners, and three on something called CRV—an anti-terrorism program developed by Kelly, in which lines of police cars with lights flashing drove around the city as a supposed deterrent that was more about public relations than terrorism and was another a constant drain on patrol manpower.

In March 2008, his supervisor wrote that Schoolcraft was "always courteous and respectful, and is actively involved in enforcing precinct conditions."

Then, between March and April, something changed. That was the last favorable comment Schoolcraft received on a written evaluation. From there on out, his sergeant, Raymond Stukes, and other 81st Precinct bosses started building a drumbeat of pressure on Schoolcraft, demanding more "activity" or higher numbers of arrests, summonses, radio runs, and stop and frisks. Schoolcraft did not feel that his productivity had particularly declined, so he was puzzled at the sudden change in temperature.

An increasing level of frustration with Schoolcraft was palpable in the monthly activity reports filed by his supervisors. In April 2008, one month after the fairly positive March review, Stukes wrote, Schoolcraft "needs improvement in areas of activity." In May, they wrote, "MOS has consistently produced substandard activity. He has been counseled repeatedly."

In June, Mauriello himself counseled Schoolcraft on his "productivity expectations."

It was around this period that Schoolcraft complained to his father about the constant harangue for numbers and the pressure his supervisors were placing on him. They went back and forth about what to do. Schoolcraft finally decided to start wearing a digital recorder. The taping of the precinct began. He wore the recorder throughout his eight-hour tour, picking up the roll calls, the precinct banter, and whatever happened out in the street. When he got home, he downloaded the day's content onto his computer, reviewed it for what might be useful, and made careful notes.

"He knew they were going to come after him because he wasn't producing," Larry said. "Brower [Mauriello's predecessor] looked the other way on him, he accepted the other qualities that Adrian had. The whole tenor of the precinct changed when Mauriello came in. He knew Mauriello was going to make him do things that he didn't want to do. I told Adrian, 'play the game.' Go out and get a couple more quality numbers a day. Let them think you are playing the game. He couldn't do that."

Meanwhile, Mauriello and his sergeants and lieutenants were hammering home to the patrol officers that they needed to bring back numbers. He was particularly focused on congregations of young African American men on the corners. He would often roam the precinct, and when he spotted these groups, he would call in his officers to arrest them. These came to be known as "Mauriello Specials." The arrestees would be held a few hours in the precinct and then released. At one of the roundups outside a particularly notorious housing project, Mauriello whistled "Danny Boy" as seven people were cuffed and hauled away.

On June 12, 2008, Schoolcraft's recorder captured a sergeant ordering cops to arrest with the intent of releasing the "suspects" a few hours later. "Guys on the corner? You gotta leave. Bounce. Get lost," he said. "You'll void it later on in the night so you'll all go home on time."

Shortly after that remark, a lieutenant discussed "productivity" and actually—and this is rare, because quotas are illegal—identified the expected numbers that cops were supposed to generate. "The XO (second-in-command) was in the other day, he actually laid down a number. He wants at least 3 seat belts, 1 cell phone and 11 others. Alright, so if I was on patrol, I would be sure to get 3 seat belts, 1 cell phone and 11 others. Pick it up a lot, if you have to. The CO [commanding officer] gave me some names. I spoke to you."

On July 1, 2008, a sergeant told his cops: "Be an asshole. They gonna do something, shine a light in their face. Inconvenience them. It saves trouble later on. Some of you with good activity are going to be moving up."

The following day, a precinct supervisor ordered cops to make an arrest, when in the past, a dispute might have been talked out. "The days of mediating between a perp and a store owner are over," a sergeant said on July 2. "If the guy is in the back with five sticks of deodorant, you gotta collar him," the sergeant said. "There's no more mediating."

The bosses also demanded stop and frisks, known as 250s for their official designation on NYPD forms. The pressure was so great, Schoolcraft repeatedly saw officers filling out fake stop and frisk forms for imaginary people. These were known as "ghost 250s." Because citizens were allowed to refuse to give their name, patrol officers could get away with omitting the identity of the person they stopped. The problem got so bad that summer that a lieutenant had to dress down officers for filing too many 250s without names. "We had ninety-six 250s, all refused," he says. "We can get some people refusing, but it can't be every 250 that you do."

Also that summer, Mauriello was on a campaign to clear the corners through quality-of-life arrests. He became a fixture in the afternoon roll calls. On July 15, he said, "They wise off, they fucking push you, I expect them handcuffed, all right?" He later added, "Anybody gets stopped and it's a summons-able offense, I want them handcuffed and brought into the precinct . . . zero tolerance."

He made a veiled threat to punish officers who didn't get their numbers. "I don't want to see anyone get hurt. This job is all about hurting. Someone has to go. Step on a landmine, someone has to get hurt."

He told them that he wanted block parties shut down after 8:30 p.m. "After 8:30, it's all on me and my officers, and we're undermanned," he said. "The good people go inside. The others stay outside."

"I'm getting rocked today," Mauriello said on another day. "Since the midnight [shift], I've got five fucking robberies already and burglary assaults.

So the game plan tonight is Operation Zero Tolerance. If they fuckin' break the law on the corner, I'm scooping them all up, putting them in the cells."

Schoolcraft continued to get poor evaluations. In September, his bosses wrote, he "does not meet activity standards. He has been in numerous meetings with the squad sergeant and the precinct commander concerning his low activity."

At the same time, Schoolcraft was picking up more and more evidence of unethical behavior on his recorder. During a September 12, 2008, roll call, a fellow cop told him that the commanders were downgrading robbery, a major crime, to petit larceny, a misdemeanor. "A lot of 61s, if it's a robbery, they'll make it a petty larceny. I saw a 61, at t/p/o [time and place of occurrence], civilian punched in the face, menaced with a gun, and his wallet was removed, and they wrote lost property."

The quota pressure continued unabated. On October 28, Mauriello told the cops he would change their tours if they didn't make their numbers. "If I hear about disgruntled people moaning about getting thrown off their tours, it is what it is. Mess up, bring heat on the precinct, you know what, I'll give you tough love, but it doesn't mean you can't work your way back into good graces and get back to the detail and platoon you want."

He added, "If you don't work and I get the same names back again, I'm moving you. You're going to go to another platoon. I'm done. I don't want to be embarrassed no more."

In the same roll call, a sergeant warned officers to make sure their appearance was within standards or else the inspections unit would come in and discipline them. "It keeps the hounds off," he said. "That includes smirks. One smirk cost the whole borough 13 CDs last week." (A CD is a Command Discipline, usually a light penalty of five vacation days for lesser misconduct.)

On the afternoon of Halloween that year, Mauriello was particularly aggressive about arresting anyone doing anything that might even come close to a crime. "Everybody goes. I don't care. You're on 120 Chauncey and they're popping champagne? Yoke 'em. Put them through the system. They got bandannas on, arrest them. Everybody goes tonight. They're underage? Fuck it."

He added, "You're on a foot post, fuck it. Take the first guy you got and lock them all up from 120 Chauncey. Boom. Bring 'em in. Log them. You're going to go back out and process it later on."

As the campaign went on into the winter of 2008, Mauriello seemed to be aware that there was some resentment in the community, but he justified the campaign by saying the "good people" were supportive. "Fuck 'em, I don't give a shit," he said on November 8, 2008. "They are going to come to a community council meeting, yell at me, whatever, I know the good people over there are happy we have officers there."

A lieutenant followed up, telling the cops to be more aggressive. "If they don't move, they are going to get out of control and think that they own the block. They don't own the block. We own the block. They might live there, but we own the block. We own the streets here."

All of Mauriello's work under the Damocles sword of CompStat paid off, for him. In October 2008, Kelly promoted him from captain to deputy inspector, based on his achieving a crime reduction of 9 percent, increasing the number of arrests and qualify-of-life summonses, and winning a unit citation. His relationships with community leaders were also lauded.

Meanwhile, Schoolcraft wasn't entirely happy with the quality of his recordings, and he bought a more sophisticated recorder. He spent $324.15 on an Olympus LS-10 Linear Recorder on Amazon.com and had it shipped to his home. His dossier on the precinct was getting thicker by the day.

Around that time, an aspiring screenwriter named Timothy Covell contacted the precinct to inquire about his complaint that he had been assaulted on October 23. Schoolcraft took the call. Covell complained that the officers seemed to discount his story. Schoolcraft asked him to supply a written account of the incident.

Covell faxed over a two-page description of what had happened on the evening in question. He said he was riding home on the J train, when four black teens got on at Marcy. The quartet left the train at the Myrtle stop, followed by Covell, who lived nearby. It was about 7:20 in the evening. Covell walked in the dark down Myrtle Avenue to Lewis, crossed the street, turned right on Pulaski, passed a bodega, and heard footsteps running toward him.

"I froze, and an instant later a male was on my back and a pair of arms was around my neck. My glasses flew off at the impact. I was hit in the face several times. I believe this was done by the male who grabbed me, while another male ran up past my right side and tore my side-bag from me. The strap snapped immediately. A male voice yelled, 'It's empty!' I was thrown to the ground, where I was punched and kicked by a number of people."

Covell screamed for help. One of his attackers tried to cover his mouth, and they struggled. People looked on at this without doing anything. While choking him, his attackers grabbed for his cell phone and wallet. Just to get them to stop, he pulled the items out of his pocket and handed them over. The quartet took off down Pulaski.

He walked home alone. He had dried blood on his nose, bloodied wrists, and blood soaking through the back of his T-shirt. Once home, he canceled his cards and emailed a friend to send police to his apartment. A few minutes later, two 81st Precinct police officers arrived. He gave his account of the incident, declining their offer to go to the hospital because he did not have health insurance.

"I was asked if I could come down to the precinct and try to identify the attackers," he wrote. "I responded that I could come down there, but I didn't think that I could actually identify anyone, because it was dark when I was attacked, and I didn't get a good look at anyone's face."

He wrote that one cop called it in, and a supervisor called back and they spoke for several minutes.

"Perhaps twenty minutes later, they called up on my intercom again," he wrote. "I went downstairs to find Officer Deck standing outside of his car. He informed me that, since I couldn't identify the people who had attacked me, his sergeant had the incident reported as 'lost property.' He apologized, saying, 'I know this sucks.' He then got back into his car, and I went back inside."

Schoolcraft learned from one of the officers that the supervisor, a lieutenant, told him, "We can't take this robbery." To Schoolcraft, this was sinister. Here was a regular person getting viciously assaulted and robbed while just walking home from the train, and the police officers ignored his attempts to file a crime complaint and instead marked it noncriminal and walked away. Here was a real-world example of how CompStat and the pressure from 1 Police Plaza led directly to an injured civilian being mistreated and criminals left on the street to commit other crimes.

"This kind of thing is occurring in every precinct in the city," said Marquez Claxton, the retired detective. "Another dodge is if the person who comes in doesn't have their ID, you don't take the report. Every precinct in the city has a crime analysis unit, and they call the victims back and try to get them to change their story. If you leave your door unlocked and you're burglarized, they'll call it lost property, or instead of burglary, it becomes trespass and a larceny.

"What you'll find is that in the current PD environment, the precinct commander has a lot more authority," he said. "Now you have precinct commanders challenging the detectives on classification. That's the mentality. There has to be an outside audit of the complaint reports to really get at the problem. If you give people a false sense of security, you create more victims."

Schoolcraft's activity report for November 2008 showed he was making an effort at the job. He took 36 radio runs, did 25 vertical patrols, and took 10 complaints. But he only wrote two parking tickets. The constant practice of pulling cops out of the precincts left him with just eight tours actually on patrol.

The drumbeat for low-level arrests continued. On November 23, 2008, he recorded: "If they're on a corner, make 'em move. If they don't want to move, lock 'em up. Done deal. You can always articulate [a charge] later." Here, the sergeant was literally telling cops to make a nuisance arrest of people standing on a corner, a public space, for refusing to move.

On December 5, Schoolcraft picked up yet another example of downgrading: A teen was attacked by a gang of thugs who tried to steal his videogame player. He took the report as an attempted robbery, but his sergeant reclassified it as misdemeanor assault. "Why didn't you call a supervisor over?" the sergeant asked. "We can't take another robbery."

In the December 8 roll call, Mauriello was extremely verbose, going on for ten minutes on various issues. "I'll say one thing. My legacy in this place, if it's another year, another week or whatever, is that I fucking, we fucking cleaned up Malcolm X, Bainbridge and Chauncey," he said, describing himself as "old school." "I'm an overachiever. I'm not an underachiever. Never will be. Never have. I'm an overachiever. Is that a curse? Yes. I expect everybody to at least try."

He excoriated officers who failed to write enough tickets for double-parking, running red lights, and disorderly conduct, and those who failed to stop and frisk enough people.

"I see eight fucking summonses for a 20-day period or a month," Mauriello said. "If you mess up, how the hell you want me to do the right thing by you? You come in, 5 parkers, 3 As, no Cs, and the only 250 you do is when I force you to do overtime? I mean it's a two-way street out here."

Later, he added, "In the end, I hate to say it, you need me more than I need you because I'm what separates the wolves from coming in here and chewing on your bones."

In the same roll call, a sergeant added, "When I tell you to get your activity up, it's for a reason because they are looking to move people, and he's serious.... There's people in here that may not be here next month. Just keep the hounds off."

In 2008, Schoolcraft worked 62 hours of overtime, did 619 radio runs and 171 vertical patrols, made no felony arrests, made 3 misdemeanor arrests, wrote 35 tickets, did 37 stop and frisks, took 81 complaints, and wrote 72 domestic incident reports. Between all the tours he was pulled away for other assignments, he worked just 88 days on patrol.

As Mauriello's career bloomed, Schoolcraft's career was rotting. In December 2008, Schoolcraft received the lowest rating of his career from his immediate supervisor, Raymond Stukes—2.5 out of 5, or below standards.

In total, Schoolcraft had written 34 summonses for the year, an average of less than 3 a month.

Stukes wanted Schoolcraft transferred. "P.O. Schoolcraft's poor activity is a direct result of his lack of innovativeness. He needs constant supervision. He performs his tasks idly. He is unwilling to change his approach to meeting the performance standards."

He added, "The performance exhibited by P.O. Schoolcraft is well below standard. He frequently disregards adherence to activity standards of a New York City police officer."

Mauriello agreed. "He has been counseled by both his squad supervisor and his platoon commander about his lack of drive. He has yet to show any improvement. I concur with the above evaluation," the precinct commander wrote.

If one happened to average the 28 individual rating categories in the evaluation, Schoolcraft should have received a 3.4. After all, he received a 4 in 16 of the 28 categories. And yet, in NYPD math, it averaged to a 2.5.

If it was not already completely clear, the rating signaled to Schoolcraft that his bosses were after his job. He was furious with the rating, refused to sign it, and sent notice that he would appeal. He had been thinking about leaving New York for another police department, possibly in Arizona or New Mexico, but the bad evaluation would pretty much kill that idea. The realization set in that he was stuck in a bad place, and he didn't know what to do.

CHAPTER 5

THE HUNTS POINT DIGRESSION

Right around the time that Schoolcraft was struggling with his commanders, a very similar thing was happening to an officer assigned to the 41st Precinct, which is in the high-crime Hunts Point section of the Bronx. His name was Adhyl Polanco, and he and Schoolcraft couldn't be more different—or more similar.

Polanco was born fifteen hundred miles from New York in a small, dilapidated town in the Dominican Republic called San Francisco de Macorís. As a boy, he recalls waiting outside the wooden two-bedroom shack where he lived for his father, Ramon Polanco, to return home. In 1986, Ramon had followed the timeworn course of many Dominicans. He had gone off to New York to make money and send it home to the family.

Adhyl was being raised by his mother, along with two sisters and a brother. Polanco said the town was home to many people who later went into the narcotics business, often in New York. Narco dollars built houses and paid for paved streets and office buildings in the town.

"We were very poor," he said. "This was when the drug dealers were in their prime. They would go to New York or somewhere in the U.S. and come back with millions of dollars. Some came back dead, including people in my family."

In 1990, after four years of hard work, Ramon Polanco finally had made enough money to bring his family to New York. They settled in their grandmother's cramped apartment in the upper Manhattan neighborhood of Washington Heights, a largely Dominican enclave that was rife with drugs, crime, and poverty. Ramon worked hard as a waiter and a bus boy.

"We had to walk through the drug dealers to get to school," Adhyl said. "There were three stash houses in the building. Everywhere you turned, there was crack—under the steps, in the alley. I saw a lot of shootings. I saw people shot, stabbed, people thrown off roofs. All of it was drug related. The thing with drug dealers is if they knew you lived there, they left you alone."

At the time, Washington Heights was the home turf for a number of extremely violent drug gangs—the most notorious of which was the Wild Cowboys, which were credited, or blamed, with at least 50 killings in those years. The fruits of San Francisco de Macorís were visible on the streets of Washington Heights.

At some point, living with seven other people became too much for his grandmother, and she ordered the Polancos to find another place to live. Meanwhile, the restaurant cut Roman's hours.

"She just didn't want to deal with all of us," Adhyl said.

Using a loan from a relative, Ramon Polanco found another apartment at 189 Audubon Avenue. But in order to get this place they couldn't really afford, he had to make what turned out to be a devil's bargain. Cheap apartments are such a premium in Manhattan that Ramon had to pay the current tenant $5,000 in cash so the tenant would turn over the lease to them. Ramon weighed the options. He had to decide whether to send his family home and deprive them of the decent schools and better chance in life, or take out a loan.

"He's deciding whether to send us back or go into debt and borrow money," Adhyl said. "Sending us back meant we wouldn't get the education we needed or learn English, which he wanted from us. He decided to do the deal, and borrowed money."

For Ramon, and for Adhyl, this was one of those important moments in life. Ramon Polanco borrowed the money from a fairly murky character, under the condition that he repay the debt in one year. This man returned not a year later, but in a week, and demanded the full amount. Ramon said he couldn't raise it. What could he do? He was supporting four children. The man replied by making Ramon an offer. All he had to do was watch a lobby and let them know if any cops show up. The man controlled an apartment in a nearby building that was being used to stash drugs.

Ramon Polanco, who had until then resisted the dark side of the street, had no choice but to agree. Thus he was drawn into the drug world, standing in the lobby of an apartment building as a lookout to warn the drug dealers above if the cops were coming. The atmosphere in his home turned tense and uncomfortable.

"That's when the house turned very frustrating," Adhyl said. "Mom and Dad were always fighting in the house. She would say, 'I don't want that money.' She knew where it was from. The kids knew about it. But for people who came from where he did, it was not a strange thing to do. He's not selling or dealing. He's making $300 to $400 a week to watch this apartment and pay off the loan."

A block away, someone tossed a bucket off of a roof and struck a police officer in the head, seriously injuring him. Two blocks away, a woman was robbed and thrown off of a fifth-floor balcony. There were three apartments in the building stashed with drugs. Kiko Garcia, a young drug dealer whose shooting death by a police officer touched off the three-day Washington Heights riots in 1992, was from the same Dominican town as the Polancos, and Adhyl went to school with his brother. During those riots, Polanco's mother came and grabbed him from the baseball field at Highbridge Park and locked him in the apartment.

In 1993, Ramon Polanco was arrested on a minor charge but was out in two days. Months later, while going back and forth to court, he met a more significant drug dealer who wanted to hire him because he had a reputation for honesty.

"He's making more money, and now he's watching an apartment with a cash and drug stash," Adhyl said. "One day, he's helping a guy load two or three kilos of cocaine into a van, and that's when he's arrested again."

The feds, it turned out, were watching the stash house and swept in on both men. Ramon posted $18,000 bail. The source of the leak turned out to be a young man who had been renting a room in the Polancos' apartment with his pregnant girlfriend.

"He had grown up calling my father 'Dad' and my mother 'Mom,'" Polanco said in an interview.

The feds wanted Ramon to take a plea that would put him in prison for six years. He couldn't handle the time. So, in 1996, Ramon fled back to the Dominican Republic. Polanco remembers the police coming to his house to search for him.

Back in the DR, Ramon disappeared into the communities he knew and lived in a little house that was falling apart. He was gone for three long years and finally returned, slipping back into the country and finding a job as a gardener in New Jersey.

Then one day, the feds came back and knocked on the door. The Polancos' former tenant, looking to cut a deal, had turned Ramon in, and he went to prison. "They wanted my dad to cooperate, and he refused, he said I have a family," Polanco said. "If I tell you guys anything, they're dead. He did five and a half years in a federal prison in North Carolina and was then deported."

Meanwhile, Adhyl had grown into a teenager, and he saw the course before him: either get sucked into the drug world, as many of his friends had, or take the alternate, straight-and-narrow path. He was attending George Washington High School, a massive public school with a notorious reputation and a few famous alums, including baseball great Manny Ramirez.

"There was prostitution on the third floor, a stash room on the fifth floor where they sold drugs, fighting and violence," Adhyl said. "Kids beating the teachers, the principal, 18- to 19-year-old kids in ninth grade, repeating the grade for four years. The gangs: Dominicans Don't Play, La Familia, Netas, Zulu Nation, Latin Kings."

He says some of his friends got professional baseball contracts, but he wasn't good enough to hope for such an outcome for himself. So, instead, he focused on work. He got a job as a janitor in the school. When he turned 18, the school hired him as a math tutor and then as a teaching assistant at elementary schools.

"In order for me to keep the job, I had to keep my grades up," Polanco said. "I had been working since I was 12 or 13 years old. It was the school that kept me out of trouble. Working from three to seven, eight, nine at night, a student in the school, and also working. I think that's what kept me away from everything else."

At 19, he met his future wife, Elizabeth. She was a young teacher. She encouraged him to go to college, and Polanco fell into a life of working and going to school at Technical College Institute, a vocational school. He would leave at six in the morning and not get home until midnight. It was around this time that he began considering a career with the NYPD. He needed 60 credits to qualify to take the academy exam.

"I had many friends dead or in jail because they turned to drugs," Adhyl said. "Coming from where we came from, we basically had three choices: drugs, the police, or working for the city. Two of my friends had become cops, beating the odds, and I thought I would try for it. I had never been summonsed or arrested as a teenager, and I thought I had a chance.

"I didn't like people who do wrong. I thought that being a cop, helping people out, wearing the uniform, especially coming where I come from where the odds weren't in my favor, I wanted to help people. But in the end, things were not like I thought they were."

Polanco applied to the police academy in 2000, when he had amassed the 60 college credits, but as often happens, his name was not initially called. In late 2001, he got the call, but by then the hiring numbers were reduced for that class, and he was out of luck again.

He used his work money to send cash to his dad in the DR and helped him find a home. He continued to work in the schools and picked up security gigs as well. About two years later, he went through the process again.

Then, during a visit to the DR, Polanco was injured in a car accident, and that delayed him again. Then on July 11, 2005, he was finally hired as a police officer.

He took his turn in the academy on 21st Street. "They didn't really teach me much in there," he said. "The floor was nasty and filthy, so bad that you couldn't put your feet down on it because you would get an infection. There were a bunch of rats. There were 2,300 of us, no room for anything. Everyone screaming at you. Some of them kept it real, some said whatever we learned was bullshit. They were more worried about our shoes not being tied correctly, our hat not straight enough. I learned nothing there that prepared me for the outside."

He graduated from the academy in January 2006. Mayor Bloomberg and a dean from Columbia University gave speeches. "I was extremely proud; it was a lot to go through," Polanco said, remembered the date with some fondness. "It was like a dream come true. And I had a newborn baby on top of it."

Like Schoolcraft before him, Polanco was sent from his academy graduation into Operation Impact, this time in the 46th Precinct, which usually had the highest crime in the Bronx. He was one of 100 cops sent there from the academy.

"There were already 400 cops in the precinct, and our job was to go out, 6 a.m. to 2 p.m., and write summonses and arrest whatever moved," Polanco said. "We were stepping on each other to write summonses, parking, urinating, drinking. Trespassing was a big arrest."

The pressure was constant. "The numbers were important," he said. "There was a sergeant over me, and it was all about activity and numbers. One day, he sent me and my partner to some building on Andrews Avenue in the Bronx where tenants were complaining about a lot of drug activity in the building. Go check it out, they said. I stepped into the building. I probably arrested 30 to 40 people in the month.

"There was a big stash house on the third floor, they kept coming by the dozen. I remember the address: 1665 Andrews Avenue. I would go to the second floor and they would whistle. They would get a big surprise.... We arrested them for trespassing. It was very easy. I was never a superstar, I wasn't there to clean up the Bronx. I remember a veteran officer told me, 'This street's been filthy since before you were born, and it will be filthy after you're gone.' I was there to do my job, to be a cop. We were shot at. We were running every night. We were always running. I was there to be a police officer. I wasn't there to put hands on someone."

In 2006, just as Polanco was settling in at the 46th Precinct, the man who had informed on his father to put him in prison was arrested again. The suspect fled to the DR and sought out Ramon Polanco. According to Adhyl, the suspect was concerned that Ramon had information that could put him in prison for a long time. He met him at a nightclub, got him drunk, lured him outside, and shot him five times. Ramon Polanco, who had devoted his life to his family but entered the narcotics world out of necessity, died there on that street corner.

"My father was my everything, even though he made a lot of bad choices, but he also made the ultimate sacrifice," Polanco said. "I had a very close relationship with him. I was extremely depressed. I sought department help for that. I was very, very depressed, and decided to try to track down this guy."

By then, Polanco was a police officer in the 41st Precinct in Hunts Point, a desperately poor neighborhood in the South Bronx, stricken with hookers and drugs and crisscrossed with highway overpasses and industrial yards. He referred to it as "the poorest square mile in the country."

The area was remote, and that made it perfect for conducting illicit deals and dumping bodies.

He used his new skills to go after the man who killed his father. His commanding officer in the 41st Precinct gave him the time to do it. "I took time off from PD to investigate my father's homicide," he said. "That was in 2008. I started calling Interpol, and I was trying to find out where he was, the extradition stuff. They were mean, they called police headquarters, saying there's a cop calling and harassing us."

Polanco believed there were witnesses to the killing and went to the Dominican Republic and searched for his father's killer for two months.

"I was finally able to track him down with the help of a DEA [Drug Enforcement Agency] agent," Adhyl said. "He put me in touch with a prosecutor, and he got the man to show up at a court hearing. He thought it was for another case. They arrested him and brought him back to the U.S."

U.S. authorities opted to convict the man on drug charges, rather than return him to the DR on the murder charge where, according to Adhyl, the corrupt legal system might have released him. "They feared if they sent him back to the DR, he would buy his way out of the case," Polanco said.

By 2009, like Schoolcraft's, Polanco's view of policing had evolved. The years of pressure from commanders, particularly involving stop and frisk and ticket quotas, had begun to get to him. He found himself essentially being forced to constantly stop young African American and Hispanic men over and over, many of them high school kids, people who reminded him of himself when he was their age. Very often, he saw, these youths were doing nothing suspicious, and it seemed utterly pointless and insulting to do what he saw as nothing more than harassment. He saw illegal searches, illegal stops, putting phony charges on people, putting them through the system.

"We'd make up a bullshit reason to justify the stop, when, most of the time, we had no reason to justify the stop," he said. "We were told to say they 'fit the description.' But that just meant you were Spanish or black. It was just for the quotas."

CompStat was the reason: "If last year we had 300 UF-250s, that means this year we have to match that number," he said. "Otherwise you will be failing. You will be under, and if you have 7 major crimes, let's say you had 20 major crimes during that time, you've got to make sure that yours stays under 20, because if it goes above, you'll get in trouble."

He spoke to his partner about the problem. "Our concern was if we keep arresting these kids for no reason, if we keep searching them for no reason, we are destroying their future," he said. "Tomorrow these kids won't be able to go to school, tomorrow these kids won't be able to apply for a job. If they are criminals, we have no sympathy for criminals, but if they're not criminals, they should not be treated as criminals."

One of the pressure techniques was called "driving a supervisor." "You will be taken off your duties as a patrol officer and you're going to be on the street looking for someone to arrest at all costs," he said. "Anybody who does any little thing, your job is to arrest him and bring him back and the supervisor is there to make sure that you do it. Only the people that didn't meet the quota will drive a supervisor," meaning that precinct bosses would pair an underperforming officer with a supervisor, and the supervisor would drive the precinct and force him to write tickets.

Polanco also objected to the constant pressure for summonses. On many tours, he would be sent to perform what was called directed ticket writing. He and another cop would set up at an intersection and write tickets, the point being to get the precinct numbers up, rather than to enforce the traffic laws. His supervisors didn't want him to use his discretion, to give warnings. They just wanted the numbers.

"I did not become a cop to be harassing people in the street," he said. "You end up summonsing innocent people. They don't go to court, and the next time you stop them, they have a warrant and have to go to jail."

"They want you to summons people for disorderly conduct, when they aren't doing anything," he said. "If the summonses are down for the month, they rush to get them up, so they'll stick you in a checkpoint just for the purpose of getting 10 summonses. What happens when you don't witness anything illegal, but still have to hit your quota?"

He said it was a common practice in the precinct for officers to be ordered to make arrests when they hadn't actually seen the misconduct: "One time, I was ordered to give a guy a summons for no dog license, but the problem was I didn't see a dog," he said.

He looked on with disgust as supervisors ordered officers to downgrade crime complaints and refuse to take complaints from civilians in order to manipulate crime statistics. "It happened all the time," he said. "The reason was CompStat. They know what they are going to be asked for in CompStat, and they have to have a lower number—but not too low."

The effect of this approach is that it strained relations with the community, he said. "A lot of the time, I would apologize," he said. "They are frustrated. They don't trust the police. They feel we're here to harass them."

In one incident, he said, he responded to a call of a burglary in a city-owned apartment. When he arrived, he noted that a window had been broken, and the occupant said cash and a video game had been stolen. He called his sergeant and a lieutenant. When the lieutenant arrived, he wondered skeptically how a guy who lived in public housing could own a 40-inch flat-screen television. He ordered Polanco and his partner to leave the scene. Even though the victim wanted a report taken, the lieutenant closed the case as "unfounded."

In a second incident, an alleged burglary, the door had been pushed in. The victim claimed that $600 in cash and some jewelry had been stolen. But a sergeant arrived at the scene and ordered Polanco to take a report for something called "unlawful eviction."

"He said, 'Don't mention the money and jewelry in the report,'" Polanco said. "He told me that the numbers were high that week. They look at the numbers weekly and compare them to the same week the previous year. What they want is to show a decline in the numbers, but not too low, because it will be harder the next year to show a decline."

In a third incident, Polanco responded to a call of shots fired. A bullet had gone through a vehicle window, but he was ordered to take the report as reckless endangerment. "I was told to write that a 'sharp object' went through the glass," he said. "They didn't have the perp, and it would look bad for the precinct taking the report for attempted murder."

Polanco said precinct supervisors routinely called crime victims back to try to persuade them to withdraw their report or change their account in some way that would allow the incident to be reclassified as a lesser crime: "They'll say, 'You know we're not getting anything back on this,' or 'Do you really want to make the report?'" he said.

If a robbery victim refused to return immediately to the precinct to speak to detectives, cops were told not to take the report, Polanco said. "If the victim couldn't identify anyone from mug shots, they would tell them they would follow up, but they wouldn't take a report," he said. "A lot of the time, they were Mexican or Chinese delivery people who don't really know how the system works." The sergeants in the crime analysis unit would call cops on the carpet to get them to explain why they took a given report, according to Polanco. There was a special bin for complaints involving the seven major crime categories, and the following day, the complaints would be reviewed and "edited."

There were also a couple of arrests that bothered Polanco. In one case, a sergeant ordered the arrest of a young man for having a warrant for an open container, even though he had been slashed across the back—a wound that required 40 stitches to close. In another case, a man who had been shot in the leg was arrested and taken to the hospital in handcuffs because he had a prior warrant on a minor charge.

Polanco started wearing a tape recorder in August 2009 to capture some of the practices he witnessed. "It was the only way to prove what was going on," he said.

In one recording, a sergeant said, "I spoke to the commanding officer for about an hour and a half. . . . They want 20 (summonses) and 1 (arrest). Next week you could be at 25 and 1, you could be at 35 and 1 and guess what?

Until you decide to quit this job and become a Pizza Hut delivery man, this is what you're going to be doing."

He taped another supervisor saying, "Things are not going to get any better, it's going to get a lot worse. If you think 1 and 20 is breaking your balls, guess what you are going to be doing? You're going to be doing a lot more, a lot more than what you think."

A third: "It's really non-negotiable 'cause if you don't do it now, I'm gonna have you work with the boss to make sure it happens."

"Twenty [summonses] and one [arrest, the monthly quota]—make sure you take care of what you gotta take care of," a supervisor told cops in one of Polanco's tapes.

When he made an issue of the quotas, another supervisor told him, "I don't give a shit. You need to take care of your business, feel me? As a cop to a cop, make sure you take care of what you gotta take care of."

Polanco also recorded two police union delegates heaping on the quota pressure. In one conversation, a PBA delegate told Polanco, "Twenty and one is what the union wants. . . . This is what the job is coming down to."

Later, another delegate told cops in a roll call, "Things are not going to get any better. It is going to get a lot worse. If you think getting 1 and 20 is breaking your balls, guess what you're going to be doing? You're going to be doing a lot more. A lot more than what you think. This was all dealt with in the last contract."

This delegate was later heard to say, "This is not coming from me—this is coming from higher up. The unions agreed on it. We're unionized here. This is what we pushed through. And let's be smart about it. You gotta be smart about it."

"Play the fucking game," a delegate said on another tape.

Those statements embarrassed the union, which had long railed against quotas, and at least one of the delegates was removed from his post.

When Polanco went to a sergeant to complaint about quotas, the sergeant told him, "It's like fighting a current. If you stick your head out there, make sure. They'll drown you."

In October 2009, Polanco contacted Internal Affairs to report the quota pressure. "I went to Internal Affairs because I grew up in Washington

Heights, and I know what it's like to sit in the park. . . . I was seeing an awful lot of people, kids, getting arrested for no other reason than being number for CompStat," he said in a deposition in *Floyd v. City of New York*, a lawsuit that challenged the city's stop and frisk campaign.

His bosses soon found out. "My supervisors knew I had gone to IAB [Internal Affairs Bureau]," he said. "They were asking me, why did I go to IAB?"

There was a larger conflict coming with his commanders. Polanco could feel it. And on December 13, 2009, that conflict came. On that particular day, he and his partner had been ordered once again to stand at an intersection and write tickets to increase the precinct's summons numbers. His partner fell ill as the result of a heart condition, and Polanco called an ambulance.

His lieutenant, a man with whom Polanco had had words previously, responded and arrived at the scene. As the ambulance prepared to transport his partner to the hospital, Polanco asked if he could accompany him. The lieutenant refused and ordered Polanco to remain on post and keep writing summonses. Polanco lost his temper and argued with the lieutenant.

The lieutenant grabbed him. Polanco pushed him away. The lieutenant ordered him suspended and demanded his gun and shield. Polanco refused, because he didn't feel safe giving his gun to someone who had pushed him. The lieutenant told Emergency Services that Polanco was to be treated as an "emotionally disturbed" person—the same label that Schoolcraft would later be tarred with.

He believed his commanders engineered the whole thing to prevent him from speaking out. For the next three years, Polanco drove to the Internal Affairs offices on Hudson Street from Rockland County, where he lived with his wife and three children, signed in, and drove home. But he didn't remain silent. He gave several interviews, spoke at a forum on NYPD quotas, and gave a deposition to the Center for Constitutional Rights for their stop and frisk lawsuit.

In July 2011, the NYPD hit him with more charges, claiming that he filed out two criminal court summonses for misconduct he didn't observe. The irony of the charge was that he himself had reported that to Internal Affairs.

As of March 2013, Polanco was still in limbo. His job status had been changed from suspended to modified, and he was working in VIPER, a unit where cops just sit at video monitors linked to security cameras and watch for their full tour.

"It took a lot of courage to do what I did," Polanco said.

CHAPTER 6

"YOU GOTTA PAY THE RENT"

The new year, 2009, began with Schoolcraft still upset about the low rating. That January he decided to hire a lawyer to help him appeal the evaluation—a step that was fairly unusual in the NYPD and likely to cause more problems for him than it would solve.

Indeed, on the day after he gave notice that he would file an appeal, a sign appeared on his locker that read, "If you don't like your job, then maybe you should get another job." He never found out who placed it there, but the message was clear.

This sort of anonymous message was not an uncommon method of intimidation. On another occasion, for example, someone posted a fake thank-you note written by a perp on the locker of another officer. The note read, "Thanks to him, I'm still on the street selling my drugs and holding my gun. PO Edouard was too busy talking shit to some chick. Thanks to him, I'll be getting some head."

At any rate, Schoolcraft decided not to go outside the precinct to complain. And his tape recorder kept rolling, tour after tour. The theme was often "You gotta pay the rent."

Mauriello and the other precinct bosses were irritated by the latest edict from the borough command, which, in addition to sending commanders downtown for CompStat, was holding its own mini-CompStat meetings. The strategy was being taken to ridiculous levels. And they weren't just reviewing crime, they were also reviewing the number of tickets each officer wrote and the number of days they called in sick. A boss called it "account-ability" on January 13.

"Robbery spikes, crime spikes, on and on and on," a sergeant later groused. "It's a lot of horseshit I gotta sit through, but it's accountability, alright?"

Mauriello continued to harangue the troops, and on January 27, he almost seemed to be speaking directly to Schoolcraft. "Be a cop, do your job," he said. "You got a problem with how I roll? My style? Too fucking bad."

On January 28, Mauriello visited the roll call again, calling for more stop and frisks. "Listen, if it's micromanaging, it's micromanaging," he said. "Just do your job."

Lieutenant De La Fuente in the same roll call then told the cops that Michael Scagnelli, a top-ranking chief, was closely questioning the command in CompStat meetings about the numbers of traffic tickets they wrote. "He says, 'How many superstars and how many losers do you have?'" he said. "And then he goes down and says, 'How many summonses does your squad write?' I want everyone to step up and be accountable and work. Don't get caught out there."

De La Fuente then mentioned the patrol borough commander, Marino, who was apparently examining the "activity" of every cop in the ten precincts he oversaw. "He's taking this very seriously, looking at everyone's evalua-tions," he said. "And he's yelling at every CO [commanding officer] about 'who gave this guy points, or this girl's no good.'"

Points means evaluation points. The significance of these two statements was that top-ranking chiefs at the thin-air end of the NYPD pyramid were reaching down from Ararat and literally looking at the "productivity" of individual police officers in a way that was rare prior to CompStat.

De La Fuente said the cops should be able to hit their numbers targets. "I told you guys last month, they are looking at these numbers and people are going to get moved," he said. "It ain't about losing your job. They can make your job real uncomfortable and we all know what that means."

He cited the declining number of officers in the department. "A lot of people are leaving the job," he said. "They aren't getting new recruits. Patrol is not getting new people. It's more accountability, it's less people. They got this catch phrase, 'do more with less,' right. And they're looking at the numbers."

He said the top bosses were pressuring the precinct commander, who was pressuring his supervisors, who then had to pressure the cops.

"Unfortunately, at this level in your career, you're on the lowest level, so you're going to get some orders that you may not like," he said. "You're gonna get instructions. You're gonna get disciplinary action. You gotta just pick up your work. I don't wanna get my ass chewed out, in straight words. I'm sick of getting yelled at."

Here again, the threat was clear: Get your numbers or get punished. And it was clear that the pressure was also on the mid-level supervisors. Though the NYPD would stubbornly deny the existence of quotas, these remarks made by a typical lieutenant in a typical precinct seem to bear out what was really happening. Schoolcraft felt like these words, said to the group, were directed at him.

On February 3, 2009, he was written up for arriving 47 minutes late to court and for improperly wearing jeans and sneakers in court. One of the ways the NYPD controlled its officers was adherence to dozens of tiny rules about appearance in the Patrol Guide. An inspections unit spent all of its time roaming the precincts, looking for minor rule violations and handing out discipline.

"Inspections," a sergeant said with evident disgust. "They pull you over like a perp and you know it's disrespectful to us, but this is what they're doing. So inspections is not really our friend. Let's leave it at that."

On one particular day, a sergeant spent an entire roll call criticizing his officers for not having whistle holders for their whistles. "That's unacceptable," he bellowed. "When I fall down the mine shaft, I'm the only one that's going to be able to call for help. The rest of you are going to have to fire off your gun, and they'll give you a CD for that."

On February 20, Schoolcraft was called to meet with Lieutenant Rafael Mascol to arrange a hearing with Mauriello about his decision to appeal the low evaluation in house. In this conversation, Mascol basically admitted what Schoolcraft had long suspected—that the whole system was completely subjective.

Mascol shuffled papers until he found a document he was looking for, and then he talked about the reality behind the evaluation system, which rated officers from a low of 1 to a high of 5.

"Nobody in this department get a 5, nobody gets a 4.5," Mascol said. "If anybody read the standards of what a 5 is, nobody could ever get it. I have no time to get to the sergeants to tell them to evaluate their personnel correctly. I'm talking about what a 4 is, what a 4.5, what a 5 is. Because most police officers are just basically meeting standards. They are basically doing what they are told to do. Very few police officers are actually going above and beyond the recommended minimum of competence, you know? Those get a 4. For the most part, most police officers are just meeting standards."

Another cop wandered by and asked, "Hey, what's going on with you, Chuck?" The unflattering nickname for Adrian referred to the horror movie *Chucky*. Schoolcraft merely chuckled, going along with the joke.

Mascol then sang along with a line from a song on his radio, "I can't get enough of your love," and added, "I was talking with someone about evaluating personnel appropriately by the department standards of what each thing should be and what each person should qualify for, and we're not even doing it.

"Unfortunately, if we like you, you get a certain thing, if we don't like you, you get a certain thing as opposed to what the department requires in the performance standards. I have no time to change the entire department mind unfortunately."

Schoolcraft listened quietly. Then Mascol told him he needed to "improve his activity."

"How do I improve it?" Schoolcraft asked.

"Maybe answer more radio runs, do more summonses, might write some more reports and stuff, be more proactive out there," Mascol replied. "If you have trouble seeing activity, maybe we can put you with an officer with high activity who could point it out to you."

Schoolcraft decided not to sign the document until he spoke to his lawyer.

Then, another officer wandered by and asked, "What's going on, Chucky?"

"Same old, same old," Schoolcraft replied.

Mascol's message was clear: Go along with the program.

His memo book provides a clipped sense of what Schoolcraft was doing during work hours in this period. On February 22, 2009, he started at 3 p.m. and spent the next eight hours babysitting a prisoner at Brooklyn Central Booking, until the prisoner was released by a judge. He then returned to the precinct and was ordered to take overtime and sent to man the SkyWatch tower at Gates and Garvey. At 2:30 a.m., nearly 12 hours after he started his shift, he wrote in his memo book that he had been "released from forced OT."

Three days later, he was called to meet with Mauriello about the appeal of his evaluation just before the start of his shift. Prior to the meeting, Schoolcraft talked with his PBA delegate, Raymond Gonzalez, who made a reference to statistics-obsessed Deputy Chief Michael Marino—and a disciplinary case against him. The appeal of the evaluation had been referred to Marino for assessment.

"Fucking steroid Marino is going to look at it, he's going to look at the evaluation, he's going to pull all your activity, and he's going to say what are you fucking kidding me? He's going to see the same. Knowing him, he's going to talk a lot of shit. What would you like to see be done?"

"Change this. The officer has been trained," Schoolcraft said. "I'd like to see documentation of it. I'll admit it's been whispered in my ear that I need to write more summonses. But there's nothing documented."

"This is based all on activity."

"If you have Joe Schmo who comes in with a box of donuts every month, then that's what they're going to rate you on," Gonzalez said. "Everyone here has a job to do. Well, let's see what they want to do," Gonzalez said.

"There's no possible way that they can say I'm not doing anything," Schoolcraft said. "I'm not going to summons a guy for open container for picking cans out of a trash can."

Schoolcraft and Gonzalez went into Mauriello's office for the meeting. Eventually six bosses joined them: Captain Lauterborn, Lieutenant De La Fuente, Lieutenant Mascol, Sergeant Stukes, Sergeant Weiss, and Sergeant Cox. Most of the meeting was taken up by the bosses trying to get Schoolcraft to agree to raise his activity and wondering why he had become inactive. Schoolcraft stubbornly resisted.

Schoolcraft asked, "What's the standard?"

"If you're out there on the street, we gotta see something," Mauriello said. "I'm not here to hurt anybody. But you can't put [these low numbers] down. Guys in your squad did something and you did nothing. Everybody has to do something. The days of 10,000 extra cops are gone. We're bare bones. They want everybody to get in the game."

"I'm contesting that I'm seeing something and not doing anything," Schoolcraft said. "I've taken action on anything I've observed, whether a summons, an arrest, or a warn and admonish."

"The last thing he wants is this to go to Marino," another boss said. "You're likely to get kicked out of the command and work in another shithole."

"No one here is looking to hurt you," Mauriello said. "The people in the community want active cops. Our job is to make sure Bed-Stuy is safe."

Mauriello added, "I've been a fighter all my life, and I've been knocked out numerous times on this job. As a captain, I thought I was never going to get a command. I busted my ass. You got a body blow. Now you're going to get up off the canvas and fight. When I'm gone, they are going to miss me in the place, all the haters. I never hurt anybody on this job. I didn't even want to have this conversation."

Mauriello went on, "With these numbers, Marino will go through the roof. His head will come through the top of Wilson Avenue. He's going to call me and ask me what the fuck was I doing six months ago that I didn't put you on paper. We go to CompStat and they want names. They already have the numbers in their computer at headquarters."

Schoolcraft then angered Mauriello by insisting on appealing and noting that he was going to get a lawyer.

Mauriello said, "When you came in here through the door, you should have said I have a lawyer and I'm gonna do what I gotta do, instead of wasting 45 minutes of us trying to talk to you and show you the results, and this is the way you are going to go out, so you know what, I tried."

"I appreciate your assistance," Schoolcraft said sarcastically.

"That's for when I get the lawsuit, you can spell my name right," the precinct commander said.

Schoolcraft said, "I'm not going to sue anyone."

Schoolcraft left the meeting feeling he had been ambushed, in an attempt to intimidate him to drop his appeal and shut up.

Later, Stukes documented the meeting, and his frustration with Schoolcraft was almost pungent. "PO Schoolcraft was counseled in regards to his low activity and the annual evaluation. He was instructed in the proper performance of his duties in the 81st Precinct and was given the opportunity to find a way to enhance his activity on a steady basis, at which time PO Schoolcraft refused any help!" (The exclamation point was Stukes's.)

Later that night, their words still ringing in his ears, Schoolcraft helped a guy who needed an ambulance, served family court papers, and responded to a call of a blocked driveway and several other calls. He got home around 1 a.m.

On February 27, he wrote his own appeal of the evaluation, noting that the Patrol Guide "makes no reference to activity levels," but instead the evaluation was based on bias against him and used other factors besides performance. He also accused Mauriello and Sergeant Stukes of falsifying documentation. He went on to ask for records, including a calculation of the "actual number of hours that Schoolcraft is available for enforcement duty." This was a shot at the fact that cops were constantly being pulled away from enforcement for various special duties.

One again has to pause and consider this. No officer, at least in the NYPD, did this kind of thing, talking back to the bosses, accusing them of falsifying documentation.

And the screws continued to turn. On March 1, in a monthly activity report, Stukes wrote that Schoolcraft's work was "unacceptable by NYPD standards." Mauriello chimed in, "Unacceptable."

A week later, Adrian's lawyer, James Brown, sent a formal appeal of the 2008 evaluation to Mauriello. In a letter, Brown argued that the evaluation was wrongly calculated and pointed out that it noted he was good at interacting with the community.

"His overall evaluation fails to correspond to his evident accomplishments as reflected in his strong ratings and the above praise," Brown wrote.

The letter charged that the evaluation was based on Schoolcraft's "activity," or numbers, and pointed out he had been given no set target for activity. Of course, it would be illegal for his bosses to start setting performance numbers, so they would be leery of doing that, but they were doing everything else short of it.

On the evening of March 13, 2009, Schoolcraft was assigned to a foot post on Reid and Bainbridge. While he was talking with another officer,

Sergeant Weiss approached him, according to his memo book, and accused him of being off post.

When Schoolcraft disagreed, Weiss said, "You're being a wise ass right now. You're off post because you're inside a building talking to PO Chan."

Almost tongue in cheek, Schoolcraft wrote in his memo book, "Sgt. Weiss wouldn't elaborate on the boundaries of my post when asked. Sgt. Weiss responds with a smirk."

Weiss then said, "You're getting a CD for being off post and Chan for unnecessary conversation, and then ordered me back on my post."

Later in the evening, Weiss took Schoolcraft's memo book, read the entries, and lost his temper at the account Schoolcraft had placed in it.

From Schoolcraft's notes: "After reading said copy, Sgt. Weiss lost control yelling while berating and belittling me in front of the 81 desk surrounded by multiple police officers because I disputed his charges that I was off post. Weiss' public tantrum was not only unprofessional and embarrassing to himself and the NYPD but conduct unbecoming a New York City police sergeant."

Of course, it was completely out of bounds for a police officer to write critically of a boss in his memo book, which is an official document. And one might think that Schoolcraft was just amusing himself. Far from it. He took his responsibility to document events on his tour seriously. But it didn't help him with his bosses.

The taking of the memo book meant that from March 13 on, the command was aware that Schoolcraft was documenting events in the precinct that didn't make his bosses look good.

On March 16, it happened again. This time Lieutenant Caughey and Sergeant Weiss found Schoolcraft off post because he'd left his post to urinate. Once again, they took his memo book and examined it, and told him they would have to watch him more closely. Schoolcraft felt he was being harassed, and so he went on his police radio and demanded that the duty captain respond to his location. A radio call of this sort was usually only used for a major incident, and it caused a huge reaction on the other end.

"The radio went crazy," Schoolcraft recalled. "In my activity log, I was documenting the retaliation, and they were punishing guys [other officers] I talked to. They were building a paper trail."

Schoolcraft claimed he was later told by another police officer that a sergeant was saying he would have to have Adrian "psyched," which meant to get him labeled a psychiatric case.

The responding captain, Theodore Lauterborn, arrived and angrily ordered Schoolcraft back to the precinct. At the time second in command to Mauriello, Lauterborn also served as a duty captain for the entire Brooklyn North Command. His personnel records contained only minor black marks. He was cleared of two missing property cases, two excessive force cases, and several other minor claims of misconduct, the record shows.

When Lauterborn first arrived at the precinct in July 2008, he later told investigators, he viewed Schoolcraft as "active" and "an overall nice guy." Over time, however, he began to believe his productivity and general disposition worsened, though there was no indication he thought Schoolcraft had any emotional issues.

Back at the station house, Lauterborn brought him into his office. What followed was a rare dialogue between two men who, viewed most favorably, had completely different ideas about policing: a commander demanding numbers, and a street officer resisting that pressure. Lauterborn thought Schoolcraft wasn't working hard enough, and Schoolcraft thought he had been retaliated against for doing things his own way.

Schoolcraft was wearing his recorder and can be heard saying at the outset, "I just feel my safety and the public's safety is being compromised because of the acts of retaliation. I assume it's because I appealed my evaluation, in fact I know it is."

"Today Lt. Caughey pulled up, asked me where I was, I was in the restroom, and takes my memo book," Schoolcraft added. "Yesterday, Officer Chan got written up just for talking to me, and I want to report it."

Lauterborn replied, referring to the February 25 meeting, "We told you when we left here, there's going to be a lot more supervision out there. People want to know what you're doing out there.... You don't call for a duty captain who doesn't know what's going on. He's running around doing 30 other things."

Schoolcraft replied, "I feel my safety and the public's safety is being compromised by the way they are behaving. I feel that other officers get in trouble because of me. I'm not working in a tire factory. I'm a police officer."

"Are you? Are you? Are you? Are you?"

"I'm a police officer, sir," Schoolcraft replied.

Lauterborn told him every time he went to the bathroom, he had to write in his memo book.

Schoolcraft, having not been treated this way before in his career, said, "For seven years, haven't had to do that."

Lauterborn replied that since his activity was down, he was getting treated this way. "For seven years, you probably weren't subject to that because no one would bother you. You were doing a good job."

"So they are bothering me now?" Schoolcraft asked.

"No we have to pay closer attention to what you're doing," the captain replied.

Schoolcraft tried to get Lauterborn to specify exactly what he was being evaluated on, but Lauterborn wouldn't do it. The captain told him that Mauriello was constantly watching each cop's activity.

"Mauriello is a fanatic about this," he said. "He is fanatically looking at what people do every single day. You want to warn and admonish everybody that's out there [rather than ticketing or arresting them]? You want to be Mr. Community? Is that what you're doing?"

"I wasn't aware I was doing anything," Schoolcraft said.

(In his subsequent notes on this conversation, Schoolcraft wrote that when he would stop motorists for not wearing their seat belts, and they had valid insurance and a valid driver's license, he would make them put on their seat belt, warn them, and let them go without a ticket. "That was driving them nuts," he wrote. "There is no official way of policing.")

Lauterborn continued, "My question to you is: Is this getting through to you? Do you understand where this office is coming from? Explain from your point of view."

"I'm out there. I don't make things happen. If something happens, I correct it. I deal with it."

"So tell me, from Adrian's point of view, you're saying you don't create anything," Lauterborn said. "When it comes to you, you address it. That's what you do. So PO Schoolcraft will not go out there, and if there are a bunch of kids sitting on a stoop in front of 229 Bainbridge, 187 Howard, you saw them sitting there, you won't stop and question them?"

"I didn't say I seen anything. I said I wouldn't going to create anything."

"What do you mean?" Lauterborn asked.

"It's a common practice here by other officers to fake 250s, or there are fake summonses being handed in, because they can't keep up with the numbers that the supervisors want," Schoolcraft said. "It's well known. I don't know if the supervisors know it. Even Inspector Mauriello brought it up in in a roll call. He said stop doing it."

(In his notes, Schoolcraft wrote that with stop and frisks for 90 percent of robberies, "It's not the guy. Just grabbing a body. Guys fake 250's more than anything else.")

Lauterborn denied he had ever heard of that practice. He asked, "Are you going to question them, and if they refuse to answer, keep walking even if those people on the stoop say 'Fuck you'?"

"That's how it usually happens," Schoolcraft said.

"Are you going to create something there?" Lauterborn asked. "I'm going to tell you if that motherfucker told me to fuck myself, yeah, is he going in handcuffs, yeah, cause he shouldn't talk to anybody like that. If you let that go because there's no violation, because he didn't break a law, then I feel bad for you. Because then you have a tough job, and maybe you should find something else to do. Do you call that creating something? Or do you call that a matter of keeping the respect because they'll step all over you when they see you out there, and not only you, but the next person in blue?"

Schoolcraft just said, "I want my activity log back."

Lauterborn went back to hammering away on the numbers. "At one time, you were a police officer and now you're not.... We want to help you. We don't want to see you drop off. You got a long road ahead of you especially because of this. Eyes and ears are out there. The Boogie Man is around. Cross your t's and dot your i's and make it all look nicey-nice. People will move on. You want to be a cop?"

"Yes."

Lauterborn asked, "Do you want to take the promotion test for sergeant?"

Schoolcraft shook his head. "The only supervisors I know are the ones here."

"Are you coming in here miserable every day?"

"Most of the time."

"Do you want to change precincts?"

"I don't know how far this is going to go. I don't want to change precincts. I feel I can do the job anywhere."

"You don't want to come to a place where you feel a pit in your stomach. You worked hard here at one point, right?"

"I just became aware the other day that I wasn't," Schoolcraft said.

In a subsequent interview, Lauterborn told Internal Affairs investigators that Schoolcraft went into a tirade that the captain and 81st Precinct officers were conspiring against him. However, the recording indicates there was no "tirade." Schoolcraft was calm and polite throughout the conversation.

On March 27, Schoolcraft and a fellow officer patrolling a sector in the neighborhood together held a remarkable conversation about the extent of crime downgrading in the precinct, the extent to which commanders would go to come up with ways to shit-can crime reports, the micromanaging and the hurdles cops would have to climb over just to get routine crime reports accepted by their bosses.

"One day I had three GLAs (auto thefts) in a row, and they said have the sector disregard," the other officer said. "They want special ops. Then he tells one of the victims at a GLA I was at, 'Maybe karma took your car.'"

"Karma? Who?" Adrian asked.

"Mauriello," came the reply. "He's like, 'Come over here, what do you mean the car was missing?' The guy said, 'I parked it there last night. I woke up today and it was gone.' He says, 'You ever been arrested before?' The guy says, 'Yeah.' I think he did six or eight years for drug and gun possession. So Mauriello says, 'You think karma woke up this morning and took your car?' He's like, 'No, no, I think it was stolen.'"

"So he didn't take the report because he's a felon?"

"Basically."

"That sucks," Adrian said.

"I'm looking at him and I say I don't really feel great about not taking the report, at least not transmitting the alarm," the cop said. "He's like, 'Alright,

alright, take it for unauthorized use. Give it to the lieutenant to see what you are going to put in the story.' So I tell the lieutenant how can we make this unauthorized use. He just looked at me."

To this, Adrian replied with an anecdote of his own. "I was with Santana. This kid got jacked on Quincy and Patchen. He's not really talking. The kid isn't talking. The sister is saying they tried to take his PlayStation. They beat him up bad. He's bleeding. I called a bus [ambulance].

"The sergeant says why did you call a bus. I say it's a robbery. She goes, 'Yeah it is, but what are we going to do about it? It's a 90Y [a case disposed as an unnecessary call].' I said, 'No, I'll write the report. It's an attempted robbery. They beat him up. He went to the hospital. They didn't succeed because he held the PlayStation like a football and they kicked the shit out of him.'

"Santana said they won't take it. I say I'm going to write the report, sure as shit. You know I had to write that report four different times. The sergeant rewrote the aided card. They finally made it an assault three. They say go back and investigate. They say you've gotta call a supervisor over. Do we have to do that?"

"You have to for a major," his fellow officer replied, meaning for a major crime of the type central to the CompStat numbers.

Surprised, Schoolcraft responded, "You do? So I said, 'What is this story that I wrote?' The sergeant says that looks like an assault three. He rewrote it for me. I said I'm not writing it again. He rewrote the aided card and the 61 [crime report]."

Back to the other cop. "Yesterday I walked into this thing. There had been a fire in a second-floor apartment on Van Buren. The firemen didn't know it had spread, so they had broken in the other doors too. The landlord and the super came and they put new locks on the door. So, the victim tells me his PlayStation's missing.

"The only people in the building were the landlord, the super, and the firemen. I'm think the fucking firemen stole the PlayStation. So I call it in and they go, 'Take it for petit larceny.' I'm like, 'How?' Whoever was in the apartment didn't have permission. It's a burglary. The sergeant says does it look like forced entry. I said the firemen forced in all the doors. The apartment is a fucking mess and all the doors are kicked in. I can't tell if the damage is from the firemen. I wrote a story this long hoping no one would read the goddamn thing. Because if you look at the story, this is a fucking burglary. How do you make it not a burglary?"

Adrian said, "What's-her-name upstairs told me they change reports. I asked her, 'Do they have to tell the investigating officer that something is being changed or augmented on the report?' She says no. That's criminal, I think. I think that's fucking criminal."

"And I got my named signed to it," the other officer replied.

"And you're signing it, that's more important," Schoolcraft said, incredulous. "Basically, you're swearing to the story and they are changing it."

He added, "It was so out in the open in December. If it was a major [crime] he would come over and call in his lieutenant. Some you can't bullshit away, so he got all puffy. December must be the cut-off [for the annual stats]. He was stressing."

Here, the other officer supplied another anecdote. "My favorite one of all is fucking is we get a cell phone snatch over on Stuyvesant. We throw the girl in the back of the car and do a canvas, and he [Mauriello] shows up and says roll down the window. He tells the girl, 'What do you want us to do here really?'"

"Who's this? Mauriello?" Schoolcraft asked.

"Yeah, he's like, 'What do you want us to do with this?' She wants her cell phone back. He's like, "What if we can't get it back for you?'"

"Is this a normal-looking girl?"

"Yeah, she just moved out here from California, nice girl," the cop said. "He's like, 'What are you going to do with this? Are you going to press charges?' She says not really. He's like, '90 yellow. Take her home.'"

"When was that?"

"That was like six months ago. It is what it is."

"Yeah," Schoolcraft replied, "but that's a pin that needs to go on the wall somewhere. Now that fucking crook, we helped him. We basically destroyed evidence or something. I don't know how to articulate it in a court of law."

"Exactly," the cop responded. "You should just be able to fucking take the major and just put down won't prosecute. This way there's a record. But this way, the detectives aren't going to look into it, nobody's time is going to be wasted on it, but you know a robbery occurred right there. So this way, if you start getting four or five of them, then you have a description of the guy."

"Exactly," Schoolcraft said. "Let's not hide it. It happened."

"They don't going to do anything with it, that's fine, but they know what happened," the other cop said.

This one conversation captured on Schoolcraft's tape recorder crystallized what was happening in the precincts as a result of the CompStat pressure coming out of 1 Police Plaza. It filtered down to the borough, to the precinct bosses, and to the cops, and in the end, crime victims were not being properly served by the NYPD, all in the name of showing better numbers. How could these same things not be happening in other precincts?

As April began, the pressure of working in the precinct was taking a toll on Schoolcraft's health. He called in sick on April 3, suffering from chest pains and an upset stomach. An NYPD doctor told him to take the rest of the week off. He was told by his bosses to get a checkup and see the NYPD psychiatric services unit. He viewed this order as an attempt to push him out.

During the exam by a Dr. Joseph Ciuffo, he told the doctor about events in the precinct and the stress he was under from what he viewed as retaliation against him. Ciuffo diagnosed him with anxiety and ordered him to see a department psychologist.

On April 13, he sat and talked with Dr. Catherine Lamstein of the NYPD Psychiatric Evaluation Services Unit. Her notes from the session characterized Schoolcraft as a police officer under a tremendous amount of job-related stress, but also an officer who was being absolutely honest and forthcoming.

Schoolcraft told her that he was only getting four or five hours of sleep a night. He told her about his low evaluation. He had bouts of chest pain, tightness in his chest to the point where he went to an emergency room in Staten Island and got medication for anxiety, which he took only a couple of times.

His diet was awful. He drank too much soda. "I eat crap." He dreamed of a better lifestyle. Of his personal life, he said, according to her notes, "No real dating, just one woman briefly, not into drinking or dancing, a chore to meet women in New York, drank a little in the navy."

He talked about his mother Suzanne's death. "My mother died of cancer five years ago. That beat the hell out of me and my father. My dad is depressed."

She asked about drug use. "No one in my family drank or smoke. Coffee or soda was my only fix," he said.

He told her about the sign that appeared on his locker. He talked about his philosophy as a cop and said he was disappointed in the reality of the NYPD. "I'm more comfortable on foot than in a patrol car," he told her. "I would rather work alone than with a partner.

"It's all about activity, they are pressuring me for activity, but other cops write fake summonses and the command won't do anything. They want lots of movers for seat belts and cell phones, they want more stop and frisks."

He continued, "I had no problems on the job until last year. My summonses are probably lower than the year before but I'm still very active. My bosses told me that I used to be a hammer, but I don't ever remember being a hammer."

"I'm on some kind of double secret precinct probation," he told Lamstein. "Few officers in the command still talk to [me] because they get written up for unnecessary conversation."

Lamstein asked if he felt any paranoia. He said no, "but the way they are treating me, I am inevitably going to jammed up and fired.

"I like police work in general, but not the neighborhood where I work, and I don't want to write a lot of summonses and 250s. I disagree with my bosses about the demands for numbers. I hired an expensive labor attorney to contest the annual evaluation."

Of the neighborhood, he said, "The black community doesn't trust white police officers. They get treated badly. I'm not a racist. Where I come from, I was white trash."

Lamstein concluded that Schoolcraft was stressed and upset, but he was resistant to accepting that he was anxious. She urged him to see a psychologist and recommended medication. Adrian declined. She left the room to consult with a supervisor and then returned and announced she was placing him on restricted duty. He would have to turn in his guns and his shield and be confined to a desk in the station house.

Suspicious, Adrian asked her what the charges were. Lamstein told him, "Restricted duty is not a disciplinary action. We want to monitor you so you can get better and get back to full duty."

Two officers drove Schoolcraft to the station house and then to his home to collect two firearms—a Sig Sauer 9 mm and a Glock 9 mm—and his shield.

Lamstein later told an IAB investigator, Sergeant Frank DeFabrizio, that she ordered him placed on restricted duty due to "symptoms of stress and anxiety, complaints of chest pains, stomachaches, high blood pressure and loss of sleep." She felt he was not ready for full duty.

Schoolcraft, however, felt her decision was another step in an effort to marginalize him and eventually push him out of the NYPD.

And on the following day, unknown to him, the appeal of his evaluation was abruptly closed out.

CHAPTER 7

DESK DUTY

When he returned to the station house, Schoolcraft was placed on the day tour desk as the telephone operator, which meant that he would answer the phone and deal with civilians who walked in to report a crime or make a complaint. Officially, at least, his bosses were unaware of why he had been placed on restricted duty, as Mauriello later told investigators. But he found himself being referred to as a "zero" or "house mouse," police code for lazy cops.

Schoolcraft's activity report for the month showed how unhappy he was. He reported sick ten days, took five vacation days, and ended up working just six days in the month. For the next six months, he answered the phone and took complaints from people walking into the station house. Occasionally, he was asked to transport a prisoner or voucher evidence. His bosses stopped even entering remarks into his monthly reports. For what it lacked, the telephone perch, he said, gave him a much more immediate picture of how crime complaints were really handled in the precinct.

Meanwhile, in the rolls calls, the daily harangue for numbers continued unabated. Even though he was on desk duty, he still had to sit through the morning briefings.

"I see 8 fucking summonses for a 20-day period or a month [the boss said]. If you mess up, how the hell do you want me to do the right thing by you?"

Another boss chimed in: "I told you last month, they're looking at the numbers. Ain't about losing your job, [but] they can make your job real uncomfortable."

The pressure for low-level arrests also continued. On March 13, a sergeant said, "Make 'em move. If they won't move, call me up, and lock them up, discon [disorderly conduct], no big deal. Leave them out there all night and come get them. The less people on the street, the easier our job will be."

On March 28, the subject of Mauriello Specials was aired out. It happened a day after there were five robberies in the precinct. The sergeant reminded officers that if Mauriello called, they had to go to the scene and arrest people. "If you don't want the collar, too bad," a sergeant added. "If he calls for a car, somebody's gotta go. That's the way it is."

On February 27, 2009, a lieutenant said, "I know you don't want to take these shitty collars, but you can't let the CO [commanding officer] go over the air and no one answers the radio," a lieutenant told the officers on February 27, 2009. "It's disrespectful and also could be a safety factor.... Unfortunately, he likes to work the majority of our tour because it's the busiest so you gotta do what you gotta do."

The other problem with these sorts of arrests was that officers were being asked to make arrests for misconduct they had not actually witnessed. When they filled out the arrest report, they were attesting to having actually seen the misconduct. That was a crime—filing a false report.

Casting around for help on April 14, Schoolcraft called the hotline for his union, the Patrolmen's Benevolent Association. He got only a recorded message from the PBA president, Pat Lynch. No one answered. Schoolcraft could be heard saying, "Hello... Hello..." into the dead line.

On April 27, Mauriello told officers to make an arrest, drop suspects at the precinct, go back out, and then come back later to process the arrests. "You bring 'em in here, leave 'em in the cells for a little while, go back out, do your job, and come back and release them outta there," he said. "If they're acting like assholes on the street, why should I rush them out of here?"

Once again, in the name of protecting public safety, Mauriello was directing his cops to make nuisance arrests, but Schoolcraft believed it frayed the precinct's relationship with the community.

Schoolcraft's role at the desk allowed him to interact with the community and see firsthand the precinct's manipulation of crime reports. On June 29, a man walked into the precinct office to get the all-important complaint number so he could file a claim with his insurance company. But the report had disappeared. When Schoolcraft reported this to the desk sergeant, he was told to make out a new report.

After he did this, Mauriello stopped by the desk and told Schoolcraft, "I'm not taking this. Have the guy come in. I've gotta talk to him."

The auto theft victim and his cousin came in and were immediately ushered into Mauriello's office. According to Schoolcraft's account, the precinct commander interrogated the two men for 40 minutes, after which the men walked out yelling and cursing. The auto theft complaint was turned into unlawful use of a motor vehicle and didn't make it into the crime stats.

In another incident around this period, an older man walked into the station house to report that someone broke the lock on the cash box in his apartment and stole $22,000. When he reported the incident in another precinct, he was told to call 311, the city's complaint hotline. It was a "civil matter," he was told. When he tried again to report the crime to the 81st Precinct, a sergeant told Schoolcraft to send him away.

According to the Patrol Guide, one of a police officer's primary responsibilities is to take crime complaints. What's supposed to happen is the crime is then given to the detectives to investigate. If they determine there was no crime, then they are supposed to charge the person who made the report with filing a false report. But, as illustrated in these examples, the pressure of CompStat was leading precinct commanders to aggressively look for ways to dismiss complaints before even investigating them. In one instance, Mauriello was calling crime victims back and trying to get them to change their stories. In the other, a sergeant was just deciding not to believe the complainant. Both methods distorted the true role of law enforcement.

Schoolcraft added both incidents to his growing file of misconduct in the precinct. Meanwhile, the precinct bosses moved to stop him from taking walk-in complaints. They posted a memo saying that the telephone switchboard operator was not to take complaints but to refer people to the complaint room. "The primary task of the telephone operator is the telephone switchboard!" the memo read.

On June 2nd, the talk turned to the media. "They don't tell the truth," a sergeant says. "I tell DCPI [public information] the color blue. By the time it gets down there, it's green. When we do something good, it's on page 17. When we do something bad, it's on page 1."

Another piece that went into his file was the constant pressure in the precinct for stop and frisks. These were supposed to be done specifically when a person who fit the description of a suspect was spotted, or when an officer believed a crime was occurring or was about to occur. But in the 81st Precinct, the stop and frisk was distorted into just another number that showed "activity." This pressure then led to more tension with the community because folks don't like to be stopped for no reason.

Throughout Kelly's tenure, the number of stops skyrocketed across the city. That increase became one of the biggest controversies of his tenure. Kelly stubbornly defended the practice, claiming the stops were in direct relation to the locations where crime took place. Activists claimed there was an element of institutional racism in the campaign.

Schoolcraft's recordings contained numerous statements from police bosses ordering cops to simply stop people for no reason, without that key legal element of suspicion. The recordings demonstrated that it was actually the pressure of CompStat that was driving the sharp increase in stops and frisks. "Anybody walking around, shake them up, stop them, 250 them, no matter what the explanation is," a sergeant said. "If they're walking, it doesn't matter."

In a third roll call, the demand was coupled with a threat that cops would be moved out of their current tours if they didn't write more summonses and stop more people. When they made stops, they should also write quality of life summonses to justify the stop. "When you do a 250, you should do C's and knock out both of those columns in your activity reports," a sergeant could be heard saying at a roll call. "Is that understood?"

Schoolcraft, watching all of this unfold, finally hit on an idea of what to do with the recordings and his notes on what was going on in the precinct. While he started taping to protect himself, he then began working on what he called "A Patrolman's Report to the Commissioner." He got the idea from *Target Blue*, Robert Daley's history of NYPD corruption in the 1970s.

On July 27, he again met with Lamstein, the NYPD psychologist. She told him that he had "anger issues" and left him on restricted duty. He said later that he told her, "I'm disappointed with the department, but not angry."

That summer, the Schoolcrafts were so troubled by Adrian's treatment that, for the first time, they reached outside of city government for help. They contacted the police union and were rebuffed. In a letter in response to Schoolcraft's inquiry, David Morris, a representative of the PBA's lawyer, wrote that "the PBA's general counsel's office does not represent police officers in disciplinary matters." Even though he was a dues paying member in good standing, the PBA rebuffed him again and again.

They also contacted the retired Detective Lieutenant David Durk, a controversial figure both loved and reviled for helping Frank Serpico report NYPD corruption in the early 1970s. In contrast to Serpico, who retired from the force soon after he appeared before the Knapp Commission to testify about widespread bribery of police officers, Durk remained on the force for many years afterward. He was so controversial that even after his death in 2012, one retired police officer posted on an electronic bulletin board, "Good riddance to the rat."

On August 18, Larry Schoolcraft asked Durk for advice on how his son should handle the bad evaluation and get his voice heard in the department. He and Adrian detailed all the things that had brought them to that point. Durk, initially sympathetic, advised Adrian to record everything. "Without audio or video, your statement won't mean crap," Durk told Adrian. This statement encouraged the Schoolcrafts to go further down the road they were on.

Six days later, Schoolcraft took another step that would put him squarely in the NYPD crosshairs. He sent a notarized letter to Charles Campisi, the chief of Internal Affairs, alleging that a sergeant named Steven Weiss and a lieutenant named Timothy Caughey—who worked as the integrity officer in the precinct—had removed records of civilian complaints from Weiss's personnel file. The supposed motive was that Weiss was up for promotion to lieutenant, and the complaints could block his rise. In the letter, Schoolcraft claimed that he found out about this from a civilian clerk working in the precinct.

One week after that, on August 31, Durk—unbeknownst to the Schoolcrafts—called Internal Affairs and spoke to a young captain named Brandon Del Pozo, a rising star in the NYPD. Smart—a graduate of the prestigious Stuyvesant High School and Dartmouth College—and ambitious, he was just in his early 30s, quite young to rise to captain. In addition to his police duties, he was chasing a doctorate in philosophy and had two master's degrees. He had been one of the first officers sent overseas by Kelly to perform counterterrorism work and he had been stationed in Amman, Jordan, and Mumbai, India, in 2006, when Al Qaeda operatives killed dozens of people in a series of coordinated attacks. Later, he would be made one of the youngest precinct commanders in the city.

Durk told Del Pozo that Schoolcraft had evidence of misconduct in the precinct, including downgrading of crime reports and pressure to make quotas. Del Pozo opened a file on Schoolcraft's claims and referred the downgrading allegation to the Quality Assurance Division, the NYPD unit that audited crime statistics. Each year, QAD produced audits of stats in each of the 76 precincts in the city and also performed special investigations. Its work was very quiet and very closely held by the NYPD. Few people outside the department even knew about the unit.

On September 2, Schoolcraft sent a letter to Mauriello asking that the appeal of his evaluation be sent to the Brooklyn North command. Mauriello apparently did nothing.

And the ball started to roll faster.

★

On August 17, a woman walked into the station house to report that her cell phone had been stolen. Mauriello wandered by the desk, according to a recording, and initially checked with Schoolcraft about his restricted duty status. Mauriello then brought the woman into his office to talk to her about the phone.

"What's he saying to her in there right now?" Schoolcraft wondered to himself with amusement, assuming that Mauriello was trying to convince the woman to drop her complaint. "It was a friend, blah, blah, blah."

The pressure for numbers continued, as August came to a close. Following a shooting during the overnight shift, a sergeant told his officers, "Do some community visits, C summonses over there, the usual bullshit."

Since "activity" was tallied on a monthly basis, the final days of August became yet another chance to harangue cops on their productivity. "It's the 26th. If you don't have your activity, it would be a really good time to get it.... If I don't have to hear about it from a white shirt (a superior officer), that's the name of the game."

And on August 31: "Today is the last day of the month. Get what you need to get," a sergeant said.

The following day, the roll-call topic ranged from a longstanding prank in which cops drew penises in one another's memo books to personal hygiene to station house graffiti.

"As far as the defacing of department property, alright, the shit on the side of the building, and pictures of people's faces, and on people's lockers, and drawing penises in people's memo books and whatever else is going on, just knock it off, alright," a sergeant said. "We're adults. It's ridiculous. It's criminal mischief and graffiti for one, which if the wrong person sees this stuff coming in here, then IAB is going to be all over this place, alright?

"It's a joke and I'm all for a good time, but when the wrong person sees it, or you do it to the wrong person that's not in on the joke, then you start bringing the heat down on this place, that's not going to be fun. So spread the word also to people that aren't in this roll call. Just knock it off, alright? You want to draw penises, draw them in your own memo book. You'll look like an artist."

The discussion then turned to hygiene. "Someone smells bad?" the sergeant asked.

A female officer said, "I tell the guys, when I think that you stink, I will tell you."

"Don't put your vest in the washing machine," the sergeant said. "As far as the vest itself, take a damp cloth and some suds and hand wash it. If you throw it in the washing machine I don't think it stops bullets anymore. Brush your teeth. Take a shower daily. This hygiene is the new training. Change your socks daily. Kicking around in these boots all day, you take these things off, your feet stink, so don't just throw your socks in the locker and come in the next day. That shit won't come out of your boots and you'll be walking around smelling it all day. Anything else that people need to be reminded to clean?

"Clean your patrol cars too. They stink also. You're leaving your sardine sandwich under the seat for the next person. Just throw it in the garbage."

"You know what, you can't have me as a partner doing that kind of shit," the female cop says. " 'Cause I'll be like, 'Can you fucking clean that shit up?' "

On September 12, Schoolcraft heard about other downgrading incidents, when a fellow officer told him, "A lot of 61s, if it's a robbery, they'll make it a petty larceny. I saw a 61, at t/p/o [time and place of occurrence], civilian punched in the face, menaced with a gun, and his wallet was removed, and they wrote 'lost property.' "

As September drew to a close, the officers once again heard about getting their numbers up in advance of the deadline. "If your activity's been down, the last quarter is a good time to bring it up, because that's when your evaluation is going to be done," a sergeant said. "We all know this job is 'what have you done for me lately.' This is crunch time," he said. "This is game seven of the World Series, the bases are loaded and you're at bat right now.

"It's all a game, ladies and gentlemen," he adds. "We do what we're supposed to, the negative attention goes somewhere else. That's what we want."

Mauriello turned to the precinct's police union delegate, Richie Brown, to advise Schoolcraft to pick up his activity. "The CO [commanding officer] wants to know if everyone is happy and he also stated he can make you work more as long as they pay you," Brown told Schoolcraft on September 29.

On October 4, the precinct bosses issued a new edict: Cops can't take robbery reports on the street. They had to send complainants to the detective squad. "Don't take robbery 61s [complaints]. Send them to the squad." Schoolcraft saw this order, which was repeated three or four times through the month, as a clear attempt to reduce the number of robberies.

In essence, the precinct was adding a procedural hurdle to filing crime complaints. When a person gets robbed, they call 911 to report the crime. Now the cops would respond by telling the victim to go to the station house to file their report. Perhaps the victim has to go to work. Perhaps they have to care for a child. Aside from the inconvenience, the other insidious thing about this order was that it delayed the start of a criminal investigation. Most crimes that are solved are solved fairly quickly. Any delay ruins the one advantage that police have.

In this roll call, cops were told to be highly skeptical of what victims were telling them—another distortion of the crime reporting process caused by CompStat. "If it's a little old lady and I got my bag stolen, then she's probably telling the truth, alright," a sergeant said. "If it's some young guy who looks strong and healthy and can maybe defend himself and he got yoked up, and he's not injured, he's perfectly fine, question that. It's not about squashing numbers. You all know if it is what it is, if it smells like a rotten fish, then that's what it is. But question it. On the burglaries as well."

That roll call also contained proof of a second questionable precinct policy: the callback, which occurred when a precinct boss called a victim back to ask more questions about the complaint with the intent of downgrading the crime that was alleged. "Whether it's CO [the commanding officer], Lt. Crawford, or Seymour, they always do callbacks," a lieutenant said. "So, a lot of time we get early information and they do callbacks."

"And then we look silly," a sergeant added. "'Cuz they're, 'Why didn't you do this,' this is really not a...a domestic violence victim, woman, says, 'Hey, my boyfriend stole my phone.' He didn't really steal the phone. It's his phone, and he was taking it. Did he snatch it out of her hand? Yeah. Is it a grand larceny? No, because I'm telling you right now the DA is not going to entertain that."

Again, a primary job of a police officer is to take crime complaints, but CompStat was forcing the precinct to come up with administrative techniques to eliminate complaints that had nothing to do with fighting crime. There was nothing in the Patrol Guide that said police should make it hard for citizens to file complaints.

Ten days later, the subject of "Mauriello Specials" came up again in a roll call. This time, it was from a police union delegate, warning the officers about signing off on arrests for misconduct they didn't witness. "Make sure you don't sign anything that says you witnessed the arrest if you didn't," he said. "There's been a lot of cases overturned, and officers now being brought up on perjury charges."

On October 11, the order to refer robbery victims to the detective squad came up again. Two officers took a report from a man who had his cell phone stolen by force. The victim didn't want to immediately come to the station house because he didn't want to be seen getting into a marked police car.

Mauriello erupted when the report crossed his desk, and since shit always rolls downhill in the NYPD, the cops heard about it from their sergeant. "OK, so he [Mauriello] was flippin' on me yesterday because they wrote a 61 and the guy talking about he not coming in to speak to nobody," the sergeant said. "He don't want nobody see him getting in the car."

She went on: "You know we be popping up with these robberies out of nowhere or whatever. If the complainant does not want to go back and speak to the squad, then there is no 61 taken. That's it. They have to go back and speak to the squad."

She suggested the crime victim was lying. "How do we know this guy really got robbed?" she asked. "He said he had no description. Sometimes they just want a complaint number, you know what I'm saying, so if he don't wanna come back and talk to the squad, then that's it."

The topic turned to stop and frisks, and once again, the officers were told to just get numbers, without adhering to the legal standards of the tactic. "If y'all try to do a canvass, try to get at least a couple of 250s and put robbery down just to say that we was out there. You stop somebody, get a 250. Go over, let them see y'all doing something about it or whatever. OK?"

A week later, the edict about not taking robbery complaints was repeated again. "If the complainant says, 'I don't want to go to the squad, I don't want to go to the squad,' then there's no 61, right?" the sergeant said. "We not going to take it and then they say they going to come in later on and then the squad speak to them and they usually don't want to come in."

The subject turned again to "activity" in the next roll call, this time a threat that cops who didn't work would get new partners. "If you're working hard, it's not going to bother you," he said. "If you're not holding your weight, chances are you probably will be working with someone you don't want to work with.

"Just make sure you get your activity because I can't defend you, and I did a lot of defending in here the other day," he said. "I can't defend anybody who can't get themselves to where it should be."

Then, a sergeant reminded officers not to smoke at crime scenes. "And don't pee in the toilet. Don't eat food from the refrigerator. Don't sit in the guy's chair when there's a DOA in the apartment."

Three days after that, the topic was the constant shortages of cops on the day tour because again they were constantly being pulled away for a host of reasons. On a typical day in the 8-1, incredibly, there were just three to nine officers to patrol the entire precinct. "Where is everybody?" a lieutenant wondered in an October 27 roll call. "This is going to be a bad month."

The precinct didn't even have enough cops to man SkyWatch, the mobile surveillance tower placed in high-crime areas to deter misconduct. "We'd like to have two people assigned there," he said. "We don't have the luxury to do that. Today, once again, we have one, so the effectiveness of the SkyWatch is not there."

A sergeant griped that his boss had told him to send a cop to guard a car where a gun had been found. "He said, 'Put a body on it,'" the sergeant said. "He doesn't live in the real world. I didn't have any extra people to have them sit on a car."

The shortage was so bad that bosses would pray for rain. "Hopefully, it will rain until 4 o'clock today," a sergeant said. "That would be a big help to us, especially due to our limited manpower."

The same month, there was a ban on bringing homeless drug addicts, who are known collectively as "bags of shit," into the station house. These people often required special handling, which took patrol officers off the street for hours because they needed drug treatment or a visit to the hospital. Previously, it wasn't uncommon for them to be arrested specifically so they would get treatment.

"If the guy murdered somebody, then that's a different story," the sergeant said. "If the guy is smoking a joint and his name is James Johnson, then you know what to do. I can't tell you not to write him a summons or don't collar him, but...that makes my freaking head explode."

He added, "Listen, don't bring Mr. Medicine into the station house, because he's going to get free medical care from us that we all pay for, OK, and plus then he gets a nice police escort the whole time that he's there."

Often, the precinct was short of patrol cars because vehicles were pulled away for "critical response"—that is, for Kelly's lines of cars touring Manhattan, lights flashing.

On October 25, the precinct actually didn't have a single car to put in the field. "I brought it to the lieutenant's attention because we don't have no cars for the day tour," a sergeant said. "It's just really, really bad.... So honestly, I'm going to call the borough [command]."

The short staffing led to what was known as "forced overtime," in which officers were ordered to take overtime hours to fill the holes. In one roll call, a lieutenant made up a list of cops who had worked overtime and those who hadn't. "If your name is not crossed off the list, and there's an opening that day and you're off, you're working it," he said. "Whether you can or can't, you'll be here."

Schoolcraft, who had frequently worked forced overtime, thought the practice was a public safety issue. "What happens is they get addicted to the overtime, and they keep doing it because it pays for their school and housing bills," he said. "But it's exhausting."

CHAPTER 8

THE LENGTHS PEOPLE WILL GO

Adrian Schoolcraft's complaint to Internal Affairs had been percolating through the system for two months. IAB was aware that none other than David Durk had been used as an intermediary, but they hadn't responded to his August letter. Finally, things started to happen. Schoolcraft received a call from a Lieutenant Michael Brill of the Quality Assurance Division (QAD). Brill wanted to speak with him about his allegations of crime downgrading . They traded phone messages, and then Schoolcraft got a notification to appear on the morning of October 7 at the QAD offices at 300 Gold Street in Brooklyn.

It would be a formal interview, which meant that Schoolcraft had to be absolutely truthful. If he lied, QAD would bring him up on administrative charges and get him fired, or worse, would file criminal charges against him for filing a false report. He was well aware of the stakes of the meeting. He had been secretly recording in his precinct for more than 18 months. He had been collecting records of crime complaints. He had been making notes in his memo book of issues in the precinct. And now, he would be breaking the blue wall of silence, going outside of his command, and reporting all of this to official investigators.

On October 6, the night before the meeting, Adrian talked over strategy with his father, and a portion of their conversation was reproduced in a subsequent Internal Affairs report.

"Let it all out," Larry said at one point. "Never let them know that you're doing this for revenge.... Don't direct it to just one supervisor. It's a problem as a whole and that you're concerned and that you want to address it that way. Get in there and tell your story. Don't show them everything. Show them a little at a time."

"That's what he wants me to do," Adrian replied. "Go crying. I would be suing the NYPD and it would be some motherfucker from Corporation Counsel handing out cookie-cutter bullshit, but you're right, this is the way to fuck him over and it benefits us because if they do something and we go to civil court and say well look, they even said he was wrong."

In isolation this comment sounds like Adrian is planning on using the QAD meeting as a way to get back at Mauriello for giving him the poor evaluation. Indeed, these statements were later used by IAB to accuse Schoolcraft of setting the whole thing up to angle toward a lawsuit.

They then talked about misclassifying complaint reports. Adrian rehearsed answers he might give. "Maybe I'm wrong, maybe this only happens in minority neighborhoods. None of these guys came to my aid. Fuck them. We just worked together so that we didn't have to work with any niggers."

This remark was included in the subsequent IAB report specifically to suggest that Schoolcraft was a racist, though it wasn't explicitly stated. Larry said later that Adrian used the word, but only in the context of imitating how other white cops spoke to each other.

He went on. "He wants to talk about bigger issues, which are chronic, systematic problems," Adrian told his father. "I'm not looking for vengeance or to get anyone in trouble or I'm not here for retaliation, it just has to stop. It's happening in minority communities where people have no voice.... I'm not looking to burn anyone; it's not coming from the bottom."

Later these excerpts were used by IAB to accuse Schoolcraft of setting up the NYPD, but both Adrian and Larry vehemently denied any such plot.

"Absolutely not," Larry said later. "There was no conspiracy to sue the NYPD. We were talking about his appeal of the evaluation and whether he would have to file court papers to get his job back if they tried to get rid of him."

The following day, Schoolcraft drove to the QAD offices in Brooklyn. There, he was greeted by one of the QAD supervisors. The two men had an informal conversation, with the QAD cop offering a frank assessment about the extent of crime statistic manipulation in the NYPD. Schoolcraft told the officer he brought some samples of crime report manipulation with him. "I don't want to come in here as a disgruntled employee," he said. "I want to fix the problem. Let's make the 8-1 an example of how to fix it."

"You're not unfortunately the first individual who's come down and, you know, presented us with information and some of those instances have been substantiated," the officer said.

When Adrian wondered whether such instances could be crimes, the officer said that prosecutors are hesitant to file charges. "I've sat down with the DAs on a couple of occasions, outlining this is what we had, do they want to proceed. More often than not, they don't want to touch it. They'll give it back to the department to handle it internally. But you're right. It's an official department record. It's falsifying business records, so to speak."

This officer added, "You know, I've been doing this over eight years, I've seen a lot. The lengths people will go to try not to take a report, or not take a report for a 7 major. So nothing surprises me anymore."

Schoolcraft was ushered into a meeting room, where he found a deputy inspector named Abramo, a lieutenant, and three sergeants. He spoke with them for three hours, carefully detailing each questionable crime report and providing the backup documents. Though the interview was not conducted under oath, Schoolcraft knew that if he lied, he could face departmental and even criminal charges.

"I've noticed this has progressively been getting worse," he said. "2008 is the year I think we really need to look at. 2009 I've seen the same thing. I've seen the walk-ins come in and say where's my report. I need this, the insurance company needs this, and we're looking for it, and it doesn't exist.

"I think this is a public safety issue, and I think it involves the safety of the police officers by these supervisors not taking these felony reports. It's a disservice to the public, and it dumbs down the police force. They twist my head. I don't know what a grand larceny is, or a robbery. I mean I know what a robbery is, but they twist it around your head so much."

Schoolcraft described how lieutenants responded to every major crime that took place in the precinct by looking over the shoulder and second-guessing officers taking reports. He related one incident where a sergeant told him to rewrite robbery complaint as a misdemeanor assault because "we can't take another robbery."

The incident in question took place on December 15, 2008. A group of thugs accosted a young man and demanded his Playstation. When he refused they beat him severely. Looking through their computer records, QAD was able to confirm that the demand for the Playstation was deleted from the final report, justifying the lower assault charge.

"I remember him shaking his head," Schoolcraft said. "I scratched out another one. I don't know what I changed if I changed anything. I gave it to him and he said, 'We can't take this.'"

The sergeant was not at fault, he added. "It's coming from the top. It's a closed environment that enables this corruption. Someone's benefitting from this. I don't know who, I don't claim to know who. I'm just a street patrolman. I get their name, number, who are you, what happened."

He told the story of a woman who needed a report for a stolen car to give to her insurance company. She called and visited the station house numerous times but never got her report. He described how, after two men filed a stolen car report, Mauriello said, "I'm not taking this," and called them into his office where a loud argument could be overheard. The men stormed out of the office, yelling and screaming. He told them about a man who reported that $22,000 had been stolen from his apartment. The police first told the man that it's more of a civil matter, not a crime. Then, they send him to another precinct.

In another incident, a victim came in to look at mug books. Schoolcraft sent him upstairs, but the detectives sent him back downstairs because he didn't have a complaint number. "They told him, you can't look at pictures without a complaint number," he said. "I don't know what that means, but that's what they said."

He described another incident in which a man was punched by three men during a robbery. Two days later, when he went to the station house, the report had disappeared.

He related how officers were repeatedly told to refer robbery victims to the detectives, rather than take the report in the street.

He talked about a 2008 case in which a patrol responded to a man who was beaten bloody. A lieutenant arrived on the scene and said, "We can't take this robbery." The case was reported as "lost property." Schoolcraft contacted the victim, who wrote up an account that said he was jumped by several men who took his wallet and cell phone.

"We get a lot of stolen computers. The first thing the desk says, how old was it? It's too old. That's petit larceny. It's not worth anything, that's not exactly the truth, because the data on the computer is also valuable."

The meeting ended with a promise from QAD to investigate the allegations. Abramo thanked Schoolcraft for his courage in coming in. "We're very serious about this and we will do a thorough investigation," Abramo said. "That I can promise you. If we're finding that they are not taking seven major crimes, I can tell you that the police commissioner, Deputy Commissioner Farrell, we take it very seriously, and there will be disciplinary measures taken. It's not taken lightly at all."

As Adrian left, one of the men in the meeting said, "Just to educate you, they fudge crime to show a reduction. That's what this whole thing is. Everyone wants to show a decrease in crime. It's what Kelly wants, it's what Bloomberg wants, which is why sometimes people have agendas to try to do what they can to avoid taking a seven major crime. Shame on them for doing what they shouldn't be doing."

That investigation was supposed to be secret, and Schoolcraft was assured that his bosses would not know the source of the allegations. But it's fairly clear that Mauriello soon found out that Schoolcraft had spoken to QAD.

Around October 13, in an effort to get precinct bosses off his son's back, Larry called a Bloomberg administration official. "I told her, listen, someone is going to get hurt," Larry recalled, the subtext being that Adrian was being retaliated against by his bosses. "They took his guns, they put him on some kind of modified duty, he's on the desk, and he doesn't know what his duties are supposed to be. This is no way to run a railroad."

According to Larry, she replied by asking what he wanted them to do. Larry responded, "Do your job."

She evidently called the police commissioner's office, because Larry got a call from a Sergeant Bonilla, who was assigned at the time to Kelly. When the call came in, Larry was walking through an Albany shopping mall.

"Bonilla calls and says the deputy mayor's office called us and now we are responding to your complaint," Larry said. "I was really ticked.

I told him something bad was going to happen. There are rules and policies. You can't just do what you want to do. If this is legit, it has to be documented."

"There doesn't have to be anything in writing, he just needs to do what he's told," Bonilla told him, according to Larry.

"Whatever he's told?" Larry asked.

"Whatever he's told," Bonilla replied.

"I was shocked," Larry said later. "Here I was trying to stop this thing before it got worse, and he wouldn't do anything."

Bonilla then called Schoolcraft and said something similar, according to his memo book notes.

In the context of this story, these conversations are extremely significant. They show that both the mayor's office and the police commissioner's office were aware of the brewing problem in the 81st Precinct. Bonilla certainly must have documented the conversation with Larry and Adrian and put it in a file somewhere, and it's not out of the question that he also probably told a superior about it. It is logical that someone in Kelly's office would have called the precinct and maybe looked into whether there were any open investigations. However, nothing changed for the better.

Instead, it got worse for Schoolcraft. The following day, the NYPD placed him on "Level 1 Performance Monitoring" because of his low activity. Technically, the decision was made by a personnel unit, but Schoolcraft suspects that Mauriello had recommended the move. Schoolcraft had been sitting behind a desk for seven months, unable to do any enforcement activity, as a result of his restricted duty designation, but that didn't seem to matter. The designation meant his work would be closely scrutinized by his bosses, and they would try to motivate him to work more.

Schoolcraft saw this move as another turn of the screws to place him under even more pressure. He walked into Mauriello's office and demanded, "What's the number?"

On October 19, perhaps because of the messages from IAB to Schoolcraft being left in the station house, Lieutenant Caughey issued a memo ordering all officers to direct all Internal Affairs contacts to him.

On October 20, Sergeant Scott of Internal Affairs called Schoolcraft at the precinct office, which is certainly not a good idea because of the danger that other officers would find out that he was talking to IAB. The same day, a sergeant from QAD also called.

That very same day, in Washington, Mauriello was honored in a speech entered into the Congressional Record by Representative Edolphus Towns. "Madam Speaker, today I rise in recognition of Steven Mauriello, Deputy Inspector of the 81st Precinct and honorable public servant." The honor is not uncommon for local politicians looking to curry favor with the NYPD and their precinct commanders.

The next day, Schoolcraft was interviewed on the phone by Internal Affairs.

Three days later, in the roll call, which Schoolcraft recorded, cops were again told not to take robbery complaints, but to make people go to the station and talk to the detectives. The drumbeat demanding activity continued, and Schoolcraft's bosses continued to keep a close watch on him.

On October 27, Schoolcraft visited Lamstein, the NYPD psychologist, again. She told him to get more medical attention and stress management counseling.

On October 28, Larry Schoolcraft called the mayor's office to report "repeated and continuing instances of corruption within the precinct." It remains unclear what happened to this complaint.

And then, it all came to a head four days later on October 31, Halloween 2009. "I was going to do my report to the commissioner, but we called Durk and Durk called IAB," Adrian said. "It was going to be professional. It became a total cluster fuck."

★

That morning, a Saturday, Schoolcraft arrived at work shortly before 7 a.m. He sat through roll call, listening to reminders to watch for rampaging teens in bandannas that evening, and then took his post at the telephone desk. About an hour into his shift, Lieutenant Timothy Caughey came by and asked for Schoolcraft's memo book.

This usually was a fairly routine request, but for Schoolcraft, it held ominous undertones because he had been using the memo book to make notes about quota pressure, lack of training, threats from bosses, downgrading of crime, and questionable orders. It was sensitive material. In the context of what had come before—the harassment, the letter to IAB, the QAD interview—Caughey's request made Schoolcraft very nervous.

For example, on August 24, 2009, Schoolcraft had written "Sgt Sawyer swearing/yelling and belittling officers at roll call." On October 4, he noted Sergeant Gallina saying, "All I want is one collar a month." On October 24, he wrote that Sgt. Huffman told officers at roll call, "Robberies, don't take 61s."

As Schoolcraft sat with his heart racing, Caughey examined the memo book. He noticed several of what he later called "peculiar" entries and decided to make copies. It seemed to him that Schoolcraft was involved in some kind of investigation, he later told Internal Affairs. One entry that caught his eye was the name of one of Schoolcraft's former partners, who at the time was assigned to Internal Affairs.

Schoolcraft was by that point very nervous because he knew that by keeping those notes, he had already violated one of the great unwritten rules in the NYPD. Caughey was also mentioned in his letter to Campisi. Could Caughey already know what Schoolcraft had done?

Caughey made two complete copies of the memo book. He put one in Schoolcraft's personnel file. He left the other on Mauriello's desk. He finally returned the memo book almost four hours later, just before noon. Caughey later made a third copy for Captain Timothy Trainor of the Brooklyn North Investigations Unit.

Schoolcraft claimed that Caughey then was eyeing him in a threatening manner. "He was standing closely to me with his hand on the gun and staring angrily at me," Adrian said later.

This scared Adrian. Uncertain of what to do, he called Larry and told him about it. Larry immediately called Internal Affairs and the office of Chief of Department Joseph Esposito, the highest-ranking uniformed member of the NYPD.

When he reached IAB, he begged them to send someone to the precinct to intervene. "I told him what happened with Caughey, that Adrian had reported him to IAB, and now this was going on," Larry said later. "I got a very cocky kind of 'fuck-you' attitude. He says, 'He's a big boy, he got to work, he'll be okay going home.'"

The conversation with an officer in Esposito's office went the same way. "They wouldn't do anything either," Larry said later. "He wouldn't give me his shield number or his first name. He wouldn't let me speak to a supervisor. He basically said the same thing, in other words, this is bullshit. Think about it: Adrian's reported serious, widespread corruption, he's being abused, and I can't even get a supervisor on the phone?"

Larry called Adrian back and told him to go home sick. Adrian later told investigators that he left the precinct because he felt that he was being "set up" by Caughey. At 2:15 p.m., shortly before his tour ended, he told his sergeant, Rasheena Huffman, that he was going home because his stomach hurt. She was on her cell phone and asked him to wait. He dropped a sick time slip on her desk and went to the locker room to change into civilian clothes.

By Schoolcraft's account, Huffman sent an officer to bring him back to her desk and merely asked him to switch the sick time request to lost time. Schoolcraft did so, and left, with the feeling that "something bad" was going to happen, but believing that he did nothing wrong in going home.

A police officer named Craig Rudy later told investigators that he was the one sent to retrieve Schoolcraft from the locker room. Rudy claimed Schoolcraft said to him, "Oh yeah, I know. I'm trying to get out of here. They told me I could leave, but now they're saying I can't or something."

Rudy: "They're looking for you at the desk."

Schoolcraft: "OK."

Rudy later said it appeared Schoolcraft was in a hurry.

According to Huffman's account to investigators, Schoolcraft ignored her order to remain in the precinct and just left. She said she told Schoolcraft he couldn't go out sick without approval. When she told him this, he replied that he wasn't going to the hospital and walked out of the precinct office. She ordered him to return. He did not. "He seemed to be on a mission to leave," she later told investigators.

Huffman told Captain Lauterborn, who followed Schoolcraft to the parking lot, but he had already left.

Mauriello walked into the station house at about 2:15, just after Schoolcraft had left. He learned of his departure from Sergeant Huffman.

Lauterborn then spoke with Mauriello. Lauterborn later told investigators he felt Schoolcraft's behavior was "abnormal," and claimed he became "increasingly uncomfortable as time passed, and he heard nothing from Schoolcraft," the Internal Affairs report says.

As Lauterborn tried to locate Schoolcraft by phone, Mauriello called his boss, Assistant Chief Gerald Nelson, the commanding officer of Brooklyn North, and told him what was happening.

Chief Nelson later explained to investigators that he told Mauriello to follow the Patrol Guide. Nelson disclosed that he had previously talked with Mauriello about Schoolcraft. He said Mauriello had told him Schoolcraft was an officer who didn't want to work.

Lauterborn then called Lamstein, the NYPD psychologist who had placed Schoolcraft on restricted duty. According to the IAB report, she told him she did not believe that Schoolcraft was an immediate threat to himself or others, and that his firearms were removed from him because of emotional distress caused by anger issues and resentment against the department.

Schoolcraft had gone home 45 minutes early, which was not really a big deal in the great scheme of things. Then Lauterborn learned from his long-time psychologist that Adrian was not a danger to himself or others.

Lauterborn called Larry Schoolcraft and left a message. He then made the key decision that caused the dominos to begin to topple. He sent Lieutenant Christopher Broschart to Schoolcraft's home in Glendale, Queens. Broschart rang the doorbell. There was no answer.

Broschart called again to say he heard footsteps in the apartment. Lauterborn told him to keep knocking. Knowing Schoolcraft was inside, Lauterborn later told investigators he became more concerned. He decided to go to the apartment himself and went out to the parking lot.

Mauriello called Nelson again to tell him that he had learned Schoolcraft was at home.

Larry called Lauterborn back that evening. According to Lauterborn's account to investigators, Larry was "angry and agitated." Lauterborn claimed that Larry alleged a "conspiracy against his son and threatens to have the captain fired."

Lauterborn claimed he told Larry he needed to speak with Adrian before his concerns could be allayed. "Tell your son to open the door and speak with Broschart so we can all be at ease," Lauterborn said.

At this, according to what Lauterborn told investigators, Larry said, "You don't want another Lieutenant Pigott, do you?" This was a reference to Lieutenant Michael Pigott, who committed suicide in October 2008, unable to cope with the public attention he received after he ordered a mentally ill man to be shot with a Taser, and the man fell from the top of an awning and fatally struck his head.

Obviously, Lauterborn was suggesting that Adrian's own father thought he could be suicidal, thus justifying a larger response at the Glendale apartment.

Larry then abruptly hung up the phone, Lauterborn claimed.

What Lauterborn didn't know was that Larry was recording the conversation, and much of what Lauterborn told investigators was contradicted by the recording, reproduced here for the first time. First of all, from the tone of his voice, Larry was calm and measured during the discussion. He was not "angry or agitated." He didn't allege a conspiracy against Adrian. He didn't threaten to have the captain fired. He didn't hang up on Lauterborn. He didn't mention Lieutenant Pigott's death.

"I didn't say anything that would make them think Adrian was suicidal in any way," Larry said later.

Indeed, the recording, which was made at 7:40 p.m. that evening, confirmed the inaccuracy of Lauterborn's characterizations. This was not a small thing, because Lauterborn's view of what happened became a key justification of how Adrian was treated later that night.

Lauterborn explained to Larry that Adrian had gone home sick without authorization, he couldn't be reached by phone, and he wouldn't answer his door.

"I have to talk to him to settle out what's going on and he has to come back," Lauterborn said. "The situation with Schoolcraft is that he has his guns removed for unknown reasons, I don't know if this is a carry over from that. I need him to go back."

"This can't be settled tomorrow if he comes back to work?" Larry asked.

"We have people standing outside his house, and in approximately an hour, we're going to do a citywide notification search for him, and this is going to get more serious as the night goes on," Lauterborn said.

At this, Larry laughed incredulously. "OK, captain, I'm at a little bit of a loss here. You said he wasn't feeling well and he left? I don't understand what's the concern."

"There's much more involved," Lauterborn said. "He just walked out. There's ways of doing this and he knows that."

Larry said, "I don't understand why tonight, what would it matter? As long as he was okay why would he have to come back tonight?"

"I don't know that he's ok. Do you know he's OK? Have you talked to him?"

"Earlier, when he went home sick," Larry said. "He told me he was going home, and he said he would call me when he got up....Again, I don't understand why he would have to come back tonight."

Lauterborn: "He has no firearms. There's issues that he has none. That's for confidential medical reasons. As far as I know if a doctor takes your firearms, you have some unstable situations. I don't know what his motive is for leaving the way he left. I need to talk to him one way or the other. We gotta resolve things. This is not a situation that will wait until the morning."

Larry asked, "Captain, are you concerned for his safety or the safety of others?" This was an interesting question, because in legal parlance, it formed the basis of whether police can take special action against someone. It also suggested that the Schoolcrafts were already aware Adrian could be (unfairly) labeled emotionally disturbed.

Lauterborn: "I'm concerned for his safety more than others and then to figure out why he did what he did. If you're working, and a worker says I'm going sick, see you, that's a little unusual."

Larry: "You just need to talk to him on the phone?"

Lauterborn: "No, in person. It's a whole different ballgame now....Mr. Schoolcraft, this is going to get to a larger scale event, like I said. When the bells and whistles go off, it's going to be a citywide search for Adrian Schoolcraft."

"Ok, and what's the purpose of that?"

"Because we don't know what kind of condition he's in," Lauterborn said. "When someone just gets up and leaves and is already on special monitoring, we don't know what he's capable of."

"I didn't know he was under any special monitoring," Larry said.

"He has no firearms and he's seeing a psychologist, a doctor, every six weeks. that's special monitoring, no? I just got off the phone with his doctor."

"So in other words, if he talks with his doctor and it's alright with her, then everything's OK."

"No, no, no, no. That's not OK. That's not going to be the end of it. That's not the way this is going to work."

"Tell me, how is it going to work?"

"I have to talk to him one way or the other. . . . Like I said, the situation is going to escalate. The night goes on. Nobody is going in or out of that house that he lives in because there's police all over it. The car is secure, too. I don't know what he's going to do. If he's in the house, we'll eventually make our way in."

"Is he under some kind of arrest?"

Lauterborn said no. "We're on the property already. Some time we're going to enter the property."

Larry tried to reassure the captain that Adrian was fine. "Captain, I can assure you as his father, at 2 p.m. this afternoon, he called me, he told me he had a stomach ache, he was going to go home and go to sleep. I said call me when you get up. He sounded fine to me, and I've known him for 34 years."

"I understand that, I wish I could take your word for it 'cause I'd just leave it as it is right now," Lauterborn said.

In other words, the train was leaving the station, and Larry wasn't going to be able to stop it.

"What's interesting about this, when they first took his shield and gun, there was a day I couldn't reach him, and I got concerned, and I called everyone on the planet, and I couldn't get one goddamn person to go over and check on him," Larry said. "But now he walks out at two, and now you're going to have a NYPD alert for the whole city for one 34-year-old patrolman that I'm telling you right now is fine?"

"I wish I could be with you on this," Lauterborn said. "Have him come out of his apartment and talk to the lieutenant."

"Ok, captain." The conversation ended, and Larry called Adrian. That conversation is not available, but they evidently decided that Adrian shouldn't open the door or talk to Broschart.

Rewind to earlier in the afternoon and Adrian's state of mind when he arrived home. Schoolcraft called Internal Affairs.

"It's October 31, 3:38 p.m. I just left work. I didn't feel safe. Something weird's going on. I'm calling IAB," Schoolcraft said into his tape recorder.

He was initially given the run-around, transferred three times, left on hold for five minutes, and cut off once. He finally was connected to an Officer Jean, an investigator in IAB.

"Something happened today where I feel in danger," Schoolcraft told her. "I made a report to IAB. There's obviously a leak somewhere. These aren't officers. These are lieutenants, captains, and a deputy inspector that I made a criminal complaint against."

Jean asked him to describe what happened.

"Today at 0805, Lieutenant Caughey, the Integrity Control Officer, asked to scratch my activity log," Schoolcraft told her. "He took it to his office and held on to it about three hours. I have already made a criminal complaint against Lieutenant Caughey and Sergeant Weiss regarding breaking into offices and taking stuff out of personnel folders. When I was looking through it, I didn't realize how much incriminating stuff which I had been observing and noting in my activity log that they now know. And I have reported not just the downgrading of reports, but flat out throwing them in the trash. I always thought they would know, but today they definitely know, and Lieutenant Caughey was acting very spooky."

"You're a little young on the job to be going through all this," Jean said.

"One of the 124 room civilians, PAA Boston, she calls me," he replied. "She says, 'What's going on? Why is Caughey acting so funny? He's looking at you.' I didn't even notice. After she said that, I started paying attention, and he was. He was pacing with his shirt, his gun. When I got my memo book back, I started to get real worried. 'Cause what are they afraid of? I definitely didn't feel safe. I felt menaced. Even the civilian noticed. He then called in Sergeant Huffman. When she came out, her attitude changed. I have documented in my memo book statements she's made regarding not taking 61s for robberies."

"Where are you?"

"At home. At 1415 I went sick. They tried to tell me I couldn't go home sick. I did not feel safe going home at the normal time. I did not feel safe. I don't know why they were behaving that way."

Schoolcraft then described how Sergeant Scott of IAB may have blown his confidentiality by leaving messages for Adrian at the station house.

"Three weeks ago, I got the first call from Sergeant Scott. He was calling for me at the desk telling them he's Sergeant Scott from IAB looking for Officer Schoolcraft. They were leaving me messages from him."

In the end, all Jean did was give him a log number of 09–55058.

"That's it?"

"This is your log number, and I'll make a notation, and the investigative unit will investigate."

"He was calling me at work. He was intentionally leaving his name at work, IAB calling Schoolcraft."

"If I have anymore questions, I'll give you a call, OK?"

Despite the disappointing end to the conversation, this exchange established a record of the reason for his departure. The whole incident of him leaving the precinct 45 minutes early, even if he was in the wrong, should have been a minor thing, handled with a reprimand, but instead it becomes a firestorm, no less perhaps because of the appearance of high-ranking chief Michael Marino in the story.

CHAPTER 9

HALLOWEEN NIGHT

Late in the afternoon of October 31, 2009, as he later told investigators, Deputy Chief Michael Marino was conducting his usual rounds, when he arrived at the 81st Precinct. Walking through the parking lot, he encountered Captain Lauterborn, who was on his way to Schoolcraft's apartment.

In 2003, Marino had been Schoolcraft's very first precinct commander, though the two men never interacted. Six years later, he had risen to the number two man in the whole Brooklyn North command, overseeing ten precincts and thousands of police officers. He was considered something of a star in the constellation of NYPD chiefs. He was a symbol of a commander whose career had flourished under CompStat. Some cops called him "Elephant Balls," and Greg Donaldson of *New York* magazine dubbed him "Captain Midnight" in a 2001 profile.

Donaldson wrote about witnessing as Marino chased down and tackled a shooter who was armed with a machine pistol and "striding into street brawls like a samurai." He portrayed him as a man who took to lifting weights to be able to take down suspects, and as a workaholic, obsessed with bringing down crime numbers. "I'd commit unnatural acts for three weeks of five," Marino said, meaning five fewer crimes than the same time last year. Marino also once decked a guy who bad-mouthed the NYPD, Donaldson wrote.

Michael Anthony Marino, born and raised in Brooklyn, graduated in 1973 from Midwood High School. He was raised by a single mother in the Flatbush area. Donaldson wrote that he could read on a college level by seventh grade. He spent half a semester at NYU as a premed student, but he dropped out because he was "repulsed by his well-heeled classmates," Donaldson wrote.

His personnel records show that instead of continuing with college, he worked construction, at McDonald's, and as a shipping clerk. After two years hanging telephone lines for TelSpan, he joined the NYPD in November 1979 and was sent to the 28th Precinct in Harlem, where he earned a reputation both for using too much force and for remarkable courage.

In 1983, he and another officer dashed into a burning apartment building at 140 West 111th Street and rescued a seven-month-old girl and a four-year-old boy. His effort earned him a nice letter from Congressman Charles Rangel, and a Harlem resident named Ms. Bullock wrote, "I cried with joy," he said. "They are brave, courageous. they deserve promotion and more pay. God bless them and their family." By then, a *Daily News* article noted, he already had 14 commendations for bravery.

In 1991, a tourist named Casey Rucker wrote the commander of the 10th Precinct to thank then Lieutenant Marino for capturing three men in the midst of breaking into his car. "Thanks to his service beyond the call of duty, I was able to get my car and belongings back completely intact," Rucker wrote.

He was promoted to sergeant in 1984 and saw his salary bulge to a whopping $35,876. He was promoted to lieutenant in 1991, captain in 1997, deputy inspector in 2000, inspector in 2001, and deputy chief in 2004. Earlier in his career, he occasionally worked side jobs in security and at a limousine company.

His work evaluations were consistently top-rate throughout his career. A 1984 evaluation read, "This officer is aggressive and highly motivated." In a 1996 evaluation when he was a lieutenant, his captain marked his work as well above standard and wrote, "His career potential is unlimited." "He is as good as they get," wrote another boss.

A sense of Marino's command style was provided in Donaldson's profile. The profile began with Marino, then the commander of Brooklyn's 77th

Precinct, upbraiding a young officer for his lack of activity. "You're not doing your job," he said.

"Marino is not a delicate man," Donaldson continued. "He tells the bald truth to five-star chiefs and community activists alike, exhorts the cops under his command like a football coach and rides the streets to make arrests personally."

Donaldson continued the anecdote, writing that when Marino accused him of being off post, the officer refused to discuss it. "You're talking to your commanding officer," Marino replied. "I have the power to take days."

"I thought we could talk about this man to man," the cop said.

"If this was man to man, you'd be on your ass right now," Marino replied.

A 2002 evaluation noted that he "constantly seeks to 'do more with less,'" a convenient reference to one of Mayor Bloomberg pet phrases. "Mike Marino is one of the finest commanders in the city," wrote Assistant Chief Joseph Cuneen.

By the time he arrives at the 81st Precinct that October day, his personnel file was thick with laudatory letters from various politicians, including Congressman Ed Towns and New York State Assembly member Clarence Norman, as well as residents and organizations. On a commendation letter dated November 13, 2000, the Chief of Department Joe Esposito scrawled, "Keep up the good work Mike!!" His file also included a thank-you from the Brooklyn Children's Museum. A letter from Francis X. McArdle, the influential leader of the General Contractors Association. A missive from the owner of a gun shop in Manhattan thanking him for catching a burglar.

After receiving a letter thanking him for listening and treating his constituents like people, Marino replied, "We go to great lengths to stress upon our officers the importance of treating people as we wish to be treated ourselves."

Despite his high evaluations, it took Marino an unusually long time to get a precinct command because of his reputation as being too rough. According to Donaldson, he was even told he would never get a command. But he had a rabbi in Louis Anemone, then chief of department and CompStat inquisitioner, who finally convinced then Commissioner Howard Safir to promote him, Donaldson wrote. Ray Kelly clearly liked Marino because, as Donaldson wrote, he promoted him twice.

In a 2005 deposition he gave in a lawsuit, Marino was asked two questions that offer some insight to his thinking about his job:

"Was there ever a time you spoke to an individual officer about the number of arrests he was making?" a lawyer asked him.

"Too many," Marino replied.

"What is CompStat?"

"The CompStat system holds commanding officers accountable for the proper operation of their commands," Marino replied.

Marino had fired his weapon in the line of duty three times—an unusually high number for a police officer, and a signal of his aggressive ways. In all three incidents, he was found to be within NYPD guidelines.

At the same time, he had been the target of 28 different misconduct allegations in his career, according to an Internal Affairs report, including nine incidents of what NYPD Internal Affairs broadly categorized as "corruption."

In 1982, he was accused of threatening to plant cocaine on a suspect and assaulting him. That was unsubstantiated. In 1989, he was charged but found not guilty of punching a suspect and pushing him into a wall. In 1991, he was charged with punching a suspect in the face but again was found not guilty.

In 1996, the estranged wife of another officer accused Marino and other officers in the 73rd Precinct of robbing drug dealers. That allegation was ruled unsubstantiated. In 2004, he was twice accused of taking property from a crime scene. Both cases were unproven.

In all but two of the allegations, IAB concluded they were either unfounded, unproven, or found to be untrue.

In 2008, Marino received what's known as a letter of instruction in his personnel file from Chief Campisi of Internal Affairs for taking nearly five hours to notify IAB about the death of a suspect in the 84th Precinct on September 1, 2007.

The only allegation that really stuck was that Marino, a bodybuilder, had been a regular steroid user. In 2007, he was accused of using illegal steroids purchased from a Bay Ridge pharmacy that had become a hub for the illicit selling of the drugs. A number of other police officers were caught up in the scandal. Internal Affairs investigated for more than a year and had substantiated the charge in January 2009. He admitted only to the use of human growth hormone for a medical condition. He was found guilty under department rules in 2010 of using steroids, but not of patronizing the pharmacy, and would initially reject a deal that would have cost him 30 vacation days and a year of probation.

And yet he was still regarded well enough by Commissioner Kelly that the steroid charge did not cost him his career. Brooklyn prosecutors considered, but eventually did not pursue, criminal charges against any of the officers caught up in the scandal, mainly because they would also have had to charge the many civilians who were buying steroids from the pharmacy.

Instead, Kelly gave Marino a second chance. The commissioner transferred Marino to a Staten Island command. After leaving a final decision unmade for nearly two years, in February 2011, he finally placed Marino on what was called "dismissal probation." If the chief kept out of trouble for a year, he would not get fired. He also would have to forfeit 30 vacation days. Other cops laughed at the penalty. It was a slap on the wrist, and a soft slap at that, for conduct that probably would have resulted in a criminal case if Marino had been a civilian.

In 2009, though, that weak penalty was still to come. There in the parking lot with Captain Lauterborn, Marino was still the second most powerful commander in Brooklyn North, and he wanted information about Schoolcraft. Lauterborn briefed him. Marino later told investigators that he shared the captain's concern, and told him to inform both the operations desk and emergency services, the unit that does hard entries into dwellings. Marino was immediately concerned that Schoolcraft might kill himself and wondered whether an "all-out response" was necessary.

By Lauterborn's account, he told Marino he did not think Schoolcraft was suicidal. He would deal with it himself.

But Marino overruled Lauterborn and decided to also go to the apartment. According to current and retired police, it was unprecedented for a chief to go to the house of a police officer who had simply left work early.

Such minor misconduct was usually handled the next day with some kind of low-level discipline or suspension. But the Schoolcraft affair was ramping up into a major thing, a perfect storm, an episode of cartoonish overkill.

Marino's decision can be viewed several ways: One, he was genuinely concerned about Schoolcraft. Two, he was a micromanager and wanted to be in control in an unpredictable situation. Three, he knew that Adrian had gone to Internal Affairs and QAD to report corruption and saw this as an opportunity to discredit him. In his comments to investigators, he insisted he was merely concerned about the officer.

In hindsight, the Schoolcrafts saw something sinister in Marino's appearance at the station house. They believe Marino was there to deal with the Schoolcraft problem once and for all.

By Marino's account, after he spoke with Lauterborn, he stopped in Mauriello's office to tell him that he was going to Schoolcraft's home. The precinct commander decided to go, too. Mauriello and Marino took separate cars to the apartment. The commanding officer of the 104th Precinct, Deputy Inspector Keith Green, was already there, along with Brooklyn North and the emergency services unit. So, for one marginally AWOL officer, there was now a deputy chief, two deputy inspectors, a captain, several lieutenants, and sergeants from at least four different units outside Schoolcraft's small one-bedroom apartment.

Marino and the others claimed later that they were concerned for Schoolcraft's safety, but when the 81st Precinct notified Internal Affairs at 7:35 p.m. that night, the message merely said that "PO Schoolcraft will be suspended for disobeying a lawful order and for being AWOL when the MOS [member of the service] is located by Inspector Mauriello."

Initially, Lauterborn knocked on the door. Schoolcraft didn't answer.

Marino decided that Schoolcraft should be treated as if he were under duress. Paramedics were called. Lieutenant Elise Hanlon, a fire department paramedic, said later she was dispatched to Schoolcraft's address on a call of a "barricaded EDP," or emotionally disturbed person. The dispatch call certainly overstated the gravity of the situation to an almost sinister degree.

Likewise, the emergency services officers had responded to a call of a "possible MOS down in home"—also a major overstatement. Marino ordered them to make a "soft" entry into Schoolcraft's apartment using a key provided by the landlord.

Marino, Mauriello, and most of the other bosses and officers—about a dozen police in all—followed them into the apartment.

By his account, Schoolcraft was sitting or lying on his bed in a T-shirt, jeans, and socks. A television was playing. He had taken a nap, but he had also been on the phone with Larry for much of evening wondering how to handle what he knew was about to happen. He also turned on two tape recorders, placing one in his pocket and the other on a bookshelf.

For hours, he had been basically lying on his bed as the police lights lit up the block outside. He could hear the police knocking on his door and could see them calling his cell phone, but he ignored them.

Larry had advised him to take off his clothes and lie in bed, pretending he was asleep and didn't hear the door. He also told him to ask to go to the hospital, but not give the real reason—which was that he wanted the police out of the apartment. Adrian proposed telling the police that he has been diagnosed with cancer. Tell them you have stomach problems and diarrhea, Larry replied. And finally, they discussed the fact that Larry, on a previous visit, left a rifle under his bed.

At some point, Adrian ignored a call from Lamstein, the NYPD psychologist who placed him on restricted duty. Her message said that the situation "would blow into a much bigger mess than you want."

The rest of the encounter was captured on the two recorders that Schoolcraft had with him. One was in his pocket, and one was next to his bed.

As perhaps a dozen police enter the apartment, Schoolcraft whispered into his recorder: "It's 10/31/2009, ESU is here." Tactical lights filled the room. Some of the officers were in full tactical gear. From outside the bedroom a voice called out, "Adrian, Police Department, let me see your hands. You alright?"

"Yeah, I think so," he replied.

Marino then strode into the bedroom, the chief confronting the wayward cop, the top of the pyramid talking to the bottom. "You haven't heard us knocking on this door for a couple hours?" he asked, clearly irritated. "Adrian, sit up."

Schoolcraft said he took NyQuil and fell asleep, which was not quite true, but he was trying to fend them off. "Not, why would I expect anyone to knock on my door?"

"If you hear someone knocking on the door, usually you get up and answer it," Marino said. "You got a million people here downstairs worried about your welfare, spending hours out here...."

"Alright, sit down. Steve?"

Mauriello now appeared. "What happened today?"

"I wasn't feeling well. I left."

Mauriello, skeptical: "The sergeant told you to stay."

"The sergeant didn't say anything. She was talking on her cell phone," he replied.

"What do you mean? You can't just walk out of the precinct."

"Alright, well, I'm fine," Schoolcraft said.

"Well, you're going to come back to the precinct with us," Mauriello said.

"If I'm forced to. It's against my will," Schoolcraft responded.

"Against your will? Okay, this is how we're going to handle this. Get your stuff on. We're going back to the precinct."

"I'm not going back to the precinct," Schoolcraft insisted.

It became a battle of wills, and Mauriello stepped out of the room, allowing Captain Lauterborn to take over.

"Adrian, you're going to go back to the precinct."

"For?"

"Because we're going to do it the right way. You can't just walk out of a precinct."

"What's going to be done if I go to the 8-1?"

Lauterborn and Schoolcraft went back and forth and then over whether he had the right to go home 45 minutes early without authorization. Lauterborn wanted to investigate why he left. The exchange was tense, but Adrian was calm and steady under the high-pressure circumstances, according to his voice on the recording.

Lauterborn accused him of just slapping a sick slip on Huffman's desk and leaving.

"I didn't do that, she's embellishing," Schoolcraft replied.

"Get your clothes on, we have to go back," Lauterborn said.

A lieutenant named Gough from the Brooklyn North Investigations Unit demanded that Schoolcraft return to the precinct.

"You're coming with us," Gough said.

"Am I under arrest? Have I been charged?"

"You're not under arrest," Gough said. "You're being ordered back to the command though. Are you refusing?"

"Why?"

Gough: "I don't have to give you an answer. I am a supervisor in the New York City Police Department."

"I'll go against my rights, my will," Schoolcraft said.

Schoolcraft reluctantly stood and began to look for his shoes. His dad then called. Adrian filled him in. "Who's in the apartment?" Larry asked. "Everyone," Adrian replied.

Larry may have advised him to say he was sick, because Schoolcraft sat back down and said he wasn't feeling well. Gough summoned the paramedics, who had already arrived. The apartment was thick with the sound of police radios.

All of that for one officer who went home a little early.

Lauterborn, on the phone with Larry, said Adrian was going to the hospital, but he wasn't not sure which one. "He's not feeling well," he said.

A paramedic then arrived in the bedroom. Adrian told him, "I was just having stomach pains. They're embellishing this."

The paramedic moved to check his blood pressure. Meanwhile, Marino entered the room and learned that Schoolcraft had said he was sick.

Marino accused him of disobeying an order. Schoolcraft denied it, and Marino's voice thickened with annoyance.

"Yes, you did. Listen to me. I'm a chief in the New York City Police Department. You're a police officer, and then you have umpteen people out here standing in the rain, and don't tell me you don't hear them knocking on your door, and they call your cell phone and you hang up.

"So this is what's going to happen, my friend. You've disobeyed an order, and the way you're acting is not right in the very least."

Schoolcraft interjected, "Chief, if you woke up in your house..."

"Stop, stop right there," said Marino angrily. "Son, son, I'm doing the talking right now, not you."

"In my apartment."

"In your apartment."

"What is this, Russia?"

"You are going to be suspended," Marino said. "That's what's going to happen. You can go see the surgeon if you're sick. We'll give you all the medical attention that you need. At the end of it. You're suspended son."

The tape captured the sound of the blood pressure monitor inflating. "Your pressure is like sky-high. 160 over 120."

"I've been feeling shitty all day," Schoolcraft said.

Marino was hovering at the doorway of the bedroom, a few feet from the bed. On the tape he could be clearly heard faintly murmuring, "He's an EDP. This cop's got an attitude."

This statement suggests that Marino had already concluded Schoolcraft was emotionally disturbed before even talking with a medical professional. Schoolcraft had jousted with Marino, but he hadn't raised his voice, cursed, or shown any violent tendencies.

Meanwhile, the paramedic said, "I gotta tell you, you gotta go to the hospital with that kind of pressure. I can't in good faith leave you here with that kind of pressure. You understand that, right? We're all looking out for your best interests. It's a different job. I need to look out for you. So my suggestion is you need to come with us. Alright? Alright, he's going to go. Jamaica, right?"

Schoolcraft said he wanted to go to Forest Hills Hospital, where he normally went.

Emergency Medical Services (EMS) Lieutenant Elise Hanlon, who was listening, said, "I think Jamaica would probably be a better choice."

Schoolcraft gave his age, 34, and the paramedic said, "A 34-year-old man should not have a pressure that high."

"Forest Hills," Adrian repeated.

Then the paramedic made a mistake. When Marino asked how high his blood pressure was, the paramedic told him—a violation of federal medical confidentiality laws.

Adrian was angry: "Can you share medical information with them?"

The paramedic backpedaled. "I'm only telling them the blood pressure. I'm not saying who."

"Can you share that with them?" Schoolcraft repeated.

The paramedic said, "I'm not using your name, sir."

"I'm in the same room, in my apartment! Thanks for looking out for me," Schoolcraft said.

Schoolcraft rose and left the apartment, bound for the hospital. He walked downstairs and reached the ambulance. When he realized he would be taken to Jamaica Hospital, he balked. "I'm RMA," he said, using the acronym for "refusing medical attention." The significance here is that Schoolcraft, like any citizen, had a right to refuse treatment and couldn't be forced to go to the hospital unless he was in dire straits, close to death.

He turned around and walked back up the stairs to his apartment.

By Mauriello's account, he saw Schoolcraft go outside and then abruptly turn and run back inside.

After three minutes of silence on the tape, there was the sound of footsteps entering the apartment again. Lauterborn stuck his foot in the door and pushed his way into the apartment.

"You refused a lawful order to begin with and you've gotta come back and straighten it out," the captain said.

"I don't feel good," Adrian said. "I'm laying down. I have high blood pressure, stomach problems." He called to the other officers sarcastically, "Go ahead, get yourselves a drink out of the fridge if you want." He talked to his father on the phone: "Fuck, I got like three chiefs in my apartment."

The police supervisors gathered in the living room and whispered, according to Schoolcraft's notes.

Lauterborn told him to get back in the ambulance.

"I'm going to lie down in my own bed," Adrian said. "I haven't done anything wrong."

"Yeah you have," Lauterborn said.

"Ok, go write it up, file it," Schoolcraft said.

Lauterborn replied, "We will."

"You don't need me there," Adrian said. "Write that I disobeyed an order from Sergeant Huffman. Write up whatever you want."

"Now it's a matter of your health," Lauterborn said.

Then Marino interceded again for the final act in the sordid little drama. Keep in mind that Marino had already remarked that Schoolcraft was emotionally disturbed.

"Listen to me, alright, son, hit the light in here. Right now, EMS is saying that you're acting irrational. This is them. Not us. And that if you don't go to the hospital..."

"Yeah, you're whispering in their ear," Adrian replied.

Marino's voice tightened. "Listen to me."

"Chief, do what you gotta do," Adrian said.

"Listen to me...they're going..."

Schoolcraft interrupted. "Do what you gotta do. If I have a heart attack, strap me up."

Marino's voice rose. "Listen to me, son, they are going to treat you as an EDP. Now you have a choice. You get up like a man and walk into that bus like a man or son, they are going to treat you as an EDP, and that means handcuffs and I do not want to see that happen to a cop."

Adrian, sarcastic, repeated, "Like a man. Do what you got to do."

"I don't want to see them cuff you and bag you," Marino said.

Adrian said, "If I have a heart attack...with your inspections whispering in EMS ear."

"Listen, son, they're not whispering to anyone. They're here because they're doing their job. You've caused this."

"I didn't cause anything."

"You have caused this. Now you have a choice. They're saying you have to go to the hospital. That's EMS. They are trained medical professionals. If you don't go—"

Adrian asked, "Why are they talking to you?"

"If you don't go, then you aren't acting rationally, and they say now they are afraid you are emotionally disturbed. So you have a choice. You get up, you put your shoes on and your coat and go to the hospital and get looked at. You said you don't feel good. You said your blood pressure is high."

"Yes, caused by you, chief."

"Caused by me? You've never seen me before in your life."

"I have seen you."

"Son, you've got a choice, what is it gonna be?"

"I'm laying right here until I feel better."

"Ok, son, he's EDP'd. He's EDP'd."

A cop asked, "Cuffs?"

"Yeah."

"Are you gonna go, are you gonna go? I don't want to see this happen to you," Marino said, getting frustrated again.

"I'm gonna go to the hospital."

"You're going now."

"When I feel better."

Marino said, "No. Now. You have no choice. Trained medical professionals are saying now."

"They're going to cuff me," Schoolcraft said into the phone to Larry. "I'm a perp."

Marino said, "No, he's emotionally disturbed."

The tape captured Larry's voice yelling through the phone.

"Adrian, you're making this choice on your own. You can get up and walk out of here," Marino said.

"I'm laying here," Schoolcraft said. "I'm laying here, chief."

"No, they say you have to go," Marino replied. "Now we're obligated to bring you for your own safety."

"I'm laying here, chief. My back hurts."

"OK, let's take him," Marino said.

"My stomach hurts," Adrian said.

Marino: "Adrian, get up."

"My blood pressure," Adrian said.

"I can't play this game, Adrian."

"I can't stand up," Schoolcraft replied. "I don't feel good."

Gough interjected, "Please stand up."

Adrian: "I don't feel good."

Gough: "Put your hands behind your back."

Adrian: "Why am I putting my hands behind my back?"

Gough: "Because you have to go to the hospital."

"So you're going to put handcuffs on me because I have to go to the hospital?" Schoolcraft asked.

Marino: "We're going you a choice Adrian. Get up and walk out."

Gough: "You're being irrational."

Adrian: "How am I being irrational?"

Marino: "Adrian, get up and walk out or we'll have to treat you as an EDP and you know what that means."

Adrian: "How am I being irrational?"

Marino finally lost his temper completely. "Alright, just take him. I can't fucking stand him anymore."

Gough: "Do me a favor and put your hands behind your back."

Marino and three other officers grabbed Schoolcraft, dragged him off his bed, and slammed him to the floor. The tape captured a thud as his body hit the floor and Adrian's repeated grunts in pain as he lay face down. The officers grabbed at his hands, trying to twist them behind his back. They ripped his clothes. "Get one hand! Get one hand! Get one hand!"

A cop finally said, "I got it."

"And the other hand."

They were cuffing him in a manner Schoolcraft later described as a "Chinese torture position." He said Marino put a boot on his face, which the chief later denied.

"They got him," Marino said.

Schoolcraft was still struggling.

Now paternal, Marino said, "Adrian, stop this, Adrian."

Schoolcraft grunted, "Fuck you." He grunted again. The epithet coming out at that moment seems like something Schoolcraft had wanted to say a long time to an NYPD boss, after all he had been through, but he had buried the emotion so deep that it took a physical assault in his own apartment to summon it out of him.

"Give him the other hand," a cop said.

Marino said, "Adrian, stop it."

Finally they grabbed his other hand. Evidently, they were sitting on top of him in some way, because Schoolcraft grunted hoarsely, "Oh my chest. Oh my chest. Oh my chest. Oh my chest."

Marino said, "OK, call the bus, let's get a chair and get him to the hospital forthwith. He's complaining of chest pains. Let's get him to the hospital."

The tape captured the sound of handcuffs scraping together.

They picked him up and placed him on the bed again. Adrian was breathing heavily.

Marino said in a lecturing tone, "We'll get you to the hospital right away, Adrian. You didn't have to do this. I don't know what your agenda is or why you're doing this. There's no need for this."

"You're too good to me, boss," Schoolcraft sputtered.

"Yeah, well."

Schoolcraft asked, "Why are you so good to me?"

"As good as you deserve, son," the chief said.

Schoolcraft could be heard on the tape sighing and trying to slow his rate of breathing. "Just want to make sure, just give him a little, quick toss," a cop said, searching him.

Marino blamed Schoolcraft for the whole encounter. "Absolutely amazing, Adrian, that you put your fellow police officers through this. Absolutely amazing."

At that point, one of the cops found one of Schoolcraft's recorders, which had fallen out of his pocket. Schoolcraft later accused Marino of seizing the recorder and other documents, but the chief appeared on the tape to tell an officer he didn't want them to seize it. The recording was not entirely clear on which version is true. The police later denied they took his "Report to the Commissioner" or anything else from Schoolcraft's apartment.

A cop said, "He's reaching down into his waist."

"I'm not reaching down into my waist. You're pulling my pants down."

The cop replied, "Why are you putting your hand in your pants?"

"You're pulling my pants down annoyed. It's a natural reaction [chuckling a bit at the absurdity of it] to a man pulling my pants down."

Marino told the officers to count his money. "I don't want him turning around saying we stole his money. He's wearing recording devices and everything else so he's playing a game here. Cute. When I came on the job a cop would never do any damage to another cop, not for all the money in the world. Things change."

Schoolcraft had $450 in cash in his pocket.

Next they wanted him to stand up so they could load him onto an orange chair and carry him to the ambulance.

"Adrian, are you going to cooperate and stand up?" an officer asked.

Schoolcraft replied, "I never didn't cooperate with you.... What's the charge?"

Eventually, they had to lift him off the bed, strap him on the chair, and then carry him down the stairs. The humiliation of the evening was complete. As he left, he saw plainclothes officers searching his apartment, looking through boxes in both the living room and the bedroom.

Schoolcraft later claimed that he saw Mauriello speaking with Paul Browne, the department's spokesman and Kelly's top aide, but Browne later denied that he was present. Police vehicles were blocking traffic.

Lauterborn, who had left the apartment when Marino arrived, had returned to the precinct and called to check in with the chief. "The update is we have the officer," the chief told him. "He's gonna to go to the hospital. I don't know which one yet. But he's fine. He's just going to go to be evaluated."

Marino was now referring to Schoolcraft as "fine," when minutes earlier he had characterized him as in crisis.

The ambulance report noted that his breathing rate was normal, he was verbally oriented and alert, and he obeyed commands. Though the report noted he was agitated and resistant when ESU entered the apartment, there was no mention of any psychiatric issues.

Contradicting other reports, the paramedics stated in their report that Schoolcraft walked back to his apartment.

As the officers left, Schoolcraft's other recorder kept rolling for another 30 minutes or so, picking up ever more faint sounds of departing police radios, and then just silence.

★

Back at the station house, Lauterborn was filling out paperwork, having left the scene to Marino. While Lauterborn would later portray Schoolcraft as unbalanced, a document he prepared that night showed just the opposite. At 9:30 p.m., Lauterborn filled out a "fitness for duty" report on Schoolcraft in which he wrote that he was "fit for duty." He noted that Schoolcraft's appearance was neat, his attitude "indifferent," his eyes "apparently normal," his balance "steady," and his speech "normal." Broschart checked exactly the same boxes in his report, except he found Schoolcraft "antagonistic," not "indifferent." In neither document was there any indication they thought they were dealing with a crazy man.

Lauterborn received an angry call from Larry Schoolcraft, who had listened to everything that happened in Adrian's apartment via the open cell phone line. He threatened to have the captain fired and indicted.

Larry Schoolcraft called Internal Affairs to emphasize that Adrian had left work because he didn't feel well. He reiterated the claim that Caughey had threatened him with the gun and claimed that police had broken into Adrian's apartment, assaulted him, dragged him out, and took personal possessions without authorization.

Mauriello called Nelson to say Schoolcraft had been suspended and psyched. Marino, Mauriello, and Lauterborn returned to the station house to discuss the events of the night further and decide who would undergo official interviews.

In subsequent interviews with Internal Affairs, the captain, inspector, and chief offered accounts that diverged from Schoolcraft's account and, more importantly, were at odds with what the digital recorder picked up that night.

In the interviews, all three men went to great lengths to portray Schoolcraft as unbalanced. Lauterborn said Adrian became confrontational and antagonistic, the IAB report said. He called him "disoriented and agitated." He claimed that when Mauriello asked a question, Schoolcraft "jumped out of his bed and charged at Mauriello as though he was going to fight with him."

There was no indication of this on the recording.

Lauterborn claimed Adrian continued to refuse to cooperate, but he admitted that he was sick. Lauterborn recommended he go to the hospital. Schoolcraft, according to Lauterborn's IAB statement, claimed that "there was a conspiracy against him, that he was being retaliated against by everyone." Schoolcraft said nothing about conspiracy or retaliation in the recording.

Lauterborn described Schoolcraft resisting three officers. "As they were attempting to handcuff him, he was moved from the bed to the floor, where he continued to resist the officers' efforts to place his hands behind his back," the IAB report said.

Lauterborn claimed he did not see anyone hit, kick, punch, or strike Schoolcraft, and he saw no injuries. He denied that Schoolcraft was hog-tied or forced to kneel. He said he didn't see anyone remove anything from the apartment.

When a tape recorder fell out of Adrian's pocket, Lauterborn claimed, he picked it up and put it on the dresser.

Lauterborn told investigators he was shocked that Schoolcraft had to be handcuffed and questioned "why a cop would want to fight with other cops."

He denied that there was ever any talk about retaliating against Schoolcraft. He denied the existence of quotas or productivity goals, but said they did expect officers to do their jobs. No officer was ever denied overtime or days off or given poor assignments. He denied threatening anyone in connection with their productivity.

He denied any knowledge about the Caughey and Weiss incident that Schoolcraft reported in August 2009 or any knowledge of Caughey threatening Schoolcraft with a gun. He did say that Caughey and Schoolcraft had a disagreement in March 2009.

Lauterborn insisted to IAB that the events at Schoolcraft's home were not excessive. Lauterborn said the ESU presence was necessary because Schoolcraft "did not appear to be acting rationally," the IAB report said.

Lauterborn also claimed that officers "had been aware of the possibility that Schoolcraft was in possession of firearms because he lived upstate in the past." This assertion came out of left field. The police don't find out about the rifle until Internal Affairs returned to search the apartment several days later.

Lauterborn conceded that he had never seen a chief respond to an AWOL officer, but he said he thought Marino's response was justified because Adrian was "potentially mentally disturbed." Lauterborn said Schoolcraft's removal from his apartment was "appropriate."

While most of his statements are negative toward Schoolcraft, Lauterborn did say that Mauriello knew about the QAD investigation—something that Mauriello denied in his interview. On Halloween 2009, the same day that cops entered his apartment, Lauterborn said he told Mauriello that Schoolcraft might be experiencing stress because of the QAD investigation, and that would explain why he was "shunned" by his fellow officers.

And he admitted that he knew, and other supervisors knew, well before October 31, 2009, that Schoolcraft had been keeping unusual notes in his memo book.

In a separate report known as a "49" that was completed that night and sent to the office of the First Deputy Commissioner, Lauterborn wrote that Schoolcraft "repeatedly exhibited irrational behavior." But he also admitted that the NYPD psychologist, Lamstein, told him she didn't think Schoolcraft was an immediate threat to himself or others.

Lauterborn put the responsibility for labeling Schoolcraft as an EDP on EMS's Lieutenant Hanlon. It was she who decided he would not be allowed to refuse medical attention. Lauterborn also noted that Schoolcraft had numerous hard copies of NYPD complaint reports with perpetrator and complainant information.

In her IAB statement, Hanlon told investigators that Schoolcraft told her he had high blood pressure and stomach pain. She described him as "irrational, belligerent and shouting." But according to the tape, the only time Schoolcraft shouted was at the very end when he was being arrested.

Mauriello also characterized Schoolcraft as unbalanced. He described seeing "boxes, animal cages and traps" in the small one-bedroom apartment. He said Schoolcraft was sitting on his bed in shorts, with white socks pulled up to the knees, and looked disheveled.

Mauriello portrayed himself as only concerned about the officer's well-being. When he said he thought Adrian might have hung himself, Adrian supposedly said, "Obviously not." Then when Mauriello asked why Adrian left work, he claimed Adrian angrily approached and said, "What are you worried about?" Mauriello told investigators Schoolcraft was unstable and his eyes were "bugged out." Mauriello, concerned about a confrontation, left the bedroom and went outside.

Mauriello did not think the response was excessive and would not have done anything differently. He did not think it was at all unusual that Marino was at the scene.

Marino also mentioned boxes, saying it looked like Schoolcraft hadn't finished unpacking. He told investigators that he found Schoolcraft sarcastic, belligerent, and argumentative. "Why would there be police at my door, Chief," Schoolcraft said, according to Marino.

Marino then brought the paramedics over to check him out. If he was not sick, he would be suspended. Marino said he was about to leave the apartment, when a paramedic remarked that Schoolcraft's blood pressure was so high he might have a stroke. Marino claimed he asked for the specifics, but Schoolcraft ordered the paramedics not to disclose them. Marino later claimed that it was the paramedics who advised him that since Schoolcraft refused to go to the hospital, he would have to be declared a psychiatric case and forcibly removed. Marino said he tried to convince Schoolcraft to go to the hospital. When Schoolcraft refused, Marino suspended him and ordered him taken to the hospital involuntarily. Schoolcraft accused him of coercing the paramedics into that decision.

Marino told Schoolcraft to go to the hospital or he would be labeled as an EDP. Schoolcraft was on the phone with his father, and Marino said he could hear Larry screaming.

Marino denied making any physical contact with Schoolcraft, especially putting his boot in his face or ordering him to kneel. He said he didn't speak with any doctors that day. He denied having any conversations with Nelson or any higher-ranking officials. He did not think it was necessary to involve Nelson.

Nelson, however, recalled that he spoke with Marino the next day. He did not believe the response was excessive, and he denied searching the apartment or taking anything from it. He denied knowing about any prior investigations. He said he recalled previously having a conversation with Mauriello about an under-performing officer, whom he later learned was

Schoolcraft. At the time, He agreed that he should be reviewed by the borough command.

Almost as an afterthought after all that had happened, Schoolcraft was given another low evaluation of 2.5. He was below standards for the second consecutive year. He was given zeros in nine categories. Lieutenant Rafael Mascol wrote, "He fails to maintain the confidentiality of department documents and cases. He breaches integrity and department guidelines and has had disciplinary problems."

For the year, 81st Precinct crime dropped 10.9 percent—well ahead of prior year declines.

CHAPTER 10

PATIENT NO. 130381874

The act of forcibly entering an American citizen's apartment is not, at least under the U.S. Constitution, something to be undertaken lightly. The Fourth Amendment reads that "the right of the people to be secure in their persons, houses, papers, and effects, against unreasonable searches and seizures, shall not be violated."

The amendment goes on to say: "No Warrants shall issue, but upon probable cause, supported by Oath or affirmation, and particularly describing the place to be searched, and the persons or things to be seized."

The police had entered Schoolcraft's home without his consent, assaulted him, and forcibly removed him. They had searched his possessions without a warrant and, he said, seized, among other things, a tape recorder and certain files and folders from his desk. (Those items were never returned.) They had kept him handcuffed in the Jamaica Hospital emergency room even though he was not charged with any crime.

The law doesn't take lightly committing a person involuntarily to a psych ward. In this instance, the standard appears in the New York State Mental Hygiene Law, section 9, subsections 39 and 41, and it is a high bar.

The more general standard states that a person can be involuntarily committed only if there is "a substantial risk of physical harm to himself as manifested by threats of or attempts at suicide or serious bodily harm" and/ or "a substantial risk of physical harm to other persons as manifested by homicidal or other violent behavior."

Subsection 41 relates to the powers of police officers: "Any peace officer, when acting pursuant to his or her special duties, or police officer... may take into custody any person who appears to be mentally ill and is conducting himself or herself in a manner which is likely to result in serious harm to the person or others."

In other words, the police and the hospital had to meet a fairly high standard to justify committing Schoolcraft—the "substantial" or "serious" threat of physical harm to himself or others.

Schoolcraft had not, either that night or at any point in the past, made any threats against anyone, nor had he ever expressed a desire to hurt or kill himself. He had never tried to hurt anyone, nor had he ever tried to harm himself, nor had he ever evinced any violent behavior. And he had zero prior psychiatric history before being placed on desk duty.

Moreover, under police procedure, a person "may refuse medical attention." Even if it is true that the paramedic believed his high blood pressure was a health issue, he still had a right as a citizen to refuse to go to the hospital.

This right is so fundamentally ingrained in law that it goes back almost 100 years to a 1914 case, *Schloendorff v. Society of New York Hospital*, in which the court held that "every human being of adult years and sound mind has a right to determine what should be done with his own body."

The case included one exception: "cases of emergency, where the patient is unconscious and where it is necessary to operate before consent can be obtained." (Schoolcraft was neither unconscious nor incapable of making that decision.)

Indeed, medical staffers can be liable for performing care without the consent of a patient.

Justice John Paul Stevens of the U.S. Supreme Court wrote in a 1990 decision, "There is no doubt... that a competent individual's right to refuse medication is a fundamental liberty interest deserving the highest order of protection."

The fact that police showed up in force at his house after he had merely left work early was another red flag. Typically, that does not happen in instances of minor misconduct. In most instances, police commanders would have simply waited until he returned to work and written him up for going home early.

At worst, the misconduct would have resulted in a suspension and the loss of some vacation days. For some reason, Schoolcraft had received the worst kind of special treatment.

Schoolcraft was like Lewis Carroll's Alice. He had been pulled through the looking glass and landed in a world where the standard rules of physics didn't apply, and things were going to get substantially worse.

★

Schoolcraft was in an ambulance on his way to Jamaica Hospital Medical Center, a private institution overlooking the Van Wyck Expressway that had benefitted greatly from both government backing and the largesse of private donors. One building in the complex was named for developer Donald Trump.

Lieutenant Broschart, who had been ordered to accompany Schoolcraft to the hospital, later told investigators that Schoolcraft's attitude changed in the ambulance. He was cooperative with the paramedics, smiling and answering questions.

Schoolcraft remembered it differently. He was still in the chair. He tried to question the paramedics, but they were only interested in checking his conduction. He asked Broschart to remove the handcuffs, but the lieutenant told him to wait until they got to the hospital.

What is striking about this is that the medical "crisis" that Marino had spun in Adrian's apartment became irrelevant. It wasn't mentioned again.

Schoolcraft reached the emergency room after 10 p.m. Other than a few hospital documents, there is no independent record of the next six days, except for a ten-page single-spaced account Schoolcraft himself wrote. There is no mention in either the Brooklyn North files or the Internal Affairs files of what took place behind the hospital walls.

Broschart took Schoolcraft to a gurney, handcuffed him to a railing, and placed him in a hallway under relentless fluorescent lights.

Schoolcraft begged Broschart to loosen the cuffs. "I kept asking them, 'Why am I under arrest, why am I not free to leave?'" he said. "'Why am

I handcuffed?'" No answer. This is who I had to protect me." Broschart smirked and said, "I bet you wish now you came back to the 8-1 like you were told." He walked away without loosening the cuffs.

An hour later, according to Schoolcraft's notes, he asked Broschart to get someone there from Internal Affairs. The lieutenant turned away. Broschart and an officer named Cruz were relieved by Sergeant Shantel James, who started her career as a school safety agent in a Manhattan high school, and a second police officer. Schoolcraft asked James to contact Internal Affairs. She, he recalled, returned to filling out her monthly activity reports. She also ignored his request to loosen the handcuffs.

At some point later, he was interviewed by a female Asian doctor, who asked him, "Do you feel like they are coming to get you?"

"They *did* come to get me, that's why I'm here," he replied drily.

She asked him to remember three words in their 10-minute talk: "blue rose, New York, and table." She asked him other questions, and then said, "This is ridiculous, you shouldn't be here much longer."

"I just want to go home," he told her. "I haven't hurt or threatened anyone, and I won't."

Schoolcraft claimed that during this interview, a police officer was directing a cell phone at them, possibly videotaping the conversation.

"The minute that Adrian shows up at the ER, the doctors aren't supposed to look at him as a prisoner, because he hasn't been arrested," Larry said. "They are supposed to objectively advocate for Adrian. They had a duty to protect him, and instead of advocating and caring for the patient, they assaulted him, too, just like the police did. They just bought right into the whole thing and allowed the NYPD to exploit their medical licenses."

The handcuffs were locked to a setting that made them painfully tight. "His hands were so swollen he was losing his feelings in his hands," Larry said, drawing off of his own law enforcement experience. "When you are in the hospital, the doctors give the orders. It's clear that he's not a threat, but they won't even tell the cops to loosen the handcuffs, let alone remove them. Adrian's not under arrest. He's surrounded by cops."

Later, the hospital tried to say that they agreed to leave him cuffed because they viewed Schoolcraft as a "flight risk." No arrest. No charges. Schoolcraft was not acting out. He was surrounded by police, but he was a flight risk?

"That makes them liable," Larry said. "For a doctor not to do that, a doctor should go to prison for it. Isn't a doctor's responsibility to do no harm? And right here, right in front of them, they are torturing him. This is what makes me sick."

Sitting there in the ER, miserable, in pain, his wrists killing him, Schoolcraft noted ruefully that a sign over the nurse's station read, "We are here to help you." He asked repeatedly to be allowed to call his father, but the requests were denied.

Up in Johnstown, Larry was desperately trying to find his son. But his name wasn't yet entered in the patient information system. He wasn't officially at the hospital. Larry wracked his brain. Finally, he had a good idea.

"It's clear that the hospital was letting the NYPD run the show," he said. "I tried the security department and got ahold of a sergeant. I asked him to check on him in the ER, and thankfully, he went up and checked. He gets back on the phone and tells me, he's in the ER, he's surrounded by police. He tells me he talked to an administrator, who told him to stay out of it."

Larry called the nurse's station in an effort to reach Adrian. James ignored Adrian's request to use the phone, so, frustrated, he rolled his gurney to the phone, picked up the receiver, and dialed Larry. He told his father that no one had seen him and he was still handcuffed, and the cuffs were causing his wrists to swell and cutting off blood flow. Larry was beyond furious. He wanted to come down from Johnstown and set everything straight. Adrian told him to calm down and wait. It would just make everything worse. Larry told him, "I'm going to get you out of there, I'm going to call everyone, I'm going to call the cavalry."

"I got some blips and bleeps from Adrian," he said later. "Adrian expected the cavalry to arrive, and I really did believe that somebody would show up. Nobody showed. If that's not an indictment of all of it, I don't know what is."

As he was talking, James appeared at his side and started yanking the gurney away from the nurse's desk, yelling, "Put down the phone!" James then pulled the cord out of the receiver. Five officers grabbed him, tossed him back on the gurney, and cuffed both his hands.

Schoolcraft asked James why he couldn't talk to his father. He said James then told the nurses, "If anyone calls here for him, don't tell him, just tell whoever they are he's at the 81st Precinct." It was as if he was owned by the

New York City Police Department. This was the first Adrian had heard that he was going back to the stationhouse.

"I'm not going to the 8-1 or anywhere with you or anyone else from the 8-1!" Schoolcraft responded.

James then called a sergeant at the precinct to tell him Adrian was refusing to go and asking when she could leave. She left, apparently to make a phone call, and then returned and walked into the psychiatric emergency room, apparently to confer with doctors.

Three ESU officers arrived at the hospital, saying they were there to help him. They loosened the cuffs. He saw James and one of the ESU officers speaking with a doctor. "The ESU officer appeared to be advocating for me," he wrote.

Up in Johnstown, Larry was calling everyone he could think of. He called PBA lawyer Stuart London, he called the FBI, he called Internal Affairs. "All of them assured me that they would respond in some way," he said. "I was hoping that it would keep Adrian calm, because as time went on, someone in his situation, knowing he did nothing wrong, would start to get angry."

In hindsight, Larry was upset with the PBA and with Internal Affairs, but he felt the most anger for the FBI. "I told them you need to go talk to him," he said. "Once they know the FBI is there, they are going to knock it off. But the arrogance that I got from the FBI agent, being admonished when I expressed my concerns. He tells me that the FBI works with the NYPD every day and they are fine. I'm getting this shit from an FBI agent who is 25 years old, and he's going to tell me everything is fine. This is not some little microcosm in Alabama. This is New York City, and it was reported to everybody. Nobody did their job.

"It would be no different than an FBI agent gets a call from his wife. She tells him that someone is in her apartment, and he calls the NYPD and asks them to respond, and the PD tells him 'Oh, it's fine, call Monday, and we'll have a committee meeting and then get back to you.' Here's the thing: If they don't have a duty to respond, then what are they in business for? I clearly reported a crime, and they did nothing. What probably happened is they called the NYPD, and were told bad things about Adrian, and they bought it. The thing is that if the PD lied to them, someone has to go to jail....If the FBI had come in, it would have been a totally different investigation. All we've seen from IAB is the illusion of an investigation."

At the same time, Larry was trying to get information out of the hospital staff. "I want to talk to the attending physician," he said. "It was very difficult. The nurses are extremely intimidated and careful of what they said. I did come across one nurse, she seemed to be mature and intelligent and had a grasp that something was not right. I told her what was going on, who I was, who Adrian was, and what this was about. I said they are going to try to hurt him. I said I am concerned about his safety. She told me nobody will hurt him while I'm here."

But no one responded. No one. Schoolcraft remained in the emergency room on that gurney for *nine* hours. He was not allowed to use the phone, get water, eat, or use the bathroom, according to a notice of claim he wrote soon after.

If the police had arrested Schoolcraft, they would eventually have had to disclose the reasons for it. By "psyching" him, they bought up to 14 days. They had discredited him, and they could also decline to discuss what happened. The truth would stay hidden behind a veil of confidentiality.

"I can't remember a time in my entire life that I ever felt so helpless," Larry said. "When I decided not to go down right way, when I tried to do it legitimately, I felt someone would go over there and moderate this whole thing, that didn't happen."

Then, the police supervisors at the hospital told him that after his release, he would have to return to the 81st Precinct for questioning. Schoolcraft refused, and he claimed that refusal led to him being transferred to the psychiatric emergency room.

He was transferred from the emergency room to the emergency psychiatric room "as an emergency status patient" for "immediate observation, care and treatment." The admission form said he could be kept up to 15 days. He was left to sleep on a gurney in the hallway of the ward.

He was then interviewed by Dr. Khin Mar Lwin, a psychiatrist, who wrote "psychotic disorder" at the top of his report, but the description that Schoolcraft gave was hardly suggestive of that. "He says this is happening because he has been reporting on his superiors. He says he knows that his supervisors are hiding robbery and assault cases to get higher positions, and has proper documentation about this," the doctor wrote. Of course, this was all true.

For an account of what happened, Dr. Lwin turned to Sergeant James, who had been sent by the 81st Precinct to keep an eye on Schoolcraft. She was not present at Schoolcraft's apartment and had no firsthand knowledge of what had happened.

She told Lwin that Schoolcraft "left work early after getting agitated and cursing a supervisor." There is a tape. He didn't curse anyone.

She said Schoolcraft "barricaded himself and the door had to be broken to get to him." Flat wrong.

Once he had initially agreed to go to the hospital, Schoolcraft "ran and had to be chased." Also wrong.

Quoting James, the doctor wrote that in the medical emergency room, Schoolcraft "became agitated, uncooperative and verbally abusive over telephone use and told his treating MDs, 'they are all against me.'" However, since Schoolcraft was not arrested, he still had rights. Someone with those rights might indeed get upset if he was not allowed to use the phone.

Lwin wrote that Schoolcraft was "coherent, relevant with goal-directed speech and good eye contact. He is irritable with appropriate effect. He is paranoid about his supervisors. He denies suicidal ideation, homicidal ideation at the present time. His memory and concentration are intact. He is alert and oriented. His insight and judgment are impaired."

Despite the obvious positives in the analysis, Lwin recommended his transfer to the psychiatric emergency room and said his observation should be continued for "unpredictable behavior and escape risk."

What these documents demonstrate is that Schoolcraft was not even remotely in crisis. Lwin did not note any kind of extreme behavior that would have justified keeping him.

Someone in the hospital appears to have simply accepted the police's version of events as justification for holding him longer. But the ball was rolling in only one direction.

When a Sergeant Sawyer and a police officer named Miller arrived, Schoolcraft was on the phone with Larry. Sawyer told James, "I thought perps weren't supposed to speak on the phone."

James replied that the nurses were letting him use the phone. Sawyer cut off the call and told Schoolcraft he couldn't use the phone because he was in handcuffs, but he gave no explanation as to why Adrian was in handcuffs in the first place. He hadn't been arrested.

At that point, four officers roughly grabbed Schoolcraft and handcuffed him to the gurney again. Schoolcraft described excruciating pain. When Schoolcraft asked again why he had to be handcuffed, Sawyer said, "Because you're a fucking rat," according to Adrian's notes.

The nurses ignored his requests for help. He asked for help from a hospital administrator. That was denied.

Miller and Sawyer wheeled him to a room where he was told to change into a backless gown. He claimed he was strip-searched. He was then wheeled into the psychiatric emergency room. He claimed that while this was happening he overheard Sawyer telling Miller, "I chose you because I can't trust anyone else. This is a big fucking mess, everyone is going to get GO-15'd." (GO-15, or General Order 15, is NYPD argot for an official interview done under oath.)

In the psychiatric ER, he was interviewed again, this time by a Dr. Tariq, who agreed to call Internal Affairs. Schoolcraft wanted photos taken of the bruises on his body. He spent an uncomfortable 24 hours in that ER among people who were truly in crisis, including a man who was combing his hair with feces, a woman who kept making herself vomit, a patient covered in bloody bandages, and an array of screamers. There were no clocks and no mirrors. On the television, he ruefully watched Greg Kelly, the police commissioner's son, host a Fox morning talk show.

Unknown to him, the NYPD teletype had spit out an order from police headquarters that he had been suspended on authority of the Chief of Department, Joseph Esposito. Consider this for a moment: Schoolcraft had filed complaints with Internal Affairs and QAD, and his father had called the mayor's office, the commissioner's office, Internal Affairs, and the chief of department's office. It was not like the senior bosses at police headquarters didn't know who he was. And yet they did nothing to take his custody away from the borough command and give it to a more independent overseer.

Early the next morning, according to his notes, Schoolcraft overheard one medical staffer ask whether he would be discharged, and a second said,

"No, no, no, Schoolcraft is not going anywhere. He's a special case." That afternoon, he was interviewed by a social worker who was retired NYPD, who called him "manicky." And then, finally, Internal Affairs officers from Group 1, the unit that investigates misconduct by high-ranking bosses, appeared. In a bit of a turnabout, one of the IAB officers had a digital recorder in a pocket.

At 3 p.m. on Tuesday, November 3, which happened to be election day, the day Mayor Bloomberg beat out Democrat Bill Thompson for a third term, Schoolcraft was transferred from the psychiatric ER to the regular psychiatric ward with the vague diagnosis of "psychosis not otherwise specified." He was listed as Patient No. 130381874. He was interviewed by Christine McMahon, a social worker. In his words, she said, "Well, being a cop is sometimes hard to deal with, isn't it, and you need help dealing with all those things...blah, blah, blah."

He wrote that he replied, "I reported police supervisors committing crimes against the citizens we were sworn to protect. This isn't me whining about the day-to-day stress of being a police officer."

Larry arrived via Amtrak early that evening. He switched to the Long Island Rail Road, arrived in Jamaica, and took a cab right to the hospital. While he was on the train, he got the first call from anyone in authority about Adrian's status. The call came from a case worker in the psychiatric ward, not from the police. It had taken nearly 90 hours to notify Adrian's dad about his son's status.

As a joke meant to amuse Adrian and reduce the tension, Larry wore a wig and a Rastafarian hat that he bought in a mall near Albany. Security searched him and then took him to a cafeteria, where they brought Adrian to see him. Adrian was still dressed in the backless hospital gown. He had no underwear. Larry brought him underwear and socks.

"He was pretty upset," Larry said. "He sat there just ruminating, saying, 'I just should have stayed at work,' and I looked at him and said, 'What are you talking about, Adrian? So now they can do whatever they want to you?' I said just be cool. It's tough to tell someone that. He's looking at me like you ain't done shit. Where's the cavalry? I said, 'Hey, look, be cool, it'll come out in the wash.' Physically he wasn't doing well, he was sick and pale, he wasn't sleeping good, or eating good. It was real hot, and it was dirty. You could just smell that it was an unclean environment. It smelled tainted."

After meeting with his son, Larry walked out into a cool evening. It was about 10 p.m. He stopped and gazed at the hospital building named after Trump. He hired a gypsy cab driver to help him find a hotel. "I saw this Iranian guy sitting in an old Lincoln, and I go up to him," Larry said. "His name is Kamal. I tell him I'm from upstate, I don't know my way around the city. My son's in hospital. He takes me to the Clarion Motel, kitty-corner off the Van Wyck from the hospital, and they give me a nice room in the basement."

Larry labored through the night. He called the *New York Times* at 1 a.m. He reached a reporter, who told him that he was working on another story but would get back to him. That reporter never responded and never answered another call from him. He left a message with a reporter at the *New York Daily News*. He didn't hear back from that reporter until a couple of months later.

"I wanted it to get out there, I wanted to put as much pressure as I could," Larry said. "I figured every hour they kept him, there was a chance that something else would happen to make it worse."

Larry had no computer, but he had a cell phone and the phone numbers of every agency that might, in a perfect world, help. His fingers were sore from pressing buttons. It was here that his son could have used a rabbi, an NYPD official who would make a call for Adrian, who would bring some sense to this bizarre situation. Of course, Adrian had none. The Schoolcrafts were on their own.

"I knew he was in jeopardy, it was only a matter of time before he started acting up," Larry said. "I knew they were trying to get him to take medication. They had tried to get him to take Risperdal [an antipsychotic used to treat schizophrenia]. How long would it be before they forced it?"

Larry kept dialing. He called the journalist Jimmy Breslin's agent. He called every PBA official he could. He finally spoke with Stuart London, the PBA attorney. London suggested that Larry call Norman Siegel, the former head of the New York Civil Liberties Union. Siegel advised Larry to call a mental health lawyer. Larry and Adrian then met with Dr. Isak Isakov, the psychiatrist who had control of Adrian's file. During the conversation, Isakov mentioned David Durk's name without prompting. To the Schoolcrafts, this suggested that Isakov was talking to people he should not be talking to.

"He's gotta be 65, nice, pleasant, not a jerk," Larry said. "He wanted to know who Adrian was. We talked for quite a while, and I saw the lights going on in his mind and it was like, 'Oh shit.' I could see the light bulbs, maybe this is legit. Maybe this is not crazy, but true. Now it all started to add up for him. I saw a change in his affect."

If the hospital was making its own decisions, that was somewhat contradicted by what Isakov said about releasing Schoolcraft. He told them he "wanted to hear from the police first, before allowing him to leave."

The second meeting that day was between Larry, Adrian, Isakov, and a Sergeant Wu from NYPD Internal Affairs. In this meeting, Wu finally took pictures of Adrian's injuries. These photos were never subsequently mentioned in any IAB reports. Isakov refused to show Adrian any records of the reasons behind his stay at the hospital.

"I am his power of attorney," Larry said. "He's in the hospital. They won't show the records to him. They claim they can't show them because it would make him more disturbed. I said show them to me. I am his heath care proxy. I said you tell me why you're holding my son who has no criminal history, he's a good person, why are you holding my son involuntarily. Isakov says he's free to leave. I said OK, Adrian get up, let's go."

Here, the sequence became mordantly cartoonish. The Schoolcrafts got up and walked down the gloomy hallway. They reached a locked door. Adrian whispered to Larry, "We're going to get arrested." Larry replied, "I'm not doing anything wrong." When they reached the security door, it was locked.

"The bells and whistles go off, and security starts arriving," Larry said. "We're just standing there. They are just standing there. I say, 'Sergeant, are we free to go? Will you open the door?' Nobody says anything. We decide that we made our point and return to the room."

In his subsequent Internal Affairs report, Wu never mentioned this; he just said the Schoolcrafts never tried to leave.

On Thursday, November 5, the status quo lingered. Schoolcraft remained in the psych unit. Larry was trying to get him out. "I think it was kind of like they ate dinner on Wednesday, on Thursday they digested it, and they knew he was going before the judge," Larry said. "They could release him at any time they wanted. They could have immediately corrected the mistake but they chose not to."

Isakov noted Schoolcraft was anxious, suspicious, and guarded, but he entered nothing in his report that suggested anything beyond Adrian's unhappiness at being there. "He was demanding to be discharged and appeared restless. He denied any suicidal or homicidal ideations, denied any auditory or visual hallucinations. His cognition and memory were intact."

On November 6, the next day, Schoolcraft was finally released. The hospital's discharge summary, written by Dr. Isakov, contradicted the NYPD's assessment of Schoolcraft. The only psychiatric diagnosis Isakov could come up with was "adjustment disorder with anxious mood related to stress at job." This description fit Schoolcraft's reality but did not add up to reason to imprison him in the psych ward for six days. Isakov added, "There were no significant psychiatric symptoms to treat with medications." The only tangible thing that Isakov did was give Adrian the name of a psychiatrist to visit. That was it, after all that chaos. As for an explanation, he received none. None. It was all as if it never happened.

On his way out of the building—in a massive example of adding insult to injury—Schoolcraft was handed a bill for $7,185. Someone in Jamaica Hospital must have had a pretty twisted sense of humor, Schoolcraft thought.

"I didn't even know they were releasing him," Larry said. "He wasn't given a reason. He had to give them the name of a psychologist to follow up with him. I found someone, and that was it."

In sum, based on the available record, it seems crystal clear that the hospital took the police at their word. Indeed, hospital spokesman Ole Pederson would later tell the *Village Voice* newspaper, "We have to take the word of whoever is coming in with him and make a decision based on what they tell us. If there is an issue, the issue is with the Police Department or whoever brought an individual in."

Even later, hospital officials decided that this wasn't the best position to take, as it obviously suggested that doctors weren't making independent medical evaluations. They subsequently insisted that doctors made the call to hold Schoolcraft.

Later that day, the Schoolcrafts met with Sergeant Wu from Internal Affairs at Adrian's apartment. Adrian's landlord told Larry that he had seen police removing manila folders from Adrian's apartment.

In the days that followed, Internal Affairs found the rifle—a "High Point Firearms 9-millimeter rifle with a laser scope, four magazines and ten live rounds inside of a clear plastic bag," as a subsequent report put it. This became more grist for the NYPD's campaign to marginalize Schoolcraft. Of course, Adrian was subsequently charged with possession of a gun. He was supposed to turn in his firearms when he was placed on restricted duty, and he did. The gun was Larry's, and it had been sitting unused under Adrian's bed since March 2007. It had never even been fired.

Larry kept calling oversight agencies and lawyers. He called the FBI, federal prosecutors' offices, the district attorneys in Brooklyn and Queens. And yet, in a sequence that would repeat itself over and over in the following weeks, no one would listen. Nobody overtly shut the door, but neither would anyone get involved. Not even the PBA, the police union, or its lawyers would get involved. Only Internal Affairs responded, and the Schoolcrafts were hardly optimistic about them.

On November 1, while Adrian was still in the hospital, Larry Schoolcraft called Michelle Cort, a prosecutor in the Public Integrity section of the Queens district attorney's office, and asked her to investigate his son's treatment at the hands of police. When Adrian was released, Larry called her again to let her know that he was out. Cort did nothing, it appears.

Likewise, the Brooklyn District Attorney got a call from Larry. That office did nothing. Much later, a reporter asked a spokesman for the Brooklyn District Attorney why it never investigated the case. "We would wait for a referral from NYPD Internal Affairs," he said. "If they refer this to us, we will certainly pursue it."

In all this, to the Schoolcrafts, it appeared that the arms of government that have the responsibility for enforcing the law, including the U.S. Constitution and civil rights statutes, had closed to them. They heard excuse after excuse, from one end of the city to the other. Outside the NYPD anyway, there always seems to be a reason to ignore the Schoolcrafts, a reason to not get involved, not even to see if there was any validity to their claims.

The Schoolcrafts began to feel that Adrian was held until after election day to prevent his story from affecting Bloomberg's chances at reelection. There is no support for this notion, but it illustrates what the sequence looked like to them. And given the circumstances, you can't blame them for suspecting a conspiracy. Schoolcraft's allegations are right in the wheelhouse of what makes New York's reputation. The crime numbers undergird every other indicator of the city's health, and the impression of a healthy city leads to jobs, it makes real estate moguls rich, it leads to tourism. The crime numbers are everything. Moreover, CompStat had made the careers not only of four police commissioners and two mayors, but countless police commanders who had risen in the department and then spread out to run other police departments. If the Schoolcrafts had no direct evidence of a conspiracy, they certainly had the indicia of one.

On November 9, Larry followed up on his complaint with the FBI. He got an agent on the phone who of course knew nothing about the case.

"I asked the FBI to intervene because IAB is doing nothing," Larry said. "My son, they kept him handcuffed for 12 hours. He wasn't allowed to pee. Nobody interceded. Not FBI, IAB, nobody. If I can't call the FBI when a cop is in trouble...I'm an ex-cop myself and I'm flabbergasted. I don't know who to call."

The FBI agent told Larry, "Well, you called us, you made a complaint."

"FBI agent Anderson said Sunday I should hear something," Larry said. "Is the FBI doing something or is it declined?"

"We have a lot of cases."

"I understand, but what's more important than a police officer dragged out of his house in the middle of night, especially a police officer?" Larry asked.

"Somebody will be in contact with you, OK?"

"Do you have any suggestions?" Larry pleaded. "I've contacted the U.S. Attorney General's office in Washington. Do you have any suggestion on who to call to have a look at this?"

By now, it was clear the agent was trying to get him off the phone. "The district attorney's office for the county...call them."

"I've already done that," Larry said. "The Queens County public corruption office and U.S. attorney's office for southern district, which also does not return my calls. The federal government totally walked away. What's it all about?"

"Hold tight," the agent said finally. "If we take it, we'll let you know, if not I'm sorry."

They spent the next week "hiding out," as Larry put it, in an anonymous motel in Queens. Adrian provided the recording from Halloween night to Internal Affairs detectives. They pledged a thorough investigation.

The PBA still hadn't lifted a finger to help him. "They definitely violated their contract," Larry said. "It all boils down to this: Basically they had a contractual obligation to protect Adrian's vested interest in his job, and they did not."

Larry and Adrian decided to alter their approach. Prior to Halloween night, Schoolcraft had gone through internal channels in the NYPD. He had approached Internal Affairs, he had approached QAD, his father had contacted the mayor's office and the office of the police commissioner. They tried to interest the oversight agencies, the feds, the county prosecutors, the FBI, the attorney general, and all of them had walked away. There was only one thing left to do: go down that road only followed by desperate men, and talk to the media.

And so on November 13, 2009, Larry and Adrian, still casting around for someone who would listen to the story, wrote to Leonard Levitt, a dean of New York City police reporters who had broken many big stories in his long career and authored a number of books, including an exposé of the long unsolved murder of teenager Martha Moxley in a wealthy Connecticut enclave. After a long stint with *New York Newsday,* Levitt was writing a column on the NYPD from his Connecticut home. Levitt and Kelly had once had a collegial relationship, particularly after Rudy Giuliani picked Bill Bratton over Kelly back in 1993. But when Kelly returned to the commissioner's office under Bloomberg in 2002, Levitt wrote some unflattering articles, and Kelly got mad. At one point, when he was still with *Newsday,* Levitt had written a column that so infuriated Kelly that the commissioner took a day to drive 45 miles to *Newsday's* Melville, New York, headquarters and meet with the newspaper's bigwigs to demand Levitt's firing. The bosses at *Newsday* wisely ignored the demand.

In the email to Levitt, Larry and Adrian detailed the sequence of the previous two months and then wrote, "We both understand if you don't believe this could really happen, either did I." This was an understatement. Levitt later wrote, somewhat regretfully, that at that point, when he received that first message, he just didn't believe the story.

And then Larry and Adrian pulled out of town. They left the hotel room behind, took Amtrak back to Johnstown, and lived in a cramped one-bedroom apartment in a small cookie-cutter complex just off North Comrie Avenue, down the street from Glenda's Florist and Greenhouse. It was a retreat, sure, but whether right or wrong, Adrian was concerned that if he remained in the city, he would be further harassed by the NYPD. But the distance didn't help him. It turned out that the arms of the department were a lot longer than he thought.

CHAPTER 11

A GAME OF CAT AND MOUSE

Under NYPD rules, an officer can be suspended for up to 30 days, but then he or she must return to work on what's known as "modified assignment," essentially desk duty, without guns or shield, until the charges are resolved. Dealing with the charges is a mind-numbing process that can easily take well over a year depending on the charges and the officer's position in the political landscape of the NYPD. The desk duty can take many forms and is very much like purgatory, the limbo world between heaven and hell. You're still a cop, but you can't really take any police action. You're still getting paid, but you have the black spot on you. In some ways, there's a mafia mentality. Your former coworkers won't talk to you because you might be wired, and they don't want your taint to touch them.

Cops on modified assignment often work bureaucratic desks in police headquarters or man the barricade detail, which involves roaming the city setting up crowd barriers for parades and public events. If you are really disliked, the department sends you to VIPER, an Orwellian unit where cops on full salary literally sit and stare at video monitors attached to security cameras in public housing. Many of these officers have been accused of serious misconduct, so you have miscreants watching for miscreants. Others just annoyed someone who was connected to higher-ups. Modified assignment can extend indefinitely, making it a punishment in itself.

Cops call it "getting jammed up," and even for officers accused of minor misconduct, it can interrupt their careers for years, end a chance for promotion, and prevent them from retiring. Modified assignment is slightly different than "highway therapy," in which officers who have fallen out of favor are transferred to units far from their homes. For example, a cop who lives on Staten Island might be sent to a precinct in the northernmost Bronx. No overt word is uttered, but the message is crystal clear.

But, as with everything else in this story, the conflict between Schoolcraft and the NYPD didn't play itself out in the standard way. Instead, it seems, the story entered a bizarre land where up was down, down was up, and all the actors were making up rules as they went along.

In the intervening couple of weeks that follow the Schoolcrafts' departure from the city, they continued to try to interest someone in Adrian's story, but there were no takers, and what happened on Halloween night remained a secret.

Back in the city, several parallel investigations were taking place within the NYPD. Brooklyn North and one arm of Internal Affairs were investigating Schoolcraft. Another arm of Internal Affairs was interviewing 81st Precinct and Brooklyn North cops about Schoolcraft's allegations. The Quality Assurance Division was quietly following up on Adrian's charges of downgrading of crimes, checking 81st Precinct crime reports, interviewing the victims whose reports Schoolcraft alleged were buried, and formally interviewing the precinct's commanders and patrol officers.

But neither the Internal Affairs unit investigating the allegations or the QAD contacted Schoolcraft again to ask follow-up questions, obtain more information, or clarify any statements. All he heard from them was silence. In fact, he had not heard a chirp from QAD since the October 7 meeting that kicked off the investigation.

In the meantime, internal NYPD records show that the department's disciplinary machine was moving hard against Schoolcraft with regard to the events of Halloween night. Perhaps never in the history of the NYPD had so many resources been directed at a single wayward police officer who went home from work 45 minutes early. This fact tends to favor the Schoolcrafts' claims of an organized and concerted effort to discredit him, but often the simplest explanation is the one that's right. In the aftermath of Halloween night, almost everything the department did seemed to tilt against him.

Through November, while he was technically serving his 30-day suspension without pay, the campaign started with phone calls about his status. Initially, Adrian claimed he was sick and couldn't come back to work.

On December 1, as the 30-day suspension period ended, the strategy changed abruptly. Larry and Adrian were making their stand in a small one-bedroom apartment just off the main drag in Johnstown. What happened next was a bizarre cat-and-mouse struggle that may be unprecedented in the history of the New York City Police Department. And it was all couched in process and procedure, as if it made some kind of logical sense.

The department sent a sergeant and a lieutenant from Brooklyn North, Marino's command, to Johnstown. They appeared outside Schoolcraft's door with members of the Johnstown Police Department and demanded that he return to work to face disciplinary charges. Schoolcraft told them he was too ill to travel. They left. They returned the following day, and this exchange repeated itself.

NYPD records from these visits indicated Schoolcraft could be heard saying through the door, "I don't know what to do." He didn't answer the door. The funny thing about these records is that they describe a series of events that are at once weird and Orwellian and even laughable, yet are conveyed in utterly serious bureaucratic language.

The police tried to get police union lawyer Stuart London to relay a message. He declined because he hadn't spoken to Adrian. Because he refused to return, Schoolcraft was suspended again. He was, at that point, technically AWOL, which would lead to more disciplinary charges.

On December 7, Larry called the NYPD's personnel office. He was told that Adrian had to come back to work. "He has to come back. If he does not come back, he will be listed as AWOL, and he'll be suspended again," a sergeant told him. "Time is precious in these instances. It's going to put him in a bad light, once he gets suspended. They will not perceive that as being cooperative."

On December 8, police arrived again at the apartment and banged on the door repeatedly. The officers could hear the Schoolcrafts inside the apartment, but they didn't answer.

They noted in their reports that Schoolcraft's sneakers had been taken inside. They could hear someone inside saying, "The car's back. That's what they do. They sneak around." The NYPD knocked again and announced their presence. Someone inside laughed. In response, the police shoved a copy of the suspension order under the door.

Finally, at about 3 p.m., Larry opened the door and spoke to the officers. They ordered Schoolcraft to report to the 50th Precinct in the Bronx. Schoolcraft did not report as ordered.

Two days later, Assistant Chief Gerald Nelson signed off on charges and specifications against Schoolcraft for failing to comply with orders not to leave the precinct on October 31 and for being AWOL on December 8.

The parallel internal investigations continued. Mauriello was investigating in his precinct. The Brooklyn North inspections unit, overseen by Chief Marino and Nelson, was investigating. And Internal Affairs was investigating. And there was the QAD investigation.

As time passed, it seemed the NYPD was looking for anything it could find with which to charge Schoolcraft. Until October 31, Schoolcraft's Internal Affairs file showed few allegations against him. From December 2 though July 20, 2010, another 14 allegations were logged in IAB, most of them having to do with his failure to show up for work.

On December 12, Schoolcraft applied for public assistance, food stamps, and housing assistance with the Fulton County Department of Social Services. When the department learned of this, they moved to block the application and eventually charged him administratively with fraud for applying for benefits even though he was technically still employed. The initial complaint, records show, was made by Lieutenant Timothy Caughey, the same guy who Schoolcraft filed a complaint about with Internal Affairs four months earlier—and the same guy who was allegedly menacing Schoolcraft on October 31.

Though it was perhaps puzzling to the NYPD, Schoolcraft strongly felt that he was in danger if he returned to work anywhere in the NYPD or moved back to his apartment in Queens. He and his father seriously discussed the possibility that police would kick in his door and once again drag him off.

On December 11, according to a recording, IAB Sergeant Robert O'Hare and Johnstown police officers banged on his door a cartoonish 186 times in one 15-minute period while shouting things like, "Adrian we know you're in there. Open the door."

O'Hare shouted through the door that he just had some paperwork for Schoolcraft to sign so he could start receiving a paycheck again. O'Hare was obviously frustrated and finally gave up. As they left, he told a Johnstown cop, "Sorry to bother you with this nonsense."

From the other side of the door, Adrian and Larry listened and whispered back and forth about what to do.

And so it went into the new year. Adrian and Larry hunkered down in the apartment, watching the long driveway for the unmarked cars, living in cramped circumstances, going back and forth over what to do next. Again and again, plainclothes lieutenants and sergeants made the long drive to Johnstown from the city and knocked on Schoolcraft's door: five times between January 8 and January 16, 2012. Not only did they pound on the door, they watched the apartment from dark-colored SUVs, sometimes two at a time, one parked near the apartment and one at the entrance to the complex's long driveway. They looked into the windows. They watched his parked car. Publicly, the NYPD later said this was only to try to get him to come back to work, but internally it was viewed as surveillance.

What the NYPD was portraying as routine attempts to serve Schoolcraft with papers seemed utterly sinister and disturbing to Schoolcraft and his father. They didn't leave the apartment without checking for the surveillance. They made videos of the unmarked police vehicles and took photographs of the cops. They were basically prisoners in the apartment.

On January 12, the specificity of the surveillance became almost ridiculous, as police noted, "The light from a possible fish tank has been turned on and a shadow of person was observed through the glass."

A January 13 memo from an IAB cop to the NYPD unit that handles internal prosecutions of officers read, "Surveillance and observation were performed on his residence. It's becoming a game of cat and mouse now and we just need to see him outside of the residence in order to notify him."

The same day, the case was reassigned to IAB Group 1, or the Special Investigations Unit, which handles allegations against high-ranking members of the department.

A January 17 memo read, "They surveilled the residence for 8 hours and PO Schoolcraft did not leave the residence. On Friday, my Lt. spoke with Larry Schoolcraft and he would not cooperate with our efforts to notify PO Schoolcraft to return to duty."

On January 20, Captain Trainor emailed the department prosecutors: "5th attempt to notify schoolcraft. They perform observations for 5 hours before knocking on his door. In addition, we have already consulted with TARU [Technical Assistance Response Unit] regarding their ability to make/alter caller ID. They have the capability to do so. Our next attempt will be to try and call his cell phone from a masked number."

Later, they talked about using TARU to conduct video surveillance to get Schoolcraft to return to duty.

The arrival of TARU in the story was in itself bizarre. TARU is a unit that conducts surveillance and also uses video cameras to monitor protests and other large gatherings. Its work is also important to anti-terror efforts. During the 2004 Republican Convention, there was a major controversy over TARU officers brazenly videotaping protesters on the streets. During a major protest in Harlem against police brutality in the 1990s, the unit provided a live feed of the protest to police headquarters. The fact that TARU was being brought into an employment dispute seemed to be more proof that the NYPD was treating Schoolcraft differently from any other supposedly wayward officer.

On January 20, 2010, an entry in the IAB file noted that a Sergeant Minogue spoke with a Lieutenant Crisalli "regarding the subject officer filing a complaint with the Queens District Attorney's office."

The following day, the IAB investigator spoke with Captain Trainor and attempted to contact Queens prosecutor Michelle Cort. Again on February 10, 2010, he tried to contact Cort.

The Schoolcrafts didn't know this as they made another attempt to interest the Queens District Attorney's office. Internal Affairs records show that on January 20, Schoolcraft called Michelle Cort to follow up with her on calls that Larry had made on November 1 and November 6. He told her he had a recording and evidence related to his complaint. It is notable that Cort had apparently done nothing since those initial calls. They scheduled a meeting for January 22, two days later. A lieutenant from Internal Affairs would also attend.

Cort later claimed in a conversation with Sergeant O'Hare from Brooklyn North Investigations that she had to cancel the meeting. On January 25, she asked Schoolcraft to forward copies of his evidence to her for review. She claimed she received nothing from the Schoolcrafts and told O'Hare that "without Schoolcraft's cooperation, any investigation by her office could not proceed forward."

Schoolcraft called again in February. This time, Cort told him she had called Internal Affairs but didn't receive a return call and figured "it had been dealt with," according to Larry Schoolcraft. The Queens District Attorney, apparently not interested in the case, disappeared from the story for more than a year.

On January 27, the Schoolcrafts took their first tangible step toward moving to sue. They collaborated on what's known as a "notice of claim." Under city rules, anyone contemplating a lawsuit against a city agency must notify the city comptroller's office within 90 days of the incident that is at the heart of the litigation. It's basically a place saver.

Their notice of claim was filed just within the 90-day deadline. In the document, the Schoolcrafts alleged that the NYPD and Jamaica Hospital violated Adrian's civil rights, slandered him, libeled him, subjected him to cruel and unusual punishment, and damaged his character. They also alleged that Adrian's rights were violated in that his confidential medical information was revealed.

On January 31, another cartoonish note was written, this time from the commanding officer of Brooklyn North Investigation to the First Deputy Commissioner: "Investigators arrived and positioned themselves near the entrance. Sgt. O'Hare utilized binoculars for additional visual assistance. At 1355 hours, Sgt. O'Hare and Sgt. Minogue observed Schoolcraft in a white t-shirt moved the living room window shade and look about. He appeared again at 1431 hours wearing a white t-shirt and what appeared to be grey sweatpants."

Meanwhile, records show Internal Affairs was secretly subjecting the Schoolcrafts—who, by the way, hadn't been charged with a crime—to the full investigative treatment as if they were perps. They checked their criminal history through the New York Statewide Police Information Network. They sealed Adrian's locker in the 81st Precinct. They ran them through a state terrorism database. They requested records on each from the FBI and the National Crime Information Center, which collects the names of crimes and criminals across the country.

Even more disturbing, the police issued Adrian and Larry NYSID numbers, which are unique ID numbers generally assigned to people who have been arrested or are imprisoned. Amusingly, the search lists Adrian's height as seven foot two.

They also ran Larry's vehicles going back to 1985, including his 1994 tan Nissan Altima and a 2000 Ford Windstar minivan, and looked for traffic violations and parking tickets.

They wrote memos about newspaper articles that appeared. They also included ten pages of vicious, derogatory, and anonymous comments about the Schoolcrafts from a newspaper website in Johnstown, obviously from people who had an ax to grind with the Schoolcrafts. The comments were written in 2008, long before Adrian was on the police department's radar. One comment described Larry as a "lawsuit happy leech sucking off yet another victim."

They visited Adrian's Queens landlords, Theodore and Carol Stretmoyer, and reported that Schoolcraft was behind on his rent. They went to the Johnstown post office and got a copy of the change of address form that Schoolcraft filled out.

Officers kept visiting the apartment complex and sitting in the driveway, writing their detailed reports essentially about nothing. A February 3 memo, for example, noted that snow on the hood of their car indicated it had not been driven for some time. "The undersigned remained vigilant, observed movement from the window at 1315. Sgt. Wilcon continued to video all movement from the unmarked vehicle of PO Schoolcraft's apartment windows. After knocking on door, returned to car. Noticed male with red camera in hand."

The Fulton County Social Services Department denied Schoolcraft's application for public assistance benefits the following day, obviously scared off by the NYPD inquiries.

Brooklyn North Inspections arranged with TARU to set up more sophisticated video surveillance of the apartment.

★

At that point, surveillance had been going on for two months. The Schoolcrafts had not been idle. They finally found a reporter willing to listen to their story in Rocco Parascandola, the police bureau chief at the *New York Daily News*. Parascandola was familiar with allegations of downgrading of crime, having helped write a groundbreaking series of articles in *Newsday* on the subject in 2004. Parascandola drove up to Johnstown, conducted interviews with Adrian, and left with Adrian's documentation of individual examples of downgrading and failure to take reports. The reporter then did the difficult legwork, reaching out to the victims in the cases Adrian cited.

Schoolcraft gave Parascandola the same questionable crime reports he gave to QAD in October. The reporter was able to reach five victims who backed Schoolcraft. The rest either couldn't be located or believed police handled their complaints correctly.

"It's just not right," Schoolcraft told the *News*. "They are taking advantage of people. A lot of crime victims don't know any better."

A front-page article was published on February 2 in the *Daily News* with the headline, "Crime What Crime: Cops Probe Whistleblower's Charges Precinct Fudged Reports to Lower Stats."

Mauriello called the allegations "atrocious."

The story was finally out there.

In his on-the-record comments, NYPD spokesman Paul Browne confirmed the existence of a probe into his allegations. "We have received these complaints, and Quality Assurance has undertaken a review. These complaints are being reviewed as to whether or not this is true and whether this was done as a matter of error or intentionally," Browne told the *News*.

Browne's office confirmed that Schoolcraft was admitted to the Jamaica Hospital psych ward but declined further comment.

Parascandola quoted an unnamed source familiar with Schoolcraft's psychiatric assessment that was completed following his release from the hospital. Parascandola wrote that this source told him, "The officer is perhaps too naive and idealistic but does not appear to be unbalanced. This is not someone talking to himself on the street. There's just a naiveté there. He doesn't understand the police culture. Is he insane? Is he psychotic? Is he manic? Absolutely not. I think he can be believed."

The article was long by *Daily News* standards and fairly reported what was known at the time as best as it could be determined. The Schoolcrafts were pleased with the top half, but it was the bottom half that irritated them.

They felt the piece spent too much space on Adrian's restricted duty, low work review, and the psychiatric element. "Schoolcraft has big problems of his own," the article read. "He received a poor work review early last year— his supervisors cited his need for constant supervision—and was stripped of his gun and put on desk duty after telling an NYPD doctor he thought work stress caused his stomach and chest pains."

And the photo that the *News* ran of Schoolcraft wasn't all that flattering. He was leaning forward into the camera, and his eyes were rimmed in red. The Schoolcrafts really didn't like the photo.

Undeterred by the media interest, the very same day, the NYPD filed more charges against Schoolcraft for failure to comply with orders and "conduct prejudicial to the good order of the department."

Reacting to the article, City Councilman Peter Vallone, the head of the council's public safety committee, said a hearing should take place. Interestingly, Vallone would make several public comments like this over the next two years, but he never would actually call a hearing. At one point, he asserted that while police officers confided to him that crime stat manipulation was a larger problem than the NYPD had acknowledged, no officers would come forward to appear in a hearing, thus preventing that public airing in the chambers of City Hall.

For a little context, the New York city council is well known for holding hearings at the drop of a hat. In this instance, it seemed, a high bar was set, higher than just about any other issue. Were the crime numbers really such a sacred cow for the city that the council couldn't muster the courage to challenge them? Was there someone at the top of the council blocking these hearings? As for Vallone's contention that he couldn't get other officers to testify, it could be true. However, there were plenty of other knowledgeable people who would testify. And at that point, Schoolcraft probably would have sat before Vallone's committee in open session. Could there have been a political component at work here? It begs the question.

On February 12, Parascandola followed up with a second article in the *News* that said investigators were looking into 1,400 crime reports at the 81st Precinct and "grilling" two dozen officers to determine how widespread the problem was. Mauriello told a community group, "I'm confident that the truth will come out. I know my character. I've got nothing to hide."

Still undeterred by the media coverage, the NYPD sent two lieutenants and two sergeants to Johnstown with more video gear. It still bears remembering that Schoolcraft had not been charged with a crime. "The original plan was to park, equipped with a Minipix dual receiver microwave video receiver/recorder in front of the subject residence."

One team, in a "less familiar" sedan, would park closer to the apartment, and the other, a more familiar Jeep, would park farther down the street.

On this particular day, Larry Schoolcraft, frustrated with what he viewed as harassment, came out of the house with a video recorder of his own and questioned the officers. "My son wants nothing to do with the department," Larry said.

Larry called the officers "Nazis," to which they asked him not to use derogatory language.

Leonard Levitt, the longtime police reporter, quoted a senior Queens law enforcement official on February 15, saying he "can't believe Jamaica Hospital would throw Schoolcraft into its psych ward simply on the word of police officers."

The following day, Parascandola reported that another precinct, the 77th in Brooklyn, was also under investigation for crime report manipulation.

While Levitt and the *Daily News* had both jumped on the story, the *New York Times* said not a word, and the *New York Post* ran a one-column story on an inside page on Saturday that no one really noticed.

The evidence that crime report manipulation was more widespread than the department admitted was bolstered by the release of a survey of hundreds of retired NYPD bosses by two professors of criminal justice—John Jay College's Eli Silverman, who wrote an early book about CompStat, and John Eterno, a retired captain who taught at Molloy College.

In the study, the retired NYPD bosses told them that CompStat increased pressure to downgrade crime complaints. Half of the supervisors who responded to the survey told them they had seen a crime complaint altered and thought it was unethical. Based on their survey, Eterno and Silverman concluded that CompStat crime statistics "warranted careful scrutiny."

"As crime goes down, the pressure to maintain it got great," a retired boss told the professors. "It was a numbers game."

Kelly's spokesman, Paul Browne, dismissed the study as biased and unscientific. He claimed, wrongly it turns out, that it was paid for by the unions. And the pro-NYPD *Daily News* editorial board attacked the two professors, writing that they had "libeled the NYPD and every police officer who worked his or her butt off in the long, hard fight to make New York City safer."

The *Daily News* downplayed the extent of statistical manipulation, as "a handful of superior officers caught in penny ante dodges." "All those she-nanigans combined are minuscule compared with the plunge in crime," the *News* editorial concluded. "Do Eterno and Silverman believe that the NYPD is hiding hundreds if not thousands of killings? If so, where are the bodies?"

Meanwhile, on February 18, IAB opened another investigation into the fact that Schoolcraft was not residing within the city. This was a violation of the residency requirement, but one that many police officers, including police bosses, violate with impunity. Again, it seemed like the department was looking for every bit of leverage with which to squeeze Schoolcraft.

★

On February 22, Schoolcraft sat down with aides of Councilman Vallone and recorded it. Also present were retired lieutenant Anthony Miranda, who was the head of the Latino Officers Association and had remained active in police issues, and another retired cop. The purpose of the meeting was to basically convince Vallone to get involved. On the recording, one of his aides told Schoolcraft that the councilman took the allegations very seriously.

"They gotta continue to show higher numbers," Miranda said. "That's where the abusive nature of CompStat comes in. It was first just to make commanders aware. Now it's about getting their numbers. All these things need to the abuse."

Miranda added, "If you, as a cop, file complaints, there's more of a tendency to refer you to psych services. If you aren't hitting the quota, that becomes part of the it. And that ruins a person's career."

Schoolcraft chimed in: "Being referred to psych services is like being thrown down into a well and trying to climb out with a shoe string."

Miranda suggested Vallone create a website where cops could provide information on downgrading. "Mmhm," Vallone's aide said. "Mmhm. We have to get ready for 5 o'clock. Thanks for coming by."

The other aide asked about Adrian's status.

"Screwed," he said. "They're probably going to fire me. But I'll probably be able to be a big help to Mr. Vallone in my civil suit in acquiring court orders. So perhaps that can be of help. I would like to have some safe guarantee. Perhaps you can ask Mr. Vallone."

"Yeah, we'll be in touch," the aide said, almost dismissively.

Despite what was said in the meeting, it went nowhere tangible. Vallone did nothing of consequence afterward, and, to the Schoolcrafts, it served as yet another example that the people and agencies who were supposed to monitor the NYPD were not willing to do their jobs. The Schoolcrafts didn't hear from Vallone's office again.

★

In late March 2010, largely because they thought the press coverage had been too narrow, the Schoolcrafts contacted Paul Moses, a former *New York Newsday* editor and reporter teaching journalism at Brooklyn College, who put them in touch with me at the *Village Voice*. Schoolcraft initially sent a cryptic email to me containing an excerpt from a tape of Sergeant Huffman telling officers not to take robbery complaints in the field but to refer them to the detective squad.

"I hope to collaborate with you on reporting the whole story on my investigations, objectively, without misquotes," Schoolcraft wrote.

In a second email, he wrote, "Nothing has changed regarding my status. On suspension, and they won't give me a department trial... Pay me or fire me... I'm never quitting... Never!"

There was an initial correspondence by email, and then I drove up to Johnstown on March 16.

The town was clearly depressed, stuck between the last vestiges of industry, a modest farm community, and the inevitable Walmart and chain stores that contrive to suck the life from any small town. The Schoolcrafts lived in a small cookie-cutter apartment complex that looked like it had been thrown up in a week.

Their one-bedroom apartment was disheveled and messy. The kitchen was piled with dirty dishes. There was something of a dog smell. The carpet was worn and pitted. A fuzzy television buzzed in the background. Larry slept on a sofa. Adrian had the bedroom, which contained a desk, a chair, a mattress on the floor, and plastic containers of papers and computer parts. After the interview, Adrian walked outside for a couple of photos. He was using a cane.

"How many recordings do you have?" I asked.

"Oh, about 1,000 hours," Adrian replied. "Roll calls, patrol, the locker room, stuff in the station house."

"Um, over how long?"

"About 18 months."

I paused to take this in for a moment. No police officer in NYPD history had ever recorded 1,000 hours inside a precinct on his own. Sure, officers involved in undercover Internal Affairs investigations had done more limited recordings. But this was unprecedented. Schoolcraft had done it alone. Most cops would have been put off by the danger of getting caught. And he wanted it to go public.

"A lot of it is personal conversations between cops about their wives and girlfriends, and stuff like that, and I don't think any of that should be put in the paper," Schoolcraft added.

There was more discussion, and then I suggested, "Well, why don't you send me the roll calls on a disk, and we'll see what's there." Schoolcraft agreed. A couple of days after this visit, a single CD arrived in an envelope at my office at the *Village Voice*. It took weeks for me to transcribe the recordings into coherent form and then make sense of them.

On May 4 and May 11, the *Voice* published the first two articles in a five-part series with the recordings as the centerpiece. The first article examined crime stat manipulation and quotas. The second article looked at whether certain orders given by precinct bosses led to civil rights violations on the street.

The articles caused a public buzz, and there was turmoil in the 81st Precinct. On May 14, 2010, records showed that an anonymous caller to the IAB reported that Mauriello was yelling at officers because of the "Schoolcraft incident." The caller went on to say that "numbers are being fudged" in the precinct and threatened to go to the *Village Voice*.

As these articles appeared, Brooklyn North Inspections substantiated 25 of 26 charges against Schoolcraft and referred their conclusions to department prosecutors. The report indicated that the unit expected Schoolcraft to be tried in absentia and fired. In all, they had opened at least 15 different investigations into Schoolcraft. But the conclusions ignored the elephants in the room: the QAD investigation, its relationship to Halloween night, and the Internal Affairs probe of Mauriello and Marino.

To understand how, on the one hand, the NYPD could be investigating Schoolcraft and building evidence that would get him fired, and at the same time could be investigating his allegations separately, one has to know something about the organization itself. Most people consider the NYPD to be a single monolithic entity that drives forward in unison. Nothing could be further from the truth. In fact, it is a rapacious battlefield in which police bosses with a range of agendas slug it out to rise higher in the agency. In this light, the Brooklyn North investigation can be seen as an attempt to discredit Schoolcraft to save the reputations of its leaders. Internal Affairs, meanwhile, may have been looking to protect Kelly. QAD, at the same time, was looking for a big case that might raise the profile of its bosses.

Since Schoolcraft was folding his arms and refusing to return to work, Kelly could order his department prosecutors to try Schoolcraft—even if Schoolcraft wouldn't attend—and then fire him. But he didn't do that. Instead, he left Adrian in a kind of employment limbo: still a cop with medical benefits but without a salary. Perhaps he was waiting for the conclusions of the QAD and IAB investigations, perhaps he viewed the Brooklyn North report as biased, perhaps he was concerned that he would take a public shellacking for getting rid of Schoolcraft, perhaps he was just following department protocol. On all these issues, he was publicly silent.

Schoolcraft was not. "They assassinated my character," he told me. "I would someday like to be a police officer again. I have no other option but to fight this. What they did was cover up what I was trying to report."

CHAPTER 12

THE SCHOOLCRAFT EFFECT

As the elements of the *Voice* article percolated and the internal investigations continued, the police department remained largely silent. Police officers themselves did not. The Schoolcraft revelations become fodder for discussions in precinct station houses throughout the city. Of course, none of those officers were willing to speak publicly. The fear of retaliation by the NYPD for making public comments was so acute that a lot of cops didn't even want to be seen in the same room with a reporter.

But there was Thee Rant, an Internet site that acted as a sort of Greek chorus for the NYPD. On this site, the issues of the day were poked, prodded, dissected, and argued over. It was probably the only place where a police officer could publicly attack Kelly and get away with it.

A favored expression in the Rant's forums, used for supporters of Kelly, is to say so-and-so "drank the Kool-Aid," or bought into Kelly's policies. It's a reference to supporters of cult leader Jim Jones, who coerced his followers to drink Kool-Aid laced with cyanide in Guyana in 1978. Dozens of current and retired cops posted to the Rant about Schoolcraft. The fallout from his recordings eventually became known on the Rant, for better or worse, as "The Schoolcraft Effect."

Some cops supported Adrian, believing it completely credible that Halloween night was retaliation for him reporting misconduct. Others call him a lying rat who betrayed his fellow officers. His case has clearly made waves.

One poster offered this more thoughtful analysis. "I can see this quickly degrading into the typical 'he's a rat' argument . . . and there is a point to that. The bigger issue here is that there is finally some definitive proof that the NYPD is engaging in the systematic corruption of report manipulation and downgrading of index crimes.

"The article is so dead-on correct in many of the examples and practices it describes, the constant pressure to meet quotas, the threats of getting your tour changed or days off denied, how we treat victims of crime by looking at them as if they are the suspect, the callbacks, the manipulation of facts, and the NYPD definitions of crimes.

"Yes, the guy was taping fellow cops, and I can't condone that. But people need to know the job is corrupt from the top down. We are numbers driven. We face the paradox of generating more activity while taking fewer reports."

Another poster, who called himself Krepke, wrote a tongue-in-cheek memo: "From the ministry of information: 'You have been made aware of the allegations of Comrade Schoolcraft. He is a good officer but has been under stress. Be assured, we will take good care of him. After a short rest, he will be sent to a re-education camp, where he can again learn to adhere to the teachings of the Organization. All would do well to learn from the experience of Comrade Schoolcraft. All would do well.' "

Another wrote, "What Chief Marino and his minions did is inexcusable. You should be outraged. If they get away with this behavior, who is next?"

A fourth: "Does the department downgrade complaints to serve statistics? Yes. Do supervisors set up cops who do not blindly follow dubious if not illegal orders? Yes. Forget your opinion of Schoolcraft and look at the issues."

Another: "At least this guy didn't roll over and die for the brass."

Another: "I've brought in a lot of EDPs who I thought would get admitted, but who the Docs cut loose. But THIS guy gets admitted for six days?"

A seventh said if ranking officers "whisper sweet nothings" in the doctor's ear, "Be assured that those docs are going to admit said cop forthwith."

An eighth: "CompStat is now totally corrupted."

A ninth: "The Feds should do a Mollen Commission or Knapp Commission on this case."

Among the posts from critics of Schoolcraft, there was this: "Schoolcraft is definitely not the hero the Voice claims he is."

Another said, "He doesn't want to right a wrong. He wants to be a Hollywood star. In the end, when his 15 minutes are up, he will be left with nothing. Not even his reputation."

A third: "He sounds like a paranoid mental patient who sucks at his job."

A fourth: "Sorry but I'll take the word of a dozen responding supervisors over the one raving lunatic."

A fifth: "This article is crap. The guy is a nut. He's looking for a big payday for being a lazy zero. I hope he gets nothing but a big lawyer he can't afford when this is over."

A sixth: "Schoolcraft is a nut who should be working at Walmart."

One Schoolcraft critic posted a photo of a dead rat caught in a trap.

The reaction outside the department, in the public arena, skewed toward Schoolcraft, but the critical mass needed to push an outside authority to step into the story didn't yet exist, if it ever would.

Once again, Councilman Peter Vallone, the chair of the City Council's public safety committee, weighed in. He said some of the comments were "clearly" telling officers to commit "illegal conduct." "You can't tell a police officer to stop them no matter what," Vallone said. "Some of it was clearly over the line."

However, Vallone added that other comments "read like good commanders struggling to win the war against crime without enough officers."

But the politician who was most incensed by the recordings was longtime City Councilman Albert Vann, who represented Bed-Stuy. He was shocked to hear Mauriello speak that way to his officers about the community he served. "It would seem to be two deputy inspectors: one that I know, who is very responsive to the community, and one who I believe, in responding to his superiors, has become overly aggressive in trying to make the statistics look good in the district."

Meanwhile, lawyers for the Center for Constitutional Rights, which was suing the NYPD over its stop and frisk campaign on civil rights grounds, immediately saw the value of the recordings, and they moved to obtain them as evidence in their case. They believed the tapes amounted to smoking-gun proof of the existence of quotas and their direct relationship with illegal stops and false arrests. The lawyers believed the recordings showed precinct bosses ordering their cops to violate the civil rights of citizens. They knew how rare it was to find an officer who was willing to speak out on these issues. They reached out to Schoolcraft and deposed him for their lawsuit.

I would publish three more articles in the *Village Voice* related to the Schoolcraft Effect, and the debate over Schoolcraft's tapes would continue through the year. For the moment, Kelly had not acted. Mauriello was still in place. Marino was still in place. The department was still insisting that any downgrading that did happen was miniscule. It was status quo.

Now, citizens from around the city began to step forward to tell their own stories of crime report manipulation. One particularly disturbing account came from Berry Hatfield, a 27-year-old film industry location scout living in the Greenpoint section of Brooklyn.

Hatfield said he was walking home on Halloween 2009, the same night that Schoolcraft was taken to the psych ward, when a would-be robber pointed a handgun at him and pulled the trigger. Hatfield took off. The gun merely clicked, he says, and no bullet discharged.

Police from the 94th Precinct arrived, listened to his statement, and then drove him around, looking for the suspect without success. Rather than taking the complaint on the spot, the officers insisted on taking him to the station. He went and was told that detectives would call him the following day.

The detectives didn't call the next day. Hatfield waited a few days and then asked the precinct for a complaint number. The clerk couldn't find it. After a month of waiting, Hatfield went to the station house to try to get the complaint number and a copy of the report. And it was like what happened to him had vanished, like it never happened. The precinct had no record of the incident, not in the computer, not in the log book. He left word for the responding officers to call him. They didn't.

Hatfield waited another two months and tried again. The result was the same. The report had disappeared.

"A couple of weeks before, there was an item in the local paper that two girls got robbed nearby," Hatfield said in 2010. "It was also a silver handgun. It was also a young black man. I was just surprised at the lack of interest in getting someone who was using a gun. It makes you wonder whether this type of thing is systemic throughout the NYPD."

On March 21, 2010, a man named Joseph Bolanos, a member of Manhattan's West 76th Street Park Block Association, reacted to the

Schoolcraft allegations. He posted on Eterno and Silverman's website about an incident on January 23, when he was jumped by ten drunken teens. He was kicked in the head, kidneys, and ribs. Police got there 25 minutes later.

"When I asked to file a complaint I was told that a detective would call me on Monday," he wrote. "Monday came and I didn't hear from anyone from the 20th. Tuesday, Wednesday, Thursday...no contact from the NYPD. On Friday I walked to the precinct and waited for an hour to file a complaint. It wasn't busy whatsoever. I just sat there. A sergeant came out and gave me a third degree asking me why I had waited so long to file a complaint! I had to convince him by telling my story in order to get my complaint taken. At least I felt that way. My complaint was finally taken and it was for Assault. I was told that a detective would call me. To date, no one has contacted me from the 20th Precinct."

When Bolanos called some time later to check on the complaint, he was told that there was no record of it.

He wrote: "One of the primary goals of Compstat was to address crime and, more importantly, quality of life issues. No matter how seemingly insignificant a crime or violation was perceived to be, it earned a place in CompStat.

"After 9/11, however, a perception developed that terrorism and some crime became the only priorities. As a result, quality of life issues fell by the wayside. Today, quality of life issues are non-issues as it pertains to the NYPD.

"And because the crime stat emphasis is on major crime, and its decrease, a systemic mindset has developed that only 'stat heavy' crimes will be pursued, investigated and reported. If crimes and violations are not reported/recorded by responding police officers, the data will never reach the precinct, and certainly not CompStat. This results in flawed or omitted data that nullifies the purpose of CompStat. Filing a police report should be the right of all civilians, no matter how insignificant a violation may appear."

In the upper Manhattan neighborhood of Inwood, 59-year-old author Debbie Nathan stepped forward to tell her story of how she was sexually assaulted, but police downgraded her report to a misdemeanor.

On February 21, 2010, she said she was walking through Inwood Park, which contains one of the last old-growth forests in the city, when she was grabbed by a young man and pushed off the path. She tried to fight him off, but he pinned his arms at her sides. He told her his name was Michael and he was 17. He was wearing a tan jacket. He was African American. He began masturbating against her body, had an orgasm, and fled.

"I was terrified for my safety and my life," Nathan said.

Nathan quickly made her way out of the park to a cafe nearby and called the police. If they could arrive quickly enough, she felt there would still be time to catch him because there were only a few ways out of the park.

She waited at the cafe for 30 minutes, but the police didn't arrive. At home, she called 911 again. No police. Another 45 minutes passed. No police. Finally after two hours had elapsed and she'd made three 911 calls, officers arrived.

Six officers went over her complaint. "I stressed that I was at all times overpowered," she said. "The female officer, I thought she was acting weird. She wasn't writing anything down."

Nathan was basically interrogated for two hours. One of the cops told her they didn't know how to classify the crime. They called the Special Victims Unit. Special Victims told them the crime was "forcible touching," which is a misdemeanor.

Nathan argued with the officers. It was an attempted rape, a felony. "I argued that the force used against me, the masturbation and the veritable kidnapping constituted far more than a misdemeanor," Nathan said.

The officers ignored her protests and left.

On February 22, Nathan called the Inwood Safety Forum, a citizens' group that monitors neighborhood safety. That group called the local state assemblyman, Adriano Espaillat, and the 34th Precinct commander to complain.

After that, Nathan's complaint was upgraded to felony attempted rape. At a packed community meeting, the precinct commander apologized to Nathan and promised an investigation.

"There were some breakdowns," Deputy Inspector Andrew Capul, the precinct commander, said at the meeting, blaming miscommunication and inexperienced officers. "It should not have happened. We are conducting a more detailed investigation, and following through on this matter."

When she got her complaint report, she couldn't believe it. "My story had been scrubbed of everything except the fact that the perp grabbed me, pushed me and mentioned sex," she said. "Almost every detail of the crime was missing from the report."

The officers had left out her being overpowered and pushed into the woods, the duration of the assault, the masturbation. The report, she said, even said she had reported no sexual assault.

"After special victims downgraded my crime to a misdemeanor, an officer from my precinct tweaked my report so it described a misdemeanor," she said. "They had written non-report to conform to a misdemeanor. They were so sloppy, they forgot to rewrite the report to conform to felony."

Nathan said she was told by Assistant District Attorney Lisa Friel, chief of the Manhattan District Attorney's sex crimes unit, that there was no question that the crime she described was a felony.

Friel, Nathan said, interviewed the police officers involved and learned that they admitted to omitting many details from the report. "It is difficult to believe the omissions were accidental," Nathan said.

Nathan said she spoke with rape crisis advocacy groups, which told her that her case was not unique, that it had been happening across the city over the past year and a half.

"The difference here was that I was a well-educated journalist, someone who knew how to get action," she said.

Harriet Lessel, the director of the New York City Alliance Against Sexual Assault, told the *Village Voice* that her group met with Police Commissioner Ray Kelly about three weeks before the Nathan story broke.

Lessel saw the downgrading of sex crimes as a growing problem in 2009 and 2010. "We have been hearing that this is something that has been happening more frequently," Lessel said. "We feel that these programs are the canaries in the coal mine and we have brought it to the attention of the Police Commissioner. We are trying to figure out how to do something about it."

She said the commissioner pledged to look into the issue and created an internal task force to study the problem.

"We're seeing it as both a patrol and a special victims problem," she said. "This is something that is going to take time. Things aren't going to change after one meeting. And it's in everyone's best interest to have accurate statistics about rape, even if the numbers go up. How can we do what needs to be done if we're not getting the right information from the start?"

Capul, the precinct commander, was transferred out of the command on May 2, 2010, and sent to Patrol Borough Manhattan North. And on this issue, Kelly actually responded to the concern: Plans were set in motion for better training, and he ordered the city's special victims unit to be involved in the investigation of every sex crime.

Other reports of crime downgrading filtered in. "This exact scenario happened to me earlier this year," one commenter said. "I was assaulted and the police who reported to the scene as well as the detective assigned to my case turned the tables on me, as if I had done something wrong. The detective who did one of those 'callbacks' was very nasty and accused me of lying. He dropped the case.

"I even have an officer on recording saying that it's not really an assault unless you're bruised bloody and broken. I asked, so you're telling me that anyone can walk up to you on the street in NYC and punch you in the face and you wouldn't investigate that?"

A man talked about a being drugged and robbed in his apartment by men he took home from a gay club. "They took an astounding majority of the material possessions that I own, including a computer, phone, guitar, Wii, most of my jackets, clothes, shoes, underwear (no joke), cologne, and toothbrush (seriously)," he said. He gave personal information on the robbers to police, but they were unresponsive. "I filled out the initial inventory report of what was stolen, listing first a MacBook Pro that was taken. The police later stated that a computer was never reported missing and they tried to knock down a clear felony to a misdemeanor. I was ignored by police, my apartment was never printed, and I had to contact my city councilman to get them to contact me back."

Meanwhile, the revelations of downgrading in Bed-Stuy's 81st Precinct led to a sudden and shocking increase in the crime rate. After logging a 10.9 percent crime decline for all of 2009, crime in the precinct jumped by 13 percent for the first quarter of 2010. Observers said this was proof that downgrading had been going on in the 81st Precinct, and that the current scrutiny of the station house had made the precinct commanders more honest.

Someone obviously in city government sends an anonymous letter to City Councilman Vallone, claiming that the NYPD did not record murders in cases in which the district attorney was unable to charge anyone, listed burglaries as lost property, and lowered assaults and grand larcenies to misdemeanors.

"This game is played by every precinct commanding officers, and Kelly is very aware, but turns a blind eye," the letter concluded. "The precinct commanders know that if they don't play they will not only lose their command, but will never see a promotion under this administration."

These allegations were of course unconfirmed, and there was no record that they were investigated. But the letter, when combined with other allegations and anecdotal information, was a symptom of a larger problem and a signal that Kelly and Mayor Bloomberg had a problem.

A retired sergeant, Sean McCafferty, said the crime analysis unit in each precinct was the source for the manipulation of crime reports. "They get the report before the detective squad, and they would call the complainant and question them about their complaint," he said. "CompStat has helped the department, but some people use it as a weapon. The commanding officers—their future depends on it."

A police officer assigned to Manhattan said, "The cop writing the report is now cross-examining the victim. This insane CompStat pressure has turned a police officer who shouldn't care about what the complaint is into a defense attorney. I'm all about letting the paperwork reflect the reality. Let's just get it done and go on to the next job."

Levitt, writing on June 21, noted that despite all the indicia of problems with CompStat over the years, Kelly had been able to "diffuse their political impact." "While some people think Kelly's greatest success lies in combating terrorism, his greatest accomplishment has actually been in closing the police department to outside scrutiny," Levitt wrote. "Just think. When four mopes are charged with plotting to bomb two Bronx synagogues in a case that smacks of entrapment [the FBI supplied the bombs and its informant promised the mopes $250, 000], the story is front page news because the plot was 'terror-related.'

"But when a cop says that crimes are systemically being downgraded and that victims are encouraged not to file crime reports and he has the tapes to prove it, the police break down his door, take him in handcuffs to a Queens hospital, where he's locked up in a psych ward for six days, a move that seems reminiscent of how things were done in the old Soviet Union.

"Where is the outcry in the media about what happened to Schoolcraft? Which politician has the guts to take on Kelly and Bloomberg and demand an outside investigation of the doctored crime stats?"

Schoolcraft's strategy was quietly being duplicated in other precincts—and once again, the 81st. On April 1, 2010, a supervisor in the 81st Precinct wore a recorder in a meeting of bosses. From the recording, it was clear that in terms of the message from precinct commanders, little had changed. Mauriello and his new executive officer, Captain Alex Perez, called out officers by name they said hadn't been producing enough summonses and arrests and noted the pressure coming down from above. Meanwhile, his executive officer identified the specific number of summonses and arrests his bosses wanted—20 per week per shift—and threatened to penalize any officer who didn't hit the number. He indicated that the quota number was being demanded by the patrol borough command.

Referring to two precinct officers, Mauriello said, "They couldn't get a collar in a laundromat, those guys."

Mauriello went on to say, "Pass the word: I got a heads-up from somebody at 1PP [police headquarters]. From now on, they gonna look at any traffic stat and CompStat, and the [commanding officer] and my XO [executive officer] are gonna get our cojones busted in for patrol's activity."

"What happens is I'm going to shake it up," Mauriello said later in the meeting. "That's coming down the pike, but to step this up is I got an irate bureau chief [Deputy Chief Michael Marino] calling me up here yelling at me two days in a row about midnights and cell phones and this bullshit initiative.

"And now he's going to grab platoon commanders and look at their evaluations and I look at the sergeants and I look at every cop in the squad and see what we're giving them. That means I have to go down there and get my balls, cojones busted by these two guys telling me I don't know how to run my command.

"So now—I will say right now—it's not good to be a boss right now if your squad ain't pulling weight," he added. "Your squad ain't pulling weight, that ain't good."

Captain Perez went on to specify the number of summonses required from each shift of officers, saying the number had been established at the borough command.

"They are counting seat belts and cell phones, double-parkers and bus stops," he said. "If the day tours contributed with five seat belts and five cell phones a week, five double-parkers and five bus stops a week, okay.

"If I get the same numbers from the third platoon and whatever the midnight kicks in, it's gravy," he added. "You as the bosses have to demand this, and you have to count it. Your goal is five in each of these categories. . . . I'm not looking to break records here, but there is no reason we should be missing this number by 30 a week. That's what your job is as bosses."

Perez then told his sergeants and lieutenants that he had little problem punishing officers who did not "pull their weight." He told them he was transferring three officers from days to the midnight tour.

"I don't care about people's families," he said. "If they don't want to do their job, their paycheck is taking care of their family. If they don't realize that, they're going to change their tour, they are going to start being productive if they want a tour that works for their family.

"When I identify who's stealing, they are going to go to a different platoon," he added. "If this job don't work for them, they can find another job. That's my attitude."

Under the law, an agency was allowed to set goals, but they couldn't tie those goals to disciplinary action or any penalty. The Patrolmen's Benevolent Association had long opposed the use of quotas in the NYPD.

Perez went on to criticize any officer who volunteered repeatedly for critical response, a special anti-terror detail ordered by Commissioner Ray Kelly that drove around the city with lights and sirens.

"If nobody cares, I don't care, either," he said. "You'll work when I tell you to work. You don't have to be happy about it. And if you don't write, that's fine. Because after I bounce you to a different platoon for inactivity, the next thing is to put you on paper, start writing you below standards and look to fire you. I really don't have a problem firing people. . . . If you don't wanna work, fine. I cut the line. I'm not going to tow you."

Mauriello also defended his tenure as precinct commander. He repeatedly demanded that his supervisors tell cops not to drive by troubled areas without getting out of their cars. He talked at length about his work ethic and noted that his father worked three jobs.

"The cops gotta know their function," he said. "You're out there to prevent violence, to prevent shootings."

Mauriello said his bosses were nervous and were increasing the pressure on the precincts. "They are panicking up there," he said. "They are worried about this. They are worried about that. Oh, crime is crime, but they are going to make sure they take your toes, your fingers, your elbows, they are going to cut one by one. Almost like the movie 'Hostel'."

The unnamed supervisor recorded a second meeting of bosses in mid-May, after the first two *Voice* articles had been published.

In this second tape, Mauriello scoffed at the QAD investigation of his precinct, calling it a bullshit investigation. He expressed frustration with QAD second-guessing the initial crime reports. He referred to an incident where, he claimed, the victim initially told police he lost his wallet, then much later changed his story to theft.

"This is how QAD fucks me," he said. "The cop thinks that he [the victim] lost the stuff. At no time did anybody touch him or anything, so when the guy calls back now, now this is two months later. QAD called back a year later and saying they are going to upgrade this to a grand larceny. But the cop is saying one thing. The guy tells the cop on the scene one thing, and now we call back two months later, the guy is fucking pickpocketed."

Essentially confirming one of the durable allegations of crime downgrading, Mauriello emphasized to cops that they should not take a report on any incident that happened outside the precinct. "We're not doing favors for people," he said. "It's a robbery in the 32[nd Precinct in Harlem]. You know what. That's it. Let the 32 call them up."

"Other commands have no problem dumping stuff in this computer without even calling us up," he added.

He referred to Schoolcraft as "that fucking asshole upstate" and warned his underlings to be careful about the rank and file. "These guys and girls are nice people, but they aren't your friends," he said. "The PBA is telling them to wear fucking wires.... There's an epidemic right now of rats coming out here wearing tape recorders and distorting the facts.... Haters, malcontents, losers. And you know we got some in this place."

Mauriello and his supervisors discussed the first two parts of the *Voice*'s NYPD tapes series and whether Schoolcraft violated eavesdropping laws in making the secret recordings. "You know, I thought it was a dead issue until the *Village Voice* came out," he said.

Of the *Voice* series, Mauriello declared, "I ain't worried.... The *Village Voice*'s got their own agenda," he added. "Anybody who would say this guy

[Schoolcraft] did the right thing by wiretapping, it is what it is. He has an agenda. It wasn't to be a police officer. It was to sue the job one way or another. So, that's what he got in the end. So what are you gonna do? I'd rather not talk about it."

Mauriello didn't talk about sending Schoolcraft to the psych ward. But he did complain about how the *Voice* got into the station house to take photographs. "How does the *Village Voice* take pictures inside the precinct and you guys don't see that?" he asked.

Later, in September, when these tapes were made public, NYPD spokesman Paul Browne insisted the media was confusing "what was being said on the tape in terms of numbers." "There's no quotas discussed.... It's absurd to think that managers can't establish goals that require minimum productivity. To suggest otherwise would mean no recourse but to let slackers do nothing. Fortunately, most police officers do their job well. Some of the few who don't cry 'quota.' In no case is anyone demanding police take action on nonexistent conditions. These are minimum productivity goals in an environment where there's still plenty of conditions that require police attention."

Since in fact there were numbers mentioned in the recording, Browne seems way off base, but this became another example of the stubborn defense strategy that Kelly had adopted. In the face of the revelations of the year, Kelly simply built a stone wall.

But Citizens Crime Commission president Richard Aborn criticized quotas on the basis that they caused "officers to make decisions they would not otherwise make. It's perfectly fine for a police department to encourage activity, but when you set a quota people are going to feel compelled to make that quota, and that's where bad decisions can be made."

Aborn wanted something that wouldn't happen: He wanted Kelly to make public the annual audits of the crime statistics. "Nothing will douse the brushfire of suspicion faster than some transparency," Aborn said. "Since the department already does these audits, and verifies the numbers, I think it would help the NYPD to release the audits."

PBA president Patrick Lynch had said nothing about Schoolcraft's treatment. His union had done basically nothing to come to his assistance. But he did offer a comment on the quota issues raised by these new recordings. "From what I've seen reported about those tape recordings, to my ears, it sounds like a quota," he said. "What separates a managerial target from an illegal quota is the punitive action for failure to achieve that number," Lynch said.

On May 26, Councilman Vann, not wanting to let the issue drop, composed a letter to Kelly that was co-signed by three other leading black Brooklyn politicians, including Congressman Ed Towns, who had previously lauded Mauriello in the Capitol. The letter called for the removal of Mauriello as precinct commander. Vann noted that he previously met with Assistant Chief Gerald Nelson, who "expressed his dismay and disappointment with the disrespect that Mr. Mauriello demonstrated to our community."

"Not only did officers treat our community as if it were the subject of a military occupation, they also were dismissive of criminal complaints made by residents," the letter read. "We are clear that Insp. Mauriello is responsible for the actions and behaviors of his officers, in addition to attitudes permeating the precinct."

Kelly did not respond to the letter. Vann, irritated, raised the issue with the commissioner during a June 3 council hearing. This hearing took place as Mayor Bloomberg was announcing that New York was the "safest large city in the county." That statement, of course, was based on the very crime statistics that were now under fire.

The exchange became tense. Kelly told Vann there was an ongoing investigation. He testified that he had received the letter but had not had time to review it.

Vann suggested that Kelly was downplaying the issue. Kelly didn't like that comment at all, saying Vann could not expect a large agency like the police department to respond so quickly. "You make allegations in that letter and I need to find out those facts before I respond," Kelly said.

Vann replied that Schoolcraft's tapes stood on their own. "We didn't make allegations," he told Kelly. "We responded to what was on the tapes. This is not hearsay. . . . You know what happened over there; we only responded to what is on the tapes; that cannot be denied."

After the hearing, Vann told the *New York Times* that the tapes showed "how innocent citizens were being victimized; innocent people were arrested for no cause at all; how some of their complaints had been suppressed."

"I mean the whole array of inappropriate and perhaps even illegal action. So we reiterated that which was on the tapes, and then we asked for him to take appropriate action."

Kelly finally responded in writing on June 4, only to acknowledge receipt of the letter. He later wrote that he had "directed a review and analysis of the assertions" in the *Voice* articles.

Meanwhile, up in Johnstown, the police returned to Schoolcraft's apartment four days later to serve more charges on Adrian, with their video cameras, listening for voices or movement.

Vann did not sit on his hands. He obtained support from four more black leaders, including three leading clergymen, and sent a second letter to Kelly. He repeated the call for Mauriello's removal and asked for a meeting with Kelly.

"We believe the residents can no longer trust the precinct to protect and serve them in its current leadership," the group wrote.

City Council member Darlene Mealy, who also represented Bed-Stuy, weighed in as well. "We have to now start protecting our constituents," she said. "Something has to be done. This is a disservice to our community. And it's up to the commissioner to do something. If we keep seeing the same things, we have to try something new or move some people out. That behavior cannot be tolerated anymore."

On one occasion, she said, she walked into the station house with a number of senior citizens to speak with the police about an arrest in which a young man had been injured. "I was told to get the F out," she said. "I told them this is our house. We pay for it with our taxes. We don't have to go anywhere. Just by that day I know something is wrong with system."

On another occasion, she said, she complained to officers who were handing out tickets to people who were double-parking during a street cleaning period. New Yorkers routinely double-park while the street cleaning rule is in effect on a given block, and elsewhere police don't give tickets for it.

"On the summons quota, I had a problem just recently," she said. "A police came and gave everyone double parking tickets. But if you don't do that in every part of the city, you can't do it here. You're taxing people $150, and that's an extra burden on people's lives."

But Mauriello also had his defenders among Bed-Stuy's black community. Butch Thompson, owner of Malcolm X Pizza, said that Mauriello not only knew the names of store owners, but he was proactive in stemming crime. "He is concerned about the community he works in," Thompson said. "He's always in the street. He puts in the work. This is a commander who gets the job done. He's a hands-on officer. His tactics are unorthodox, but he gets the job done."

In conversation, Thompson said he has no problem getting searched by police because he did nothing wrong. "It's a hot area," he said. "I don't mind bending the rules a bit because of that. If you are innocent, it's not a problem.

"What do you want him to do? Let it continue or change the tactics, and a few of us get caught up in the fire. The cops can't do more than they do if the community don't get involved. And you can't blame cops for everything."

Community activist Brenda Fryson says Mauriello's initiatives got results. The police and other agencies, aided by business and block associations, targeted two buildings along Malcolm X and were able to reduce problems there, Fryson said. "You could hardly walk on Malcolm X," she said. "They were throwing garbage off the roof.

"So many negative articles in the press revolve around what's happening in Bedford-Stuyvesant, and this is a case where we have cause on a number of levels where we can point to a success," she said.

Precinct officers, Fryson said, often do their jobs well, but there are also those who don't. Mauriello, meanwhile, had shown the willingness to work with the community.

"Our expectation is that when these officers come they are trained on how to discern what is criminal quality of life that is a threat, and differentiate that from police harassment," she said. "They expect that in Bay Ridge, Boro Park, and wherever else in the city. Over the past couple of years, I think that culture is slowly changing. He's been willing to work with the community on several different levels. He's demonstrated at least the willingness to do that. That's very important."

In an extremely closely held move, later that June, the commander of the Quality Assurance Unit passed the conclusions of the QAD investigation into Schoolcraft's allegations to his boss, Deputy Chief Mary Cronin.

Cronin passed the report to Deputy Commissioner Michael Farrell and certain other select bosses. Farrell briefed or passed the report on to the Chief of Internal Affairs, the Chief of Patrol, the Chief of Department, and, presumably, Kelly's office. And then it went into a safe. It did not reappear in the public consciousness for more than 18 months, its conclusions viewed by a few top brass and no one else.

A source familiar with the report said there was deep concern in the upper echelons of the department that the conclusions of the report were so explosive that if it were leaked, it would damage the department's reputation. Some officials thought too many copies have been made. So all copies of the report were very closely tracked, the source said.

"There was serious concern that it would get out," the official said.

★

Indeed, when I sought the results of the probe later that summer, the NYPD rejected my Freedom of Information request. When I appealed, that request was also rejected. The NYPD was basically daring me to file suit.

The thing is, the report was simply about the operations of a governmental agency. It would not contain particularly sensitive material, and anything that was confidential could have been redacted. What the NYPD was doing in withholding the report was a clear distortion of the state's public records law. As a result, the report did not reach the public for another 18 months, leaving questions about Schoolcraft's credibility unanswered.

Then, three weeks after QAD sent the report to police headquarters, Kelly sent a signal about its contents. Kelly likely was also reacting to the pressure from Vann and other black politicians and clergy. Just before the start of the July Fourth weekend, he ordered Mauriello removed from command of the 81st Precinct and transferred to Bronx transit as an executive officer. Browne, Kelly's spokesman, called the transfer "routine."

Mauriello found out in a call from the chief of patrol, who told him he had been doing a good job in the 81st Precinct. As he later testified in an unrelated trial, Hall portrayed the move as a promotion, but Mauriello didn't feel that way.

"I considered it a transfer," Mauriello testified, going on to defend his record in the precinct, including the material on the Schoolcraft tapes.

"We want activity," he testified. "So it's not about numbers. It's about the officer working. If there is a crime happening, I expect him to make an arrest. There was no pressure. It was just 'do your job'."

From Mauriello's point of view, a lot of the statements on the tapes were legitimate efforts by supervisors to motivate cops to correct crime conditions in the precinct.

He talked about the challenge of covering the rougher spots in the precinct with fewer officers by putting footposts in those areas. "We had three very violent buildings that were at war with each other, and this goes back for years and years like the Hatfields and McCoys," he said. "Of course, if they observe a crime I expect, you know, if you have probable cause, arrest somebody. If they observe a quality of life infraction, I want the condition corrected. If there is reasonable suspicion to stop somebody, I expect someone to be stopped. That's their job.

"The people in the community loved it. They complimented my officers out there. And also it kept the criminals from committing crimes."

Two weeks after the transfer, in a memo to the First Deputy Commissioner, QAD Deputy Chief Cronin recommended disciplinary action against Mauriello, two sergeants, and two police officers for improper crime reporting. However, this recommendation, too, stayed secret.

In the confidential memo, Cronin wrote that her investigators had confirmed that during Mauriello's tenure, "complaint reports for index crimes are being improperly downgraded, and not being entered into Omniform [the NYPD's complaint tracking system]."

Cronin also charged that Sergeant Matthew Ferrigno failed to take an assault and attempted robbery complaint on July 16, 2009. Further, she alleged that Sergeant Timothy Rodgers had failed to make sure a robbery report had been taken on October 17, 2009. She also charged that Officer Fernando Vasco and Officer Jason Surillo had failed to take that complaint and didn't record it in their memo books. She recommended lower-level discipline for the two sergeants and the two officers. She made no recommendation in Mauriello's case. In other words, Cronin did not seek to limit the potential case against Mauriello. That would come later from another unit. QAD, at least, had done its job.

On July 30, Sergeant Raymond Stukes—one of Schoolcraft's main critics in the precinct—and Officer Hector Tirado were charged criminally with making a false arrest as part of an IAB sting. The charges would be eventually dismissed.

CHAPTER 13

THE WASHINGTON HEIGHTS DIGRESSION

In late May 2010, I received an email from a retired detective living in Florida named Harold Hernandez. Hernandez was 43 years old and had retired in 2007 after more than 20 years as a cop. In 2006, he was promoted to detective first grade, the highest and most exalted rank in the brotherhood of investigators. Typically, in the whole police department, at any given moment, there are fewer than 200 detectives first grade among more than 30,000 officers. Allowing for a few political promotions, the majority were merit based. Hernandez had made more than 400 arrests in his 20-year career and assisted in many others, and he earned 19 excellent police duty awards, four meritorious police duty awards, and three commendations. In other words, one could argue about whether Schoolcraft had been a good cop, but Hernandez had undisputedly been a very good cop. No one would say otherwise. And he had spent most of his career in drug- and violence-ridden parts of upper Manhattan, the same neighborhood where Adhyl Polanco was raised all those years ago. It was not a soft assignment.

Hernandez sent me an email, having read the *Voice* articles. He was moved by some force to reach out to me. Such moments were rare in the scheme of things. The NYPD was many things, maddeningly bureaucratic, bad, good, poor, excellent, indifferent, committed, appalling, heroic, brave, but one thing it inspired was a hard, enduring loyalty. Even when a man was not loyal to his commissioner or commander, he would be loyal to the men and women he worked alongside. Even when he was not loyal to them, he would be loyal to his own accomplishments, to the perception his family and friends had of him. Even if a cop had left on bad terms, he would often refuse to discuss a thing, if discussing that thing would bring dishonor to the people with whom he served.

Moreover, the diaspora of the NYPD was vast, nationwide, and they were a sort of chorus that would in the quiet moments, over drinks, in small groups, on the fishing line, on the phone, over the Internet, either excoriate or exalt for sins or virtues real or imagined. In short, it took a lot for retired Detective First Grade Harold Hernandez to write the email, to talk with me, to agree to speak for the record. It was a big reach. He had never been quoted in any media in his entire distinguished career. And that, in this world of over-sharing and lack of loyalty, screamed integrity and honor. On the other hand, there was a powerful force pushing Hernandez to speak—his conscience, his mission to correct what he saw as misdeeds, a final attempt at correcting a record that had been buried for so many years. Sometimes a man can't quite put something to rest until he has dealt with it. Closure is like that. Even when the waves have passed over a stretch of sand so many times that it is obscured, there is still evidence of its passing, and there in that passing is where integrity sits.

And the story told tells when he came in from the warm was this:

In 2002, a predator was stalking and attacking women in a leafy section of upper Manhattan, along Riverside Boulevard, known more for its stately pre-war apartment buildings than its crime rate.

The man was named Daryl Thomas. He was 32 years old. He worked in a law firm, managing a computer system. He had a wife and a daughter. And he lived in the same neighborhood.

He began trolling the darkened streets of his neighborhood sometime in August 2002. He would follow women—he preferred white or Asian women whom he thought would be more reluctant to fight back—home from the subway and accosted them at the door of their buildings. He would show a knife from behind and try to force them into the building. If they screamed or resisted, he fled.

His victims included a light-skinned Hispanic woman, a waitress in a cop bar down the street. A German tourist. A Japanese woman. A musician, who long after she had recovered told a reporter that Thomas accosted her as she entered her apartment. He followed her into the building and into an elevator to her floor. He grabbed her and put the knife to her throat. She screamed and struggled. They both fell to the floor. He snatched her purse and fled. She chased him down and grabbed the purse. He punched her in the face. She went down but kept a solid grip on the purse. He then fled for good. She suffered a bruised face and a cut on her throat.

"He was trying to get me into my apartment," she later said. "This turned my life upside down for more than a year. I had panic attacks. I didn't sleep. There were days I couldn't leave my apartment."

Then, at 4 a.m., on November 3, 2002, a woman heard noises in the hallway of her building. Through her peephole, she saw a man pushing a woman into an apartment. She immediately dialed 911.

Officers Luke Sullivan and Patrick Tanner kicked the door in and found Thomas hiding in a closet. The things he had with him: a knife in his pocket, a backpack containing two pairs of women's panties, and a length of rope. She was tied to a chair. She had been beaten. The equipment fairly shouted that Thomas had planned the assault; this wasn't a drunken, spur-of-the-moment attack, and he intended to keep her there all night.

Thomas was left in a holding cell overnight and then brought to an interview room for what police call a "debriefing," which is really an interrogation. Hernandez arrived with a cup of coffee and entered the room. At that moment, Hernandez knew only about the arrest on the previous night. Before he started in on Thomas, he bought him breakfast—an egg sandwich. Court records tell us that Thomas, for some reason, waived his Miranda rights and never asked for a lawyer.

And the conversation began. Hernandez recalled that Thomas didn't need a lot of prodding. He launched into a story about one particular assault but not the one from the night before.

"Listen, you've done this in the past, haven't you?" Hernandez asked.

"Yeah," Thomas replied.

"How many times?"

"I don't know. . . . Seven or eight times."

"Where did these incidents take place?"

Thomas replied, "Pretty much in this area," referring to the Fort Washington section of Washington Heights.

Hernandez paused the conversation there and left the room. He was puzzled. If there was a sexual predator working the neighborhood, the 33rd Precinct Detective Squad should have heard about it. There should have been added patrols. The suspect's description should have been put out at roll calls. And yet there was none of that. He searched but could not find a record of any recent prior attacks.

There was one report, a sexual assault and robbery from September 23. Hernandez knew about that one because he had done the report himself, classified it as a robbery and attempted rape, and sent it on to the Manhattan Special Victims Unit for investigation. Maybe Thomas was responsible for that one. But his next thought was worse: Where were the others?

He then thought, "Maybe Special Victims forgot to notify the precinct that they have a pattern." He asked and learned that no, there was only the one case. There was no indication of a what police call a pattern, a series of crimes fitting similar facts.

The declaration of a pattern would have triggered special attention from the police: patrol, detectives, plainclothes anti-crime unit officers, the sex crimes unit, and the robbery unit would all be on alert looking for a man fitting the description of the attacker. Since Thomas lived in the neighborhood, it would have been more likely that he would have been caught had a pattern been declared.

And then Hernandez figured out the problem. "It dawned on me that they [the precinct bosses] are fudging numbers and misclassifying cases," he told a reporter years later. "So I start looking."

He went back into the interview room and asked Thomas for the dates, times, and locations of the other attacks. He didn't remember them offhand, but he said he could pick them out from the street. So Hernandez and Detective Barry Felder drove him through the neighborhood and had him point out the crime scenes. He pointed to 647 West 172nd Street, 779 Riverside Drive, 156–08 Riverside Drive, 560 West 170th Street, 620 West

171st Street, and two others. Hernandez returned to the station house and paged through every complaint report for the previous four months and finally unraveled the mystery.

Precinct patrol bosses had classified the prior incidents as criminal trespassing, which was a misdemeanor, except for one case, which was classified as criminal possession of a weapon. Hernandez read the actual "narrative," or what the crime victim said had happened, and he saw the cases should have been classified, at a minimum, as first-degree burglary.

"The minute he grabs you in the hallway armed, that makes it a burglary in the first degree," he later said. "They used every non-felony you could think of" to classify the cases. "If you read the narrative, they are describing some kind of sexual assault or attempt. He came up behind them, grabbed them, placed the knife to the neck, or displayed it. He would demand money or their cell phones. If they didn't put up resistance, he was either going to fondle them or commit some other kind of sex crime to them."

But supervisors had written the reports to downplay the seriousness of the crimes. "They look to eliminate certain elements in the narrative. You change one or two words, and you can make a felony into a misdemeanor."

Back in the interview room with Thomas, Hernandez talked more. He asked him, "Weren't you ever afraid that you would get caught in any of these locations?"

"Nah, I looked around, I never saw any cops," Thomas said, adding that with each new assault, his brazenness and level of violence increased.

Within a week after Hernandez was able to put Thomas's crimes together, the Manhattan District Attorney's office charged the same incidents that had been classified as misdemeanors as serious felonies: first-degree robbery, burglary, sexual assault, and attempted rape. A Manhattan grand jury indicted Thomas in five of the assaults, charging him with numerous counts of first-degree attempted rape, robbery, sexual abuse, and burglary. But even as the evidence mounted, Thomas rejected plea deals that would have jailed him for 20 to 30 years. He went to trial in November 2003, testifying that he had been in a kind of "dream state" during his crime spree. He was convicted of all 18 counts in the indictment and sentenced in February 2004 to 50 years in a state prison in Romulus, New York. His earliest release date is 2045. He will be 75 years old.

In the aftermath, Hernandez said prosecutors were furious about the handling of the Thomas investigation. They complained to their superiors, who in turn raised the issue with the NYPD. Rather than facing the issue head-on, however, they buried the whole sordid mess, he said.

"Once this thing blew up, the job made sure the press did not find out about this case," he said. "It was very high profile within the department because they thought the women were going to run to the press."

None of the victims ended up going to the press—a fairly bizarre outcome when one considers the number of reporters in the city. It's also fairly amazing that no one in law enforcement leaked the story, and prosecutors were able to keep it away. On the other hand, prosecutors' first priority must have been to send Thomas away for a long time and worry about the cover-up later. In 2010, I tracked down one of the victims, Jennifer Krupa. By then, she had long left the city. She was shocked at what had happened behind the scenes in one of the worst experiences of her life. "If there was a chance they could have caught him earlier, that is absolutely infuriating," she told me. The effect of the attack lingered with her for years. "Anytime I'm in a corner or in an elevator, I'm very aware of what's going on around me."

As the fallout from the case swirled, Hernandez learned that one of his supervisors, a detective sergeant, had spotted a similarity in some of the incidents. When he told the squad commander and the precinct commander, he was rebuffed.

"I told them, 'You have a predator out there,' and they said, 'Keep your mouth shut,'" the sergeant told Hernandez. "I said, 'You keep on believing that, it's going to blow up in your face. And it's gonna get ugly if people find out.' They didn't listen."

According to Hernandez, the precinct commander, then Captain Jason Wilcox, was afraid of being disciplined for the handling of the case. But Hernandez earned praise for his work. Despite that, he said, "Everybody overlooked the fact that they allowed this predator to remain on the loose."

In the end, the whole incident was covered up. No one was disciplined. No newspaper ever wrote about it. It was as if it never happened. Wilcox, meanwhile, was promoted at least twice, including to inspector in charge of the Manhattan Transit Bureau.

Years later, in conversations with me, Hernandez blamed Wilcox and his crime analysis sergeant. (The crime analysis sergeant is responsible for double-checking complaints against the facts. The job was an outgrowth of CompStat, and critics of CompStat say these officers are central to the manipulation of crime reports.)

"Anybody who continues to allow this stuff to go on is pathetic," he said years later, adding that the NYPD had become more concerned with crime statistics than actually solving crimes. "They've lost sight of what they were supposed to be doing out there. They've lost sight of their oath."

He said he would have stayed 30 years, but the constant struggle over classifying crime complaints led him to retire in 2007. "I gained the most coveted position in the detective bureau, but I couldn't deal with it anymore," he told the reporter. "It was battling on a daily basis. You are providing a disservice to New Yorkers when you do this stuff. I used to think, 'What if it happened to a family member or a friend?' God forbid that someone could have stopped this, but was worried about careers and numbers and percentages."

CompStat did great things for the department, but under Police Commissioner Kelly, the system became distorted into a contest for the right statistics—a drop in crime complaints, with a corresponding rise in quotas for summonses, stop and frisks, and arrests. "As time passed, there came a time for upper management officers to attain higher rank, and they began to demand higher quotas to beat the next guy's decrease in crime. They began to make their demands known and force officers to make these quotas with the promises of choice assignments or better working conditions."

"This is going on in all 75 precincts. This is the culture for the young cop coming into the department. He doesn't see the bigger picture. If it's going to allow him to have a day off and they won't ride or harass him, he'll go along with it. And New Yorkers are being victimized, and no one responds to their complaints."

In the end, the Thomas case was the tipping point for Hernandez. He had already experienced other examples of downgrading crime stats, and they frustrated him and added to his incentive to retire. In one instance, he nearly got into deep trouble as a result.

Someone had downgraded a robbery case and forged Hernandez's signature to make it appear that he had downgraded the crime. Prosecutors discovered the forgery after the case file was delivered from police headquarters to the Manhattan District Attorney's office prior to trial.

The file contained a detective's memo, known as a "61," which reclassified the robbery to a petit larceny, and at the bottom was the forged Hernandez signature.

"It was a robbery, but when it goes downtown, it shows up as a petit larceny," he said. "The DA is pissed at me. She asks, 'Are you perjuring yourself?'"

Hernandez examined the report and was able to prove it was not his signature. "I'm saying, 'What are you talking about? This isn't my handwriting. Look at all my reports,'" he said. "Somebody forged my name. That's a crime. She agreed with me and she was livid. And I was livid because my integrity had been questioned."

There were other instances. Again and again, Hernandez came across evidence that sergeants and lieutenants in patrol had changed what patrol officers had written in a complaint. The effect was that the detective squad might never learn about a major felony because it had been purposefully misclassified. "If you classify a robbery as a petit larceny and mark it closed, it won't be assigned to the squad, and I'll never see it," he said.

In the old system, the complaint went from the patrol officer to the desk sergeant to the clerks to the squad. Under CompStat, each precinct was ordered to appoint a "crime analysis sergeant" to monitor the accuracy of crime reports. That sergeant worked out of the "124 room," a secure room where the crime complaints were kept. Now, that sergeant would also review complaint reports. This unprecedented micromanaging of accounts of crime obviously had the effect of placing a subtle downward pressure on crime statistics.

Hernandez went as far as to contend that the crime analysis sergeant's actual job was to downgrade as many complaints as possible. Other techniques to keep the stats down evolved. For example, if the numbers were high in a given week, a complaint wouldn't be entered into the system until the following week so it wouldn't count in that week's stats.

"Sometimes, you would get a robbery or a burglary or one of the seven majors a week later because they do their stats on a weekly basis," he said. "If one week was too high, they would hold on to it and push it to the next week. The thing is, they are supposed to be assigned on a daily basis. That's a week of a case sitting dead, no one running down leads."

And as Schoolcraft had experienced in the 8–1, Hernandez also witnessed commanders calling victims to get them to change their complaint. Repeatedly, he took calls from aggrieved victims about lost reports. "The victim says, 'I've been calling for a week,' and I had to say, 'I understand you're upset'."

At times, he saw grand larcenies classified as something called "theft by deception," a charge that didn't even exist in the penal code.

Hernandez began entering complaints into the system himself so he would be sure cases had been properly classified. Even then, sometimes, precinct bosses went into the system again and altered the reports. "Or they would come to me and tell me to change it, and I would refuse because that's not a lawful order," he said. "If that didn't work, they would complain to the squad lieutenant and try to manipulate him."

In short, the downgrading of the assaults to trespassing, likely for the purpose of manipulating the stats, allowed Thomas to commit six sexual assaults, to victimize seven women total, over about two months before he was caught in the seventh attack. And that was only a lucky break: a vigilant neighbor calling police on a hunch.

An article detailing Hernandez's story ran in the *Village Voice* on June 8, 2010, and the reaction was sharp. The NYPD was of course publicly silent on the matter, but within a few days, two Internal Affairs detectives appeared on Hernandez's doorstep in Florida. They wanted him to disclose more information. Hernandez refused. He said, "I've said all I have to say. I'm retired."

In a footnote to the *Village Voice*'s article on Hernandez, I wrote that I had spoken to more than a dozen current and retired police officers of various ranks who had their own stories about the downgrading of complaints, quotas, and civil rights violations stemming from the stop and frisk campaign. And yet the NYPD still denied the extent of downgrading.

CHAPTER 14

"WE'RE NOT GOING TO SETTLE"

Through the first eight months of 2010, as all of this was happening, Adrian Schoolcraft largely remained sequestered in Johnstown with his father. He wasn't working, and the two men were living hand-to-mouth between the little apartment and Larry's barn-like house, which was in danger of falling apart. As Larry later said, the house was cluttered with the contents of his parents' home, items from the house he shared with Suzanne, and Adrian's things. He was worried about the county foreclosing on the home.

Since Adrian wasn't earning his police salary, they had no income beyond Larry's modest pension. Adrian tried repeatedly to find a job. He sent out more than 90 resumes, but he was living in one of the most depressed regions in the state, and the jobs were scarce. There were two other barriers to work: Anyone could Google his name and see that there was no way the NYPD would give him a recommendation, and the Schoolcrafts were preparing a lawsuit. . . . What would happen when he had to take time off work to go to the city? At least, that's the way the Schoolcrafts felt.

The NYPD could justify not paying Schoolcraft since he refused to report to work, but the message from the PD had been only negative, giving Adrian no incentive to cooperate.

Some observers questioned why Adrian remained in Johnstown, given the potential PR bump he could get by being more present in the city. He never really moved to capitalize on this high profile, but that wasn't really his style. But whatever else they didn't have, the Schoolcrafts did have a reservoir of strength, of innate hardheadedness that gave them, even in the midst of the economic hardship and the pressure from headquarters, the motivation to press ahead in their campaign against the most powerful law enforcement agency in the country and the most powerful police commissioner in NYPD history.

Within the NYPD, there were discussions among the brass about just what to do with this recalcitrant officer whose recordings were damaging the NYPD's image. At some point that summer, a decision was made to try back channels to bring Schoolcraft to the table. The frontal assault definitely hadn't worked. Nor had the threats. For this odd mission, they turned to Captain Brandon Del Pozo, the same man who David Durk spoke to about Schoolcraft back in August 2009, when Durk called Internal Affairs.

By then, Del Pozo was in his second command, having moved from the 50th Precinct in the Bronx to the 5th Precinct in lower Manhattan. His career had only continued to rise. Since Schoolcraft wouldn't talk to the police, the department asked Del Pozo to reach out to me. He called me and asked me to reach out to Schoolcraft.

Del Pozo said the goal was to broker a deal that would bring Adrian back to work. Schoolcraft would be assigned to an out-of-the-way unit— maybe the canine unit, which would appeal to his interest in animal rescue. In exchange, Schoolcraft would agree to testify against Mauriello, and maybe Marino, if Marino was charged.

Someone familiar with the NYPD's thinking said that at the time, department bosses didn't believe Schoolcraft had done anything to get himself fired from the job, but he had to show up for work. That piece was non-negotiable. And Internal Affairs Group 1 wanted Schoolcraft as a witness.

"They want him to accept charges for being AWOL, and then be a witness, and say what he saw and heard," the source said. "They want to try to find him a place in the department. They wouldn't stick him in a place where cops would constantly bother him. It would be as comfortable a working environment as possible."

This source said, "The fact that Kelly took Mauriello and buried him in Bronx transit says a lot. [Schoolcraft] can come back, be a witness, he can discuss Mauriello and Marino, then stand trial on department charges and still turn out to be someone who is an asset to the department."

Len Levitt, the police columnist, offered a slightly different account subsequently, which he got from Schoolcraft's newly hired lawyer, Jon Norinsberg. Norinsberg told Levitt that the offer came from Julie Schwartz, the deputy commissioner overseeing the NYPD's prosecutor's office, and people working for Michael Farrell, the deputy commissioner for strategic initiatives. Farrell, interestingly, was the man who had two months earlier received the still-secret investigative report into Schoolcraft's allegations of crime downgrading in the 81st Precinct. That the report was even complete has not been acknowledged, but Farrell knew what was in it. Was it possible that he was trying to end the matter to avoid possible embarrassment about what the report said?

Either way, the fact that the NYPD, so reticent of the press to be almost opaque, would go through a reporter with an offer to Schoolcraft signaled just how concerned the agency was over his allegations.

On the plus side, the deal would have allowed Schoolcraft to get a paycheck again, cooperate in the investigations, and still continue his lawsuit against the city.

The benefit to the NYPD was that it would essentially bring Schoolcraft back into the fold. But Schoolcraft wasn't having any of it. He refused the offer right away, and Norinsberg called it "ridiculous." Schoolcraft felt that returning to the department would expose him to more retaliation and make him vulnerable to even more disciplinary action. The offer was a nonstarter.

At any rate, he had other fish to fry. On August 8, lawyers for Schoolcraft filed a $50 million lawsuit against the city, Mauriello, Marino, Paul Browne, other officers, and various Jamaica Hospital medical staff. Larry and Adrian worked long hours with their lawyers—Norinsberg, Gerald Cohen, and Joshua Fitch—on the wording of the complaint.

The complaint was 63 pages long—a book by routine tort case standards. "This action seeks redress for a coordinated and concentrated effort by high ranking officials within the New York City Police Department to silence, intimidate, threaten and retaliate against Adrian Schoolcraft for his documentation and disclosure of corruption with the NYPD," the complaint began.

The complaint went on to accuse the NYPD of having an illegal quota policy and claimed that police bosses were instructing cops to "suborn perjury" on police reports in order to distort CompStat statistics. In order to discredit Schoolcraft, police unlawfully entered his home and had him forcibly removed in handcuffs, "seized his personal effects, including evidence he had gathered documenting corruption and had him admitted to Jamaica Hospital against his will under false information that he was emotionally disturbed."

The complaint, which prominently featured the recordings, alleged that Jamaica Hospital "conspired" with the NYPD to deprive Schoolcraft of his rights for six days. As a result, he was "constructively terminated" from his position as a police officer.

It alleged that the performance evaluations were entirely tied to the quota, and Schoolcraft was in essence threatened to make his quotas or else. The precinct commanders "were so obsessed with making their numbers that they literally instructed officers to make arrests when there was no evidence of any criminal activity whatsoever.... Defendant's myopic obsession with quotas came straight from the highest ranking officials in the department."

Doctors with Jamaica Hospital failed to properly examine Adrian, failed to follow state mental hygiene law, and entered into a conspiracy to deprive Adrian of his rights. "In allowing the NYPD to dictate the medical policy at JMHC, and in utterly disregarding the legal requirement of Mental Hygiene law by ignoring objective medical evidence that [Schoolcraft] was not a danger to himself or others, JMHC departed from good and accepted medical practice by unlawfully confining him."

The complaint also referred to Marino's steroid case, noting that he was buying steroids from a pharmacy that was at the center of a criminal investigation that netted some $7 million in illegal proceeds. The document claimed that the NYPD ignored Marino's "violent propensities and explosive temper" but was never disciplined for it.

The complaint also aired out Brooklyn North chief Gerald Nelson's dirty laundry, alleging that Nelson, in a 2005 address to school safety agents, called parents "bitches who should be knocked over and handcuffed when they interfered." Kelly, the complaint said, reprimanded Nelson but left him in place.

The complaint also alleged that Nelson tried to intimidate two officers who had filed internal affairs complaints, saying, "We have friends on the IAB, and you're full of shit. If I see this in the paper, I will discipline you again. I don't need this in my career." Once again, Kelly did nothing.

It was all dramatic language, and the Schoolcrafts were fairly proud of the document. For once, it seemed as though things were going to turn around and go in a positive direction. But to their chagrin, the *Daily News* headline on the following day read, "Want My 50M Stat!"

The Schoolcrafts were ambivalent about the inclusion of a financial amount in the lawsuit, and now they felt they were being portrayed as only interested in getting rich. Nothing could be further from the truth, they said. They were also annoyed that the *News* used the same old unflattering picture of Adrian.

"It's not about the money," Schoolcraft said at the time. "We want this to get to court to get the truth out in the open. We're not going to settle. People may not believe me but we're not going to settle."

Among the wags who covered police issues and were familiar with the often brutal and life-consuming paths of these cases, many were skeptical. "He's not going to settle? Yeah right. He'll take his money, and walk away when he can't stand waiting anymore," one reporter said.

The most controversial allegation in the lawsuit, at least among reporters, was that NYPD spokesman Paul Browne was present when Schoolcraft was dragged out of his apartment on October 31, 2009. Schoolcraft was convinced he saw a large bearded man who looked just like Browne speaking to Mauriello on the street.

Browne's aides denied it right away, and at least in the media, the allegation tarnished Schoolcraft somewhat. In a revised complaint filed later, the allegation was removed, but the Schoolcrafts still believed it to be true.

As for the reaction to the lawsuit, the city offered a standard no comment. But there was this interesting comment on The Rant from a cop calling himself "Blue Trumpet": "Schoolcraft's allegations have gone un-rebutted for months because nobody is willing to put themselves on the record to refute what more and more appears to be the truth," this officer wrote. "Multiple felonies, both state and federal, appear to have been committed against a cop who wouldn't knuckle-under to official pressure and submit to the demand to flake citizens who hadn't done anything wrong. Every cop should be disturbed by this case and the Soviet-style tactics conducted against one of their own."

★

That summer also saw the Schoolcrafts pick up a new ally in the form of Frank Serpico, the most famous whistle-blower of them all, the retired cop who sparked a major police scandal in the late 1960s when he and David Durk reported widespread bribery of police officers, a practice known as "the pad." This was the same Durk who went to IAB on Schoolcraft's behalf in the summer of 2009.

When Serpico could not get the internal machinery of the NYPD to listen to his allegations, he went to the *New York Times*, which published a devastating account of the corruption. That led to the Knapp Commission and a series of supposed reforms.

One of his big moments came in his October 1971 testimony before Knapp, when he said, "The problem is that the atmosphere does not yet exist in which honest police officers can act without fear of ridicule or reprisal from fellow officers." Perhaps Serpico felt a kinship with Schoolcraft because during his long-ago ordeal, as Levitt reported, then-Mayor John Lindsay urged the *Times* publisher not to publish any of his allegations and called him "bizarre," a statement that suggested the mayor was trying to paint Serpico as crazy.

Serpico was shot in the face during a drug raid, and there were always suspicions that his fellow officers failed to come to his aid. He retired soon after that and collaborated with author Peter Maas on the bestselling *Serpico: The Cop Who Defied The System*. The book led to an iconic movie, *Serpico*, starring Al Pacino in the title role. The film pretty much cemented his name in the American consciousness. There was even a television series starring David Birney.

Despite his success, Serpico's ill feelings over his treatment by the NYPD lingered on. As he often said, he was still upset that his follow cops never called a 10-13—officer down—after he was shot. The only call that was sent was "shots fired." He had never gotten a full accounting of the shooting and many other issues from the NYPD.

Even though he was vindicated in the popular media, he still held to the belief decades later that the circumstances around his shooting had never been fully investigated by the NYPD. Incredibly, he still hadn't gotten a full look at the NYPD internal investigative file on him. Nor was he all that impressed in the end with the outcome of the Knapp Commission, as he wrote in an essay for Room for a View in August 2002:

> Mayor John Lindsay, embarrassed by my revelations, appointed the Knapp Commission to look into police corruption, and a few small fish got fried," he wrote. "Ultimately, as is usually the case with large scale corruption, the real culprits of my story were never brought to justice. They went on to become judges, politicians, commissioners and university professors. Men of base character are elected to the highest offices in the land. Such behavior may explain why we find ourselves in the mess we are in today.
>
> I discovered corruption among my fellow officers, not realizing how widespread or institutionalized it was. No matter how high I went, the response was always the same. The concern was not how to eradicate the problem, for I was soon to discover they were all await of its existence, but what kind of threat would my revelations pose to the system itself.

At times, he wrote about current events and on some occasions about NYPD matters. In 1994, he wrote President Clinton asking him to open a federal investigation into police corruption and brutality.

In 1997, at age 61, calling himself "Citizen Serpico," he told the New York City Council that America's leaders were at the heart of the nation's problems. That same year, learning that Giuliani was going to create a police-community relations panel in the wake of the police torture of Abner Louima, he said, "It's just talk until they start doing something about it and stop lying about what really happened."

In 1999, he spoke to the *Village Voice*'s legendary columnist, Nat Hentoff, about the continuing danger of retaliation against officers who spoke out. "Nothing has changed," Serpico told Hentoff.

He created a website devoted to encouraging people to "do the right thing, and keep them going when they decide to take that lonely road."

At the time Schoolcraft came forward, Serpico was living fairly quietly in upstate New York, a local celebrity, often holding court in a favored cafe.

On June 9, 2010, he weighed in publicly on Schoolcraft. "The NYPD had Officer Adrian Schoolcraft manacled and taken to the psycho ward for exposing the Police Department's fudging of statistics," he wrote. "Perhaps NYPD Commissioner Kelly is going to Israel to compare notes with Netanyahu on strategy to show the world how well they investigate themselves."

On July 29, 2010, Serpico compared Schoolcraft's treatment to what took place in the Soviet gulag. "The treatment of a cop who blows the whistle is the same in the Iron Curtain or the Blue Wall. . . . Welcome comrade."

And so, after talking at length on the phone, Schoolcraft and Serpico finally met in person at Frank's home. They spent a day together and shared a meal. Serpico later visited the Schoolcrafts and cooked them salmon for dinner.

Serpico would become an unofficial adviser to the Schoolcrafts.

As part of their strategy, Norinsberg created a website, SchoolcraftJustice. com, and other officers contacted him with their own allegations. One officer, from the 8-1, called him and claimed that Mauriello was given advance warning that Schoolcraft had gone to Internal Affairs. Another officer, assigned in the Bronx, claimed that the downgrading of crime reports was a consistent practice that he called "shitcanning." Like Schoolcraft, this officer found reports that were questionable and followed up with victims. He claimed that his precinct commander would file legitimate crime reports as "unfounded" so they wouldn't appear in the all-important precinct crime statistics.

At the end of August, the Schoolcrafts had a pleasant surprise when federal prosecutors in Brooklyn expressed interest in interviewing Adrian about his allegations. Schoolcraft traveled to Brooklyn in mid-September, sat with members of the office for more than an hour, and shared pizza as they talked. Nothing came of the meeting. It seemed to be yet another mirage in the desert of government oversight. Even two years later, a spokesman for the office declined to discuss what, if any, decision they made.

At around the same time, an NYPD judge ruled that Deputy Chief Michael Marino—the man who ordered Schoolcraft into the psych ward—should be suspended for 30 days and serve a year on probation for using human growth hormone. Marino remained in place in Brooklyn North.

On September 9, the *New York Times* weighed in with a front-page story on the second batch of tapes that came out of the 81st Precinct. And the syndicated radio program, *This American Life*, aired a segment on Schoolcraft, which received dozens of sympathetic comments from listeners around the country.

One listener in Philadelphia described how NYPD officers handcuffed his wife on some specious three-year-old unpaid traffic ticket. "I can only assume that some officer was trying to reach his quota," the listener wrote. A woman started a Facebook campaign in support of Schoolcraft.

In late September, as Bloomberg was defending the NYPD against quota allegations, and new allegations about downgrading were reported in the 66th Precinct, Schoolcraft reiterated his intent to stay the course in an interview with the *Daily News*. "This is not about money," he says. "There's not enough money in the state to get me to settle this suit. It's going to trial and there's no way around that."

★

Over the final quarter of 2010, Kelly and his top staff finally made several concrete moves aimed at blunting the controversy. First, on October 7, according to internal police reports, Charles Campisi, chief of Internal Affairs, forwarded the "interim report" on the Schoolcraft investigation to Kelly. Campisi was a long-serving IAB chief, and his opinions carried a lot of weight in the NYPD. The document was interesting almost less for what it contained than for what it omitted or left murky.

Campisi wrote in a cover letter, also dated October 7, that the investigation into Schoolcraft's allegations had been hampered by "his lack of cooperation on the advice of his attorney. . . . All efforts to enlist his continued participation have not been successful and the investigation will continue regardless of his participation."

Charitably, this claim was suspect. IAB didn't talk to Schoolcraft after November 2009, even though the Schoolcrafts were more than willing. "We never got another call from them," Larry said. "If they had called, we would have talked to them."

As for Marino, Campisi wrote that the chief had characterized the response to Schoolcraft being AWOL as "not a big issue." Campisi disagreed, writing, "This was more than a routine AWOL investigation," as indicated by Marino's involvement.

Campisi rejected Schoolcraft's claim that his tape recorder was stolen. "He was able to provide a recording. It should be noted that Schoolcraft has recently stated there were two recording devices in his residence and one is missing."

The investigation concluded that Mauriello was aware of the QAD investigation and of Schoolcraft's potential participation. "He denied both at his PG 206–13 hearing," Campisi wrote. Mauriello would receive charges for impeding an investigation and for failure to ensure that a complaint report was accurately prepared.

Campisi concluded that charges were still being considered for Marino for failing to notify IAB about "an allegation of corruption or serious misconduct against himself, as well as other MOS who were present in on the date in question and for impeding an investigation."

The 37-page interim report that followed Campisi's letter to Kelly was a curious one because it appeared comprehensive, but a close reading revealed much that was either distorted, omitted, or contradictory.

For one thing, it was biased against Schoolcraft and granted much more space to Marino, Mauriello, and Lauterborn.

Schoolcraft's claim that aide Monique Carter told him that Weiss and Caughey removed records of civilian complaints from Weiss's personnel folder was rejected, along with just about every other of his allegations.

The report concluded that there was no link between Schoolcraft reporting misconduct and the events of Halloween night. However, the report also said both Lauterborn and Mauriello knew that Schoolcraft had gone to QAD. Mauriello denied knowing anything about it, but Lauterborn told investigators he had briefed the precinct commander about it.

The report claimed, "PO Schoolcraft refused to go to the hospital and clenched his fist while backing up into the corner of his bed," while the recording of Halloween night didn't indicate that.

A total of 32 officers were interviewed, and none of them felt pressured by anyone regarding summonses and arrest quotas. They all, fairly incredibly, denied the existence of a quota system in the precinct. None of them alleged they had been punished—denied vacation, overtime, or a bad transfer— for failing to hit any quota. None of them said they heard a specific quota number in any of the roll calls.

All fell in line, except for one officer, Sylvia Nowacki, who disclosed that officers were "expected to generate 15 summonses every month and one arrest every quarter."

Mauriello denied ever retaliating against Schoolcraft. He also denied any knowledge that Schoolcraft had informed on the precinct. He claimed he never knew that Caughey had copied pages from the memo book or that he had seen those copies. He also denied knowing why Schoolcraft was placed on restricted duty. He denied any quotas and denied officers were punished for low activity.

The report used Schoolcraft's recording against him, making a priority of the fact that Adrian used the word "nigger" during the October 6 conversation with Larry and charging that the Schoolcrafts cooked up the whole thing.

"A review of the tapes provided by Schoolcraft demonstrates that he was being coached on what to say to QAD by his father, and the two individuals appear to have orchestrated the AWOL event," the report said. "The subject officer was observed to be on his cell phone during this entire incident and appeared to be coached as to his irrational behavior and refusals to comply."

Even though he had credibly reported downgrading of crimes, IAB said the charges against Schoolcraft were "a just result of his own misconduct by leaving the 81st Precinct before the end of his tour without permission."

In closing, the report blamed Schoolcraft for the unfinished nature of the investigation. "Without his cooperation, questions remain unanswered regarding his motivation for the AWOL incident and subsequent events."

This claim that the Schoolcrafts cooked up the whole thing is the most damning allegation in the report. It was known that Larry Schoolcraft had also sued his department—a fact that was leaked to me in August 2010 with the obvious intent to undermine the Schoolcrafts.

Later, the Schoolcrafts disputed the allegation that they had conspired to come up with an incident that would allow Adrian to sue the department. "We didn't start talking about suing the department until after Halloween night," Larry said. "There was no conspiracy even though some of what's on the recordings might sound like it. We were talking about an Article 78 over his evaluation, not some big lawsuit against the city."

The use of the word "nigger" is taken completely out of context, the Schoolcrafts said.

The report claimed that Adrian was free to leave the hospital at any time and said he did not attempt to leave. However, Adrian did at one point try to leave. Larry was present for that. But he was blocked. Moreover, hospital medical records showed that he was held as an "escape risk," suggesting he in fact was not free to leave.

Captain Lauterborn's statement made reference to something that no one in Schoolcraft's camp believed: During the summer of 2009, he told investigators, Schoolcraft was aware of an ongoing QAD investigation into downgrading of crime statistics.

He claimed that several officers had complained that Schoolcraft had asked them about what they had said. Lauterborn said he told Schoolcraft not to ask officers about the investigation. Lauterborn claimed he told the officers to call IAB if Schoolcraft continued to speak with them.

Lauterborn told investigators he "began to believe" Schoolcraft was involved with the QAD investigation. He said he spoke to Mauriello about it. Eventually, the whole precinct knew about the QAD investigation, and "it was commonly believed that Schoolcraft was involved."

This statement is puzzling because it's clear from the recording of the October 7 QAD meeting that that day was the first time Schoolcraft had spoken to anyone from the crime audit unit.

Finally, nowhere in the report did it mention the many other questions about the conduct of police officials other than Marino and Mauriello.

Since it was known that Nelson had been consulted, it strained credulity that they acted without the approval of their commanders, or that Nelson did not reach above him for the green light to handle Schoolcraft as they did. It was as if headquarters had drawn a circle around a set of names, and none other shall cross that line.

★

The next day, October 8, IAB signed off on charges against Mauriello for "conduct prejudicial to the good order of the department," in that when he was interviewed in August 2010, he told investigators that he wasn't aware of the QAD investigation until long after Halloween night. "In fact, the investigation disclosed that he was aware prior to those dates," the charges read.

The second count alleged that Mauriello denied that he knew about the entries in Schoolcraft's memo book, when in fact he did, according to the charge. Third, he was accused of failing to take a crime complaint report for the theft of Darryl Sweeney's car on June 30, 2009 (this was when he made the karma comment).

Fourth, he was charged with "providing inaccurate and misleading facts surrounding the circumstances" of the Sweeney incident to investigators. Fifth, he was charged with falsely claiming that he did not review complaint reports every day, when investigators found that he did.

This move had an element of politics as well. In essence, the department opted to charge Mauriello with just one incident of crime report manipulation, when QAD's July report suggested the misconduct was much broader.

Mauriello denied the charges. Mauriello's union representative, Captain Roy Richter, told the *New York Times* that Mauriello "feels abandoned by the department he has faithfully served for over two decades."

Two sergeants and two police officers were charged with failing to file a robbery complaint. Of the charges against the two sergeants, their union representative, Ed Mullins, told the *Times*, "In a nutshell, this is bogus."

Browne described the issues at the 8-1 as isolated. While the filing of the disciplinary case was important, it was treated in isolation, and no broader review of the accuracy of the crime statistics was allowed.

It would have made sense if, presented with a major problem in one precinct that had not been picked up in a routine investigation by QAD, Kelly had ordered a broader review, if not a full-blown investigation, or recommended that an outside agency look into it to avoid the appearance of a conflict. But he didn't do that, and Mayor Bloomberg backed him.

What Kelly did do at that point was appoint a deputy inspector named Daniel Carione to examine misconduct in the 81st Precinct, following on the Internal Affairs interim report. Carione had been the commanding officer of Queens Internal Affairs. He was tasked with reinterviewing 81st Precinct officers and listening to Schoolcraft's recordings. Strangely, Carione was forced out of the NYPD the following year because he needed a hearing aid to continue working. His review of the 81st Precinct was never seen by the public. Carione sued the NYPD for wrongful termination. Kelly, by the way, wore hearing aids but was exempt from NYPD policy.

On October 10, the Associated Press finally got around to publishing its own story about Schoolcraft. In that story, police officials said Schoolcraft's allegations about ticket quotas and fudged stats were taken seriously, but he was uncooperative in an investigation of them. They also viewed his case as an isolated incident, not a brewing corruption scandal.

On November 7, the *New York Daily News* published clear evidence of the existence of quotas in a different Brooklyn precinct. Memos from the 77th Precinct, which includes Crown Heights and Prospect Heights in Brooklyn, showed that the precinct bosses were demanding 75 summonses a week for moving violations. An NYPD spokesman called the memos "unauthorized" and still insisted quotas did not exist.

This obviously was yet more proof that under the pressures of CompStat, precinct commanders were either getting the message from police headquarters or coming up with their own methods to deal with the demand. Either way, the effect was the same, and it showed the pitfalls of CompStat.

The following day, Mayor Bloomberg pledged to investigate the quota memos, saying, "Commissioner Kelly will look at it." He also denied the existence of quotas. Once again, as with the Carione probe, nothing came of it. It was another blip that faded with the news cycle.

On November 8, Levitt distilled the open questions surrounding Schoolcraft, writing, "In the past year, no one from the police department has offered an explanation for Schoolcraft's forced incarceration inside the mental ward. No one has been held accountable. No governmental agency has begun an investigation. Neither Kelly nor Mayor Bloomberg has uttered one word. No one has even offered an apology. Not one governmental official has called for an investigation into what may be a blatant department crime: systemic statistical abuses throughout the city's police precincts."

★

And then Kelly dealt with the questions swirling around Marino, who remained in place despite the Schoolcraft claims and his human growth hormone disciplinary case. On November 24, Internal Affairs concluded that Marino had failed to tell them that Larry Schoolcraft had accused him of taking documents, a recorder, and other property from Adrian's apartment. Personnel records show that he has admitted to the allegation and agreed to the fairly minor penalty of the loss of six vacation days.

To put this NYPD minutiae in context, police officers are obligated to tell Internal Affairs of any allegations made against them, and Marino was a chief in the department, obligated to uphold every rule as an example. Once again, Kelly had given Marino a slap on the wrist. A cop who did the same thing—failed to report a serious allegation—would likely have been sent to Siberia. Just compare this to how Schoolcraft was treated for going home sick 45 minutes before the end of his tour.

As a result, Marino was still in place as number two in Brooklyn North three weeks later when he was heard threatening cops in the 79th Precinct who were planning to refuse to write summonses. "Just try it," Marino said, according to the *Daily News*. "I'll come down here and make sure you write them."

Then, as he did with Mauriello, Kelly picked another holiday weekend to address the Marino controversy. Two days before Christmas, Kelly ordered Marino transferred out of Brooklyn North and sent to a Staten Island command. The *Daily News* portrayed the transfer as related to the 7–9 allegations, not the handling of the Schoolcraft affair. Indeed, it had been more than a year since Marino's confrontation with Schoolcraft, and only now was he transferred.

The same day, the *New York Times* filed a lawsuit against the NYPD, saying that Kelly had repeatedly violated state Freedom of Information law by hiding information from the press and public. Things had sure changed since Kelly's pledge of "transparency" at his appointment way back in January 2002.

On January 5, 2011, Kelly took the final step during this period to blunt allegations of widespread crime report manipulation. He named three former federal prosecutors to investigate the accuracy of crime statistics— Robert Morvillo, a distinguished defense attorney, David Kelley, a former U.S. Attorney for the Southern District of New York, and Sharon McCarthy, a former special counsel to then-Attorney General Andrew Cuomo. Kelly stated, with a straight face, that the panel would complete its work in three to six months.

In a statement, Kelly said that the annual misclassification of crime reports was just 1.5 percent. "Nevertheless, every system can be improved and our goal is a misclassification rate of zero," he said. "By empaneling experienced, independent, objective experts to review our crime reporting system and the quality control mechanisms we have in place, I hope to establish the overall reliability of our statistics and identify any areas in need of improvement."

Kelly's use of the word "independent" in his statement was a direct slap at critics who were demanding an outside investigation. His timeline was charitably optimistic, but the gambit became yet another move that disappeared behind the walls of police headquarters.

In sum, Kelly had transferred and charged Mauriello and four other 8-1 cops for downgrading a grand total of *two* crimes. He had transferred Marino and taken six vacation days from him. He had appointed Carione to do a review that never saw the light of day. He appointed a panel that would disappear into the mist. The Internal Affairs Bureau had concluded that Schoolcraft cooked up everything with his dad and implied that Adrian was a racist. Kelly charged no one with any misconduct for their actions on Halloween night. He had blocked outside investigation, or no one has the cojones to investigate on their own. And the conclusions of the QAD report were still buried in some anonymous drawer in police headquarters. Those would not see the light for another year.

In short, it appeared, he was running a four-corners stall, right out of North Carolina basketball coach Dean Smith's playbook, trying to wait out the Schoolcraft allegations. The Bloomberg administration had three years left in office. It could just work.

CHAPTER 15

SMOKING GUNS AND "HAM AND EGGERS"

There are thousands of lawyers in New York City. In buildings along Park Row alone, across from the wrought iron gates of City Hall, hundreds of barristers pay for their summer houses and put their kids through school on money earned by suing the very municipal agencies they can see through their windows. Wags whimsically called them "ham and eggers" because that's what they ate, out of deli paper and aluminum foil, with their cart coffee, as they scurried to court from the subway.

In 2012, the city spent hundreds and hundreds of millions to settle lawsuits, an amount that was more than the budgets of entire municipalities. Thanks to laws favorable to tort lawyers and the relative vagueness of federal civil rights law, the New York Police Department actually was kind of easy to sue. All you needed was an aggrieved plaintiff and some modest corroboration—proving that a given officer was at a given scene was often enough. Because of the sheer volume of lawsuits, the city had no choice but to try to settle the majority of claims.

The other side of the coin was that police officers often seemed to do things that violated people's civil rights. Take January 2012 alone. In that single month, 40 people filed lawsuits solely alleging that a stop and frisk violated their rights. Extrapolated out, that's 360 such lawsuits in one year. Let's say those lawsuits settle for an average of $30,000 apiece. That's a $10.8 million bill to the city just because cops aren't following the rules for stops. Taxpayers foot the bill, and not one dollar comes out of the NYPD's budget.

Over the five years between 2007 and 2012, the number of lawsuits filed against the NYPD grew to more than 2,000 a year. The number of claims exceeded 8,000. There were so many federal civil rights cases being generated that the court created a special set of rules in an attempt to expedite the cases. Plaintiffs' lawyers claimed the rules were meant to strong-arm them into settling for lesser amounts.

Oddly, the city rarely examined these cases for commonalities and trends to identify problematic officers and lead to policy or procedural changes that would reduce the amount flowing out City Hall's doors.

If an officer's actions on the job kept costing the city money, shouldn't there be some kind of examination of the reasons and steps taken to stop it? Instead, the city just wrote the checks, the lawyers took their cut, and the officer went on doing what he was doing before. In some ways, if you strip away the rhetoric, it was a perfect circle, a good racket in a tough city.

But the Schoolcraft lawsuit was hardly a routine case. Back in 2010 when his profile was the highest, Schoolcraft and his father started searching for a lawyer. He would have preferred that an outside agency, like the feds, were at that moment knocking on doors and sending out subpoenas. But that wasn't happening. The only option they had left was to sue. Father and son, as was their way, nattered at each other endlessly over who to choose for what looked like it would be the final act in their struggle with the NYPD.

At first, someone recommended Norman Siegel, a well-known civil rights lawyer who had run the New York Civil Liberties Union for years. But that interaction didn't go so well, and the Schoolcrafts kept looking.

By then, Adrian had given a deposition to the Center for Constitutional Rights in its budding class-action lawsuit against the police for their endless stop and frisk campaign. One of the lawyers attached to that case, Jonathan Moore, seemed appealing.

Schoolcraft recalled that at one point in their talks, Moore told him to settle in for a long fight. The city wasn't going to go easy on him, Moore said.

But the Schoolcrafts, after a short while, decided to move on from Moore as well and discontinued their representation agreement with him.

Next came one of those very lawyers encamped across from City Hall. Norinsberg and his associates, Gerald Cohen and Josh Fitch, were working on the Stinson case, a class-action lawsuit over quotas—on behalf of New Yorkers who felt police ticketed them just to fill demands from their precinct commanders and not for some law enforcement reason. Schoolcraft's testimony and his tapes were perfect to aid in their case.

Schoolcraft, giving his second deposition of the month, sat and talked with them for that case and told them what he knew about the quotas in the 81st Precinct. Seeing the opportunity, Norinsberg began talking with Schoolcraft about representation, and they finally signed an agreement. He assured the Schoolcrafts that their case would be at the very top of their agenda, and that the firm has the finances to fight the city in what was certainly going to be a no-holds-barred contest that would span years before it was resolved.

"This is what you go to law school for, to fight a case like this," Norinsberg told me. "There was a terrible injustice, there were important Constitutional issues that involved an actual police officer."

At the moment, in the summer of 2010, Norinsberg was flush with the prospect of a major new case, and he and his associates, Fitch and Cohen, set about writing the massive complaint that would hold both the NYPD and Jamaica Hospital liable for what happened to Adrian.

After the civil complaint was filed in the Southern District of New York, U.S. District Judge Robert Sweet was assigned to the case on August 19, 2010. Robert Workman Sweet, at age 88, was one of the oldest judges in federal court. He attended Yale Law School, graduated in 1948, and then worked as a federal prosecutor. He was a deputy mayor for the city of New York from 1966 to 1969, coincidentally during part of the period of the Serpico investigations, and had also worked for Skadden Arps, a white-shoe law firm. President Jimmy Carter appointed him to the bench in 1978. Among the clerks, the most famous was Eliot Spitzer, a former New York governor.

Sweet had presided over many big cases, including the McDonald's obesity case and the case of journalist Judith Miller, who was accused of violating federal law for refusing to name her Bush administration source for articles about weapons of mass destruction in Iraq. He also had spoken out against harsh mandatory minimum sentencing policies on drug cases, calling them unconstitutional. He once said that the war on drugs was "expensive, ineffective and harmful."

Three weeks later, Dr. Isak Isakov, one of the doctors who examined Schoolcraft in the psych ward in 2009, was the first to respond to the complaint. His lawyer, Brian Lee, filed a boilerplate denial of every claim in the complaint. Lawyers for Jamaica Hospital followed with similar boilerplate denials. The hospital moved for dismissal of the case on October 12, arguing that it was not an arm of the government, and that the doctors in the case were not technically employees of the hospital.

On December 2, the city filed its own answer to the complaint, again essentially denying every allegation in the Schoolcraft complaint. After this initial flurry of activity, the case slowed down as 2011 began.

As the new year started, the Queens District Attorney's office reappeared in the story, having been absent, at least publicly, for a year. The office requested the recording of Halloween night and medical records from Schoolcraft's file. His lawyers complied. Once again, there was some sign of an outside investigation, but its purpose was opaque to the Schoolcrafts. Later in the year, Adrian met with prosecutors from the office for about 90 minutes. After that, the DA's office fell silent again.

The following month, the Schoolcraft recordings were used for the first time as evidence of quotas in a trial involving a Brooklyn woman who claimed she was falsely arrested. In awarding the woman $75,000, the jury found that the police had a policy "regarding the number of arrests officers were to make that violated plaintiff's constitutional rights that contributed to her arrest."

And yet another supervisor was caught on tape pushing quotas. The NYPD of course continues to deny their existence.

That May, Schoolcraft won a partial victory in court: Sweet ruled that while the federal claim against the hospital would be dismissed, the state claim would survive and stay in the case. And he ordered discovery to proceed, meaning that both sides would finally have to show their documents and then depose each other's witnesses. Regarding the hospital, Sweet ruled that Schoolcraft had sufficiently argued that the hospital and police "collaborated in depriving him of his Constitutional right." For the rest of the year, little of substance was added to the case file.

Separately a police officer named Vanessa Hicks sued the city, alleging she was fired for not writing enough tickets and not stopping and frisking enough people.

And Kelly finally closed the book on Marino's human growth hormone case, ordering him to give up 30 vacation days and serve probation for a year. It had taken three years for the case to come to a resolution.

A few weeks later, Kelly's crime statistics panel reached that magical six-month point that the commissioner touted in his statement. No report appeared.

In July, another lawsuit was filed that included material from the Schoolcraft recordings. This one was filed by Scott and Stephen Faine, who claimed they were arrested in the 81st Precinct as part of a quota. Their lawyer, Cynthia Conti-Cook, called the arrests concrete evidence of the effect of the police campaign to clear the streets that emerged in the Schoolcraft tapes.

"There is a strong connection in this case between the orders given to 81st Precinct officers in the tapes to 'clear corners' and the motivation these 81st Precinct officers had to arrest these men," Conti-Cook said. "There was no reason, but for the motivation to 'make numbers,' in either case for the officers to stop, question or arrest Scott."

The stop and frisk class-action lawsuit that had been filed against the police department now began to gather real steam. The case was potentially a massive problem for the city, which had fought it at every juncture for more than two years. That September, U.S. District Judge Shira Scheindlin issued a major decision, denying the city's motion to dismiss the lawsuit.

The Center for Constitutional Rights filed the lawsuit on behalf of New Yorkers, alleging "a widespread pattern and practice of suspicion-less and race-based stops and frisks by the NYPD."

Central to her decision, she said, were the Schoolcraft recordings, which she described as "smoking gun evidence." The decision paved the way for the recordings to be used during trial.

"Plaintiffs have presented the smoking gun of the roll call recordings, which considered together with the statistical evidence, is sufficient circumstantial evidence for this claim to survive," Scheindlin wrote.

Meanwhile, in the Schoolcraft case, discovery had finally begun a year after the lawsuit was filed. On September 28, the lawyers in the case agreed to a stipulation that all documents in the case would be kept out of the public eye. In other words, they couldn't be shared outside of the court, the plaintiffs, and the defendants. The city often insisted on agreements like this, supposedly to protect "confidential records." Plaintiffs' lawyers often agree because it lets them see documents without a big fight.

"This was a conventional stipulation," Norinsberg said. "It's done in every single case involving the city."

The Schoolcrafts said later that Norinsberg didn't tell them about this stipulation, and the stipulation went against their wishes. Months passed before they learned of this document, they said, and when they did, they were angry. From the start, they had wanted the entire injustice played out in the public arena, and their lawyer appeared to have gone against that hope and then had failed to tell them.

In October, there came yet more grist for the quota debate. A detective named Stephen Anderson testified that cops made up drug charges against innocent people to hit arrest quotas. The judge in the case, Gustin Reichbach, was so startled by the testimony that he asked Anderson how many times he had done it. Anderson replied, "Multiple times."

Four days after Anderson's testimony, Kelly issued a new order reminding officers of the difference between quotas and "activity reports."

As December came to a close, the *Times* published yet another article about someone whose crime report was not taken. A 34-year-old school-teacher said she was groped twice, but when she told a police officer, he said filing a report would be a waste of time. "His words to me were, 'These things happen'," she told the *Times*.

★

By January 2012, the fight had turned to the NYPD's internal audits of the crime statistics for the 81st Precinct. The department was refusing to turn over those records to the New York Civil Liberties Union, even though the department had released the data for every other precinct. Bed-Stuy City Councilman Al Vann jumped into the fray, demanding their release.

"Given the past controversy in the 81st Precinct, it is especially important that the NYPD be forthcoming and transparent with respect to what occurred in the precinct over the past decade," he said in a statement. "By concealing this public information, the NYPD is not only violating the law, but jeopardizing the significant progress made in rebuilding the relationship and trust between the Bedford-Stuyvesant community and the 81st Precinct."

On January 17, Kelly issued what would be at this writing the final of his steps to blunt criticism of the crime statistics: a departmental order essentially reminding officers that they can't ignore civilians who want to report a crime.

It had now been a year since the crime statistics panel was created—and its report was six months overdue. There was no mention of any findings by the panel that would have triggered the order. It was simply released without comment or reference to the panel. Nothing was heard from the panel a year later either.

At any rate, the order went on to address other CompStat dodges—sending folks to another precinct or another police agency, ordering them to go back to the scene of a crime and then call 911, taking a complaint only if the victim fully cooperates, shit-canning a report because it can't be solved or prosecutors won't indict on it, or delaying the filing of a report into the next reporting period.

He told cops to take reports even if the suspect couldn't be identified, the victim refused to look at photos, a grand larceny victim had no receipts, or the victim wouldn't speak with detectives.

True to form, Kelly's spokesman Paul Browne called the order "routine" and said it had nothing to do with crime report manipulation. Observers said this move was thin gruel if it was meant to address the mass of questions that had cropped up since 2009.

★

As March approached, the QAD report containing the conclusions of the Schoolcraft investigation remained secret, as it had for the previous 20 months, tucked away in some drawer at police headquarters. All who came near the NYPD asking for the report were rebuffed, as if the document contained the nuclear launch codes. In fact, the NYPD hadn't even acknowledged publicly at this point that any such report even existed.

At this point, Schoolcraft had been suspended for 27 months and had been living hand to mouth for that entire time. For him, the ordeal was turning into a long war of attrition, as if the city was testing him to see when he would crack.

Like Schoolcraft, Mauriello had also been in limbo. He was charged in October 2010, and now 18 months had elapsed, and very little had happened in the case. He, too, was getting the four-corners treatment. "The guy's been put out to pasture for 18 months, and he wants to get this done," his lawyer said, calling Mauriello a "fall guy." "I don't know if it's done for political, or litigation reasons. It's a big question mark. But he wants to move on. He's saying take me to the trial room....Any police officer who is awaiting an administrative trial is basically a man without a country."

And then on March 7, as if stepping out finally from behind a curtain, the conclusions of the QAD report emerged in an article I wrote for the *Village Voice*. One could immediately see why the NYPD didn't want to release the document.

Most of the allegations that Schoolcraft made in October 2009 were confirmed by the QAD investigators, as detailed in the 95-page report. For 25 months, Schoolcraft had been viewed by his critics as a man of lesser credibility, but this report pretty much vindicated him.

Eleven of the thirteen cases he brought to investigators were substantiated. Complaints were downgraded in an attempt to avoid index crime classification, investigators concluded. Reports were never filed. Reports were delayed and rewritten. Victims were ignored and pressured.

Rather than just stopping with Schoolcraft, the investigators interviewed 45 officers and examined hundreds of documents. They found a range of other instances in which crime reports had been altered, rejected, misclassified, gone missing, or not even been entered into the computer system. These involved a Chinese food delivery man robbed and beaten bloody, a man robbed at gunpoint, a cabdriver robbed at gunpoint, a woman assaulted and beaten black and blue, and a woman beaten by her spouse.

"When viewed in their totality, a disturbing pattern is prevalent and gives credence to the allegation that crimes are being improperly reported in order to avoid index crime classifications," investigators concluded. "This trend is indicative of a concerted effort to deliberately underreport crime in the 81st Precinct."

Crime complaints were changed to reflect misdemeanors rather than felony crimes, which kept the incidents out of the crime stats. The investigators said that "an unwillingness to prepare reports for index crimes exists or existed in the command."

There was an "atmosphere in the command where index crimes were scrutinized to the point where it became easier to either not take the report at all or to take a report for a lesser, non-index crime," investigators wrote.

Precinct commander Mauriello "failed to meet [his] responsibility." As a result, "an atmosphere was created discouraging members of the command to accurately report index crimes."

Most importantly, the report drew that bright line between the CompStat pressure from above down to the borough, to the precinct, to patrol officers, creating a situation that led bosses and cops alike to find other ways to reduce crime that had nothing to do with crime fighting. And if the 81st Precinct was a typical station house, then crime manipulation was certainly more widespread than city officials admitted.

Among the more egregious examples cited in the QAD report:

- A 2008 attempted robbery classified as misdemeanor assault. Schoolcraft had alleged in this instance that a sergeant in the precinct ordered him to downgrade the report, saying, "We can't take another robbery."

- A 2008 robbery wrongly classified as a report of lost property. Schoolcraft had given investigators an email from the victim who claimed he had been beaten and robbed of his wallet and cell phone by three men. But the crime complaint was changed to "lost property [because] the victim doesn't feel he was a victim of a crime." This could have been charged as perjury because the victim in this case wanted a complaint filed.

None of the precinct officers interviewed in that incident could explain how the report was changed to lost property. The complaint was upgraded to robbery. Two officers were disciplined.

- A 2009 attempted robbery for which the precinct somehow "lost" the complaint. Schoolcraft had said in the past that he subsequently wrote a new report after the initial one couldn't be found.

  A precinct sergeant told the victim that he would have to return to the precinct to look at mug shots, a process that would take "several hours." The victim said he had a job event to attend. The complaint disappeared after that. The complaint had languished for three days—a violation of a requirement that reports be "finalized" within 24 hours.

  A sergeant was facing department charges over the incident.

- A car theft that the precinct commander ordered cops not to take. Here, the victim ran into several barriers to filing her complaint. First, an officer told her to wait a few days to see if the car reappeared. That advice delayed the investigation for two days. In addition, Schoolcraft had alleged that Mauriello ordered the female officer not to take the complaint.

  The officer lost five vacation days as a result of the investigation.

- A 2009 incident in which an elderly man said he was a burglary victim. When he showed up at the precinct to file a report, a sergeant told him to go to another precinct to file the report. Again, this was a violation of the NYPD's own policy. It was only after a newspaper article appeared months later that a report was taken.

- A 60-year-old retired traffic agent made repeated visits to the precinct to get a complaint number for her stolen vehicle from May through June 2009. The investigation showed the report was never entered into the NYPD computer system, preventing it from being counted in the crime statistics. Investigators concluded nothing would have been done if the woman hadn't been a traffic agent and pressed the issue.

- Another auto theft, where the victim got frustrated because she had to wait hours to file her complaint. The report was never entered in the computer system. When she went to the 81st Precinct, she was told she had to go to the 79th Precinct. When she contacted the 79th Precinct, she was told she had to go to the location where the vehicle disappeared and report it to the 81st Precinct.

"She waited an inordinate amount of time, her was complaint was never investigated, nor was a complaint report ever generated," investigators concluded.

- A man who walked into the station house to ask for his complaint report in June 2009. The report had disappeared, and a new one was made. Schoolcraft claimed that precinct commander Mauriello refused to accept the report.

  A month later, two men were arrested for stealing the car. It was only at this point that 81st Precinct cops entered the report.

  The victim subsequently confirmed that he felt that Mauriello was "interrogating" him and doubted he was telling the truth.

  The report should have been an auto theft, not an "unauthorized use of a vehicle." They also found that Mauriello's account contradicted that of the victim and his cousin and wasn't credible.

- Investigators also recommended charges against a sergeant who told officers on Mauriello's orders not to take robbery reports if victims refused to return to the station house. Though the remark was on the Schoolcraft recordings, she initially denied ever saying that. Mauriello denied issuing any such order.

  Investigators learned that no report was ever taken for the incident that led to the sergeant's order.

- After a woman reported a knifepoint robbery, another precinct sergeant told cops, "If no surveillance cameras show her getting robbed, she's going to be locked up." In essence, cops were pressuring her not to file the complaint. She got frustrated, and no report was filed.

  Investigators concluded that two officers failed to take the report, and the sergeant failed to follow up. All three cops are facing possible charges.

As to Schoolcraft's claims that Mauriello and one of his lieutenants repeatedly ordered cops to downgrade index crimes, investigators examined hundreds of complaints and found several dozen misclassified reports.

In their interviews with QAD, Mauriello and precinct supervisors still denied there was any extensive manipulation of crime reports. Another signal of the obsession with CompStat in the precinct was that Mauriello was reviewing crime reports on a daily basis—not really the job of a commanding officer.

For his part, Mauriello denied the allegations and denied calling crime victims to question them on their reports.

When the precinct upgraded complaints, and that was rare, they usually waited a month, making it highly unlikely they could solve the crime.

"This represents a severe delay in accurate crime reporting and calls into question the motive for changing the classification" after so much time had passed, the investigators wrote. "This was more than just administrative error."

Overall, investigators wrote that they found "severe deficiencies in the overall crime reporting process as a whole."

"The investigation revealed the lengths that some members of the command went to, in order to avoid index crime reports," investigators concluded, going on to describe a "reluctance" to submit index crime reports. Since it was Mauriello's ultimate responsibility, investigators cited a "serious failure" in his command.

Schoolcraft should be credited with bringing to light a series of issues related to crime reporting, a police source said.

"Mauriello saw it as a numbers game," the source said. "There was no evidence he gave direct orders, but he was influencing members not to take reports or would fly off the handle at them."

Overall, the practice was certainly more widespread than the department admitted, this official said. "It really falls on the supervisors to follow the rules," the source said.

The general rule? "Even if the victim does not cooperate, you still take the report. It's wrong not to take the report."

In the aftermath of the report's disclosure, the problem that confronted the police department, given the new revelations, was that it had already sharply limited the charges against Mauriello, the two sergeants, and the two officers to misclassifying just two crime reports. Even as they did that, someone in the agency had to know that the problems were more widespread in the precinct based on the QAD report. And logically, then, it was likely to be happening in other precincts. Yet no broader review was ordered. This was a stunning contradiction that has yet to be explained at this writing.

The revelations of the QAD report caused a stir. "In our view, the results of the 81st Precinct investigative report completely vindicate Adrian Schoolcraft," said Norinsberg. "The report leaves no doubt that crime statistics have been flagrantly and deliberately manipulated so as to create an utterly false portrait of crime levels in the 81st Precinct....And this is no isolated incident.

"The fact that the NYPD knew about a report that wholly vindicated Adrian's claims, but never released to the public—much less acknowledged its existence—is disgraceful and a complete betrayal of the trust of the people of New York," he added. "Rather than attacking Adrian's credibility, the NYPD should have commended this officer's courage in coming forward— at great risk to himself and his own career—to expose the dishonesty and fraud which was taking place at the 81st Precinct."

Anything Kelly had done to date, he said, was "nothing more than window dressing." Neither Kelly nor his spokesmen responded to these statements.

Mauriello's union representative, Roy Richter of the Captains Endowment Association, pointed out that the former precinct commander was charged with obstructing the taking of a single auto theft report, the point being that if there was anything worse, he would have been charged with it.

"It's important to note that Mauriello was not charged in any administrative action, related to the broad conclusions that are contained in the report," Richter said. "Prior to the investigation, his command was rated very highly in previous crime statistics audits. We will challenge the charges against him. We feel he's been wrongly charged."

And then we come to the reaction from John Eterno and Eli Silverman, the two criminologists whose surveys of retired police commanders on CompStat had been attacked not only by the NYPD but by the *Daily News* editorial page as well.

"How in good conscience NYPD could continue to attack Adrian Schoolcraft and our research is beyond shame; it is revolting," they wrote. "The evidence of a problem with NYPD culture is obvious to any person who looks at the mountains of evidence. Apparently, the NYPD and Mayor Bloomberg are in complete denial. The NYPD needs a complete overhaul. A neutral outside investigative body with subpoena power and the ability to grant immunity is needed. Let's stop the charade and get it done."

Browne, in keeping with his practice, told the *Daily News* that it wasn't unusual for such reports to stay confidential. He insisted that the report was proof the NYPD took Schoolcraft's claims seriously. He said nothing else.

When he learned about these conclusions, Schoolcraft did not react quite as dramatically as everyone else. He was actually a little bit disappointed in the result. "What I was giving them were just examples of things that had happened," he said later. "I was hoping they would do a lot more to really examine the problem and correct it."

The report was picked up by numerous media outlets. On March 8, 13, and 15, 2012, the *New York Times*'s Pulitzer Prize–winning columnist Jim Dwyer wrote three pieces about the case. They were headlined, "For Detained Whistleblower, a Hospital Bill, Not an Apology"; "An Officer Had Backup: Secret Tapes"; and "Telling the Truth Like Crazy."

The *Times* also moved to unseal documents in the case, arguing the sealing order was too broad and out of line with established precedent. "Sealing is especially inappropriate when a lawsuit is the subject of immense and legitimate public interest and deals with the practices and policies of a critical public agency," wrote *Times* lawyer David McCraw.

Opposing the motion, Suzanne Publicker, a lawyer for the city, wrote, "There is no right of public access to discovery materials." She suggested that the *Times* file a Freedom of Information request for the documents. That was a laughable idea, because the NYPD had basically shut down that avenue for those seeking public records. The *Times* was already suing the NYPD over its lack of transparency.

Eventually, Sweet ordered the parties to create a list of the documents that he would review to make decisions about which should be released. (As of this writing, no documents have been released.)

The disclosure of the report created a firestorm in the lawsuit. The city assumed someone in the case leaked the document and asked Judge Sweet to order an investigation into the source. Norinsberg denied having leaked it and even asked the *Village Voice* to swear in an affidavit that the lawyers did not leak it. The *Voice* declined to provide an affidavit or discuss its sourcing. The city also brought discovery to a grinding halt, refusing to provide any more documents until it conducted its own investigation.

In June, lawyers for Schoolcraft moved to amend the complaint by adding a first amendment claim.

★

Toward the end of March, another officer had stepped forward to claim that he, too, was retaliated against for alleging the downgrading of crime. Sergeant Robert Borrelli, who had been part of the NYPD for 19 years, said that the practice was going on in the 100th Precinct in the Far Rockaways section of Queens. When he complained about it, he said he was transferred to the other side of the city, the Siberia of the Bronx courts. The NYPD disclosed that four complaints were reclassified after Borrelli filed his allegations but denied his transfer was punitive. The NYPD painted Borrelli as a disgruntled officer and said most of his reports were "unfounded."

In April 2012, nine officers claimed they were given lower evaluations as retaliation for griping about a quota system in the precinct. PBA chief Pat Lynch told the *Daily News* it was a department-wide problem.

"There are some unscrupulous bosses in the NYPD who use the evaluation system as a weapon," Lynch told the *News*. "Instead of providing constructive criticism some use it to extract retribution for personal petty differences. The PBA will use every tool at its disposal, legal and otherwise, to ensure that our members are treated fairly and with respect."

The following month, Judge Sweet allowed *Stinson v. City of New York*, the lawsuit filed by 12 New Yorkers alleging they got tickets because of an illegal quota policy, to go forward as a class action. The plaintiffs, also represented by Norinsberg, used the tapes made by Schoolcraft and Adhyl Polanco in their complaints.

Sweet quoted statistics that showed that more than 25 percent of the 3.6 million summonses issued between 2004 and 2009 were dismissed before trial, and 50 percent of the remainder were dismissed at trial. In other words, more than half the criminal court summonses that received a hearing were dismissed. This finding meant that a lot of criminal court summonses—for open container, pot smoking, blocking the sidewalk, etc.—were not worth the paper they were written on.

On May 7, the Patrolmen's Benevolent Association paid for a newspaper ad attacking the NYPD on quotas. "Don't blame the cop," it read. "Blame NYPD management for pressure to write summonses and the pressure to convict motorists." The ad claimed the department was using its personnel powers to punish officers who don't write enough tickets.

In early June 2012, the two criminologists, Eterno and Silverman, published their latest survey on crime statistics, which they announced with this headline: "Smoking Gun Emerges."

In big, bolded print, they wrote that the survey, "strongly substantiates pressures to play numbers game, and confirms crime report manipulation and quotas."

The survey contains "glaring evidence that central problems prominently emerged during the Kelly-Bloomberg era." It "substantiates our long-standing position—that CompStat was initially a positive development but morphed into a numbers game."

"These new findings clearly debunk the NYPD's rotten apple theory of isolated crime manipulation," they wrote.

Based on almost 2,000 responses from NYPD retirees, including nearly 900 who had retired during the Bloomberg/Kelly era, these were their main conclusions:

- 60 percent had little confidence in the accuracy of the crime statistics.
- Nine out of ten felt crime went down less than the NYPD claimed, and most of them believed it dropped by only about half as much as the NYPD claimed.
- Just as Schoolcraft's tapes showed, pressure for stop and frisks grew much more intense in the Bloomberg/Kelly era.
- 38 percent felt pressure during Bloomberg/Kelly to downgrade crime complaints. Half of the retirees in the period had direct knowledge that stats were changed, reports weren't taken, and reports were changed to downgrade crime. Close to nine out of ten had personal knowledge of three or more such incidents.

In their comments, retired police bosses confided to the professors a series of disturbing comments:

- "I was ordered not to review complaints because I often raised the charges and refused to lower false classifications. False reporting is endemic in the police department."
- "Assault becomes harassment, grand larceny becomes petty larceny....All with editing/creative writing on complaint reports by supervisors after submission."
- Another boss blamed CompStat. "COs [commanders] were belittled, humiliated, ambushed and embarrassed in from of (and by) the brass....After one beating, you'd have to be a consummate idiot to report higher crime stats next time."
- "Sometimes the report that is entered into the system is not what the street officer had written and it is changed without the knowledge or consent of the officer. Many times, 61s (crime complaint reports) were totally re-written. The average person is totally discouraged and a report will be taken to placate them only till they leave and another report will be done downgrading the original report."

And finally, there was this comment: "Heard Deputy Commissioner [name withheld] say in a pre-CompStat meeting that a CO should just consolidate burglaries that occurred in an apartment building and count as one, make crime reporting difficult to discourage victims, shred reports for those with no insurance, value theft from stores as wholesale not retail prices, reckless endangerment used instead of attempted assault...." This last phrase sounds a lot like an order coming not from a precinct commander but from the very top of the department.

Eterno and Silverman larded their comments with a couple of shots at the NYPD's criticism of their prior survey—a "barrage of spin" and an "impotent response" as they called it. And in a bit of grandiosity in closing, they quoted Frank Serpico in his remarks 40 years ago in the Knapp Commission hearings, calling for "an independent permanent investigative body to deal with police corruption."

The survey got a day or two of media bounce and then faded. Browne, Kelly's spokesman, sniffed at the survey and dismissed it, citing other research.

Meanwhile, here and there, more evidence of police downgrading of crime surfaced, yet it did not seem to affect the public debate.

In an article published on September 16, 2012, the *New York Times* reviewed more than 100 police reports from the preceding four months and found a number of cases in which the police classified a crime as a misdemeanor despite a narrative that suggested a more serious offense.

Joseph Goldstein's article quoted an anonymous police supervisor who said that it was common for sergeants and lieutenants to "tweak complaint reports" or "change the facts of the situation to make it a non-felony crime."

This allegation provided additional confirmation of what Schoolcraft had asserted more than 18 months before.

Goldstein also quoted a retired detective first grade, Wilford Pinkney. "Do I feel that supervisors based on some real or perceived pressure may reclassify crimes? Yes," he said.

Pinkney told Goldstein he did not believe there existed a "concerted effort" from police headquarters to misclassify crimes, but he said that among lower-level supervisors, there was "a pressure people feel" to not exceed last year's crime numbers.

Kelly's panel on the crime statistics, formed in January 2011, still had not issued a report. It was now 19 months overdue. While those close to the commission insisted that its work was proceeding, with the mayoral election just over a year away, it continued to seem like the police commissioner was trying to run out the clock.

It was as if the police department's upper echelon was merely playing whack-a-mole each time someone came forward with evidence of quotas ("productivity goals"), downgrading ("minuscule"), and stop and frisks ("based on crime locations, not race"). Nothing seemed to really stick despite years of revelations about these matters.

That is what remains so odd about this story. By the end of 2012, there had been dozens of reports of issues surrounding Schoolcraft's treatment, numerous officers had stepped forward, the NYPD's stop and frisk campaign was under fire, there was a lot of evidence of quotas, and yet the only entity powerful enough to take on the city—the U.S. Attorney's office—sat in the grandstand watching it all unfold.

On the other hand, as 2013 loomed, there were two factors that were beginning to build that could ultimately really bring these issues front and center in the political landscape. First, four major lawsuits were working their way ever closer to trial. The first was the Center for Constitutional Rights's stop and frisk class action, known as *Floyd v. City of New York* (expected to trial March 2013). The second was *Stinson v. City of New York*, the quota class action, and the third was the Schoolcraft case.

The fourth was a lawsuit filed by Craig Matthews, a police officer assigned to the Bronx's 42nd Precinct, who alleged that he was punished and his free speech rights were violated when he complained about a quota system in his precinct. Matthews claimed that his commanders actually used color-coded computer reports to track productivity of officers. Cops who weren't making their quotas got red ink. The pressure led to unjustified stops, summonses, and arrests, he alleged, and "pitted police officers against each other, straining professional relationships and diverting resources away from law-enforcement activities."

The case had been dismissed six months earlier in district court, but the appellate court overturned the decision. Now it would return to district court and proceed—setting up the potential for a series of similar challenges by police officers.

"Accepting Matthews' allegations as true, it is undisputed that his speech addressed a matter of public concern," the appellate court ruled.

The second factor was related to an upcoming election. In November 2013, the city will elect a new mayor for the first time in 12 years, as Bloomberg's third and final term comes to an end. It has been 25 years since the city last had a Democratic mayor. A bill to create an NYPD Inspector General with subpoena power was introduced in June 2012 by 22 council members. The Inspector General, under the proposed bill, would have substantial authority to review policy, conduct investigations, and most importantly, would have subpoena power to compel testimony and production of documents. Not surprising, Bloomberg and Kelly were violently opposed to it. A few months later, the bill was said to have close to a veto-proof majority.

As the Schoolcraft case lumbered along, really not very much happened after the controversy over how the QAD report became public in March. Part of this was because of the city and the hospital's strategy to delay, delay, delay. String out the case until the Schoolcrafts can't handle it, and force them to settle, if for no other reason than they need the money. Cases often start out with high expectations and lofty language, and after three years of bickering, it becomes just about the number of zeros on the check.

Outwardly, the Schoolcraft lawsuit was progressing slowly through the court. Behind the scenes, trouble was brewing in the Schoolcraft camp. Adrian was becoming disgusted with the pace of the litigation and upset with some of the decisions his lawyers were making. So, during the summer of 2012, Adrian went silent, refusing to speak with anyone, even me, even the lawyers. He barely spoke to his father. This was understandable given the strain he was under, but it also caused some frustration from Norinsberg.

The central issue in the struggle over the case was that the Schoolcrafts wanted to issue broad subpoena and document demands on the city, while they thought Norinsberg wanted to narrow discovery and limit the case. The Schoolcrafts wanted to go to trial, but they felt their lawyer just wanted to settle the case and move on.

Norinsberg later told me nothing could be further from the truth. "We never had any discussion internally or externally about settlement," he said. "This case was 100 percent going to trial from day one."

In August, the two sides met in Albany and called a truce. "They vowed to do what Adrian wants them to do," Larry said.

The truce was short-lived. Over the next six weeks, there were a series of shouting matches over the phone between Larry and the lawyers. On August 28, Larry told Norinsberg, "A lot of things we discussed in the meeting on the ninth aren't coming true," he said.

By September 10, 2012, Larry was angry again, especially about the push back from their lawyers on discovery requests. "The stuff that we asked for two years ago that Jon shot down, we would have now if we had asked them back then and Jon knows that," Larry fumed. "You can't have this subjective garbage. It will boomerang on you in court. You want to be as prepared as you can and you don't want to let people wiggle out of it."

Norinsberg later said, "We did have differences in strategy, mainly about higher level city officials. Preparing a 7-hour deposition takes two weeks. It's not a gimme. I don't know if they [the Schoolcrafts] understood that."

And then something happened that really pushed the Schoolcrafts to the breaking point. On September 18, Norinsberg asked Judge Sweet to extend the discovery deadline another 120 days, effectively delaying the case further. He noted that he, Cohen, and Fitch had been involved in five other trials since that April.

At that point, the Schoolcrafts were getting antsy for movement. The lawsuit was two years old, and not much of consequence had happened between the legal wrangling and the constant delays.

On the following day, Norinsberg did a second thing that infuriated Adrian and Larry. He agreed to an "attorney's eyes only" stipulation regarding the discovery documents in the case. In other words, neither Adrian nor Larry would be able to examine any documents in their own lawsuit. According to Larry, Norinsberg didn't tell them right away that he had signed this agreement. When they found out, they were livid.

They never wanted a protective order in the first place, and now they themselves couldn't read the documents. "How can Adrian mount his case without being able to read the documents?" Larry asked. "It's outrageous."

But Norinsberg saw it as a strategic necessity. "When the QAD report came out, the city stopped cooperating," he said. "Our solution was to have an attorney's eyes only stipulation so we could keep moving forward with discovery. It was just a temporary measure."

This was the final straw in a relationship that had been souring behind the scenes for months. And all the negative feelings came spilling out.

Norinsberg's SchoolcraftJustice.com website was initially supposed to be used to bring attention to the case, gather more evidence of downgrading and quotas, and promote reform ideas that Adrian had. But the Schoolcrafts complained that the site was just a way to promote the firm and garner more business.

And after that initial glow of publicity following the filing of the lawsuit, Norinsberg, Fitch, and Cohen largely stopped cooperating with the media, Larry said. "Norinsberg cut everyone out because he wanted control of the flow of information, control of the story, he wanted a one-way street,"

Larry Schoolcraft said. "We lost some momentum there, but we didn't really noticed that until much later."

By October 1, the Schoolcrafts were so frustrated they were talking about firing their lawyers. "They haven't done shit for two years, and now they just want to rush everything," Larry fumed on October 1, a coolish Monday afternoon. "They want to barebones it and shove it in front of a jury. They keep saying this case is not an indictment of the NYPD, but it is."

They were also upset that Norinsberg couldn't stop Sweet from ordering Adrian to be deposed for a third time.

"It all comes down to communication," Larry said. "This case is too important."

Schoolcraft, having already been deposed once, was set to be deposed twice more on October 11 and October 25. Meanwhile, not one of the city's witnesses had been deposed by Norinsberg.

On October 14, after Adrian returned from that second deposition with the city, father and son had had enough of their lawyers. That Sunday afternoon, they sat down and drafted a letter firing Norinsberg, Fitch, and Cohen from the case.

On Thursday, November 7, Adrian finally finished editing the letter to Norinsberg into a single terse paragraph and sent it to his lawyer via certified mail. Larry gave me and Levitt, the highly regarded police reporter and author, a heads up.

Levitt, the next morning, immediately called Norinsberg and asked him for comment. Norinsberg had not yet seen the letter, and he was furious. According to Levitt's subsequent column, Norinsberg said, "The father wants us to go after Kelly [Police Commissioner Ray Kelly], Bloomberg [Mayor Michael Bloomberg], the FBI, everyone under the sun. We've had a complete communications breakdown."

"This comes completely out of the blue," Norinsberg continued, ignoring the conflict of the previous months. "Adrian has stayed in my house and we've never had a bad word. Until I hear otherwise from Adrian, I'm still representing him."

Levitt, paraphrasing, wrote that Norinsberg had told him "the Schoolcrafts' behavior has become increasingly bizarre."

"They have disappeared three times in the last six months," Norinsberg told Levitt. "We literally had to have [Frank] Serpico involved to track them down."

For his part, Larry told Levitt that Norinsberg "doesn't tell us anything. He makes deals behind our backs. We need a leader. We need an architect."

Levitt went on to write that allies of theirs "expressed concern that they may be alienating the very people they need to hold the police department accountable."

"Nobody denies that whistleblowers can be difficult," he noted. "Anyone who singlehandedly takes on a gigantic organization like the NYPD, as Adrian has, comes under tremendous psychological and emotional pressures."

Levitt then quoted Serpico as saying, "The department wants to undermine all that they stand for by painting them as malcontents, nuts, psychos. The danger for Adrian is that his message may be lost and the department let off the hook."

Norinsberg later said he was caught off-guard by Levitt's call. "That was the first time I heard about it," he said. "I was enormously disappointed and very frustrated not to be part of the case."

In the aftermath, Adrian and Larry suffered one of their worst arguments yet. As Larry described it, Adrian blamed him for these events. Larry responded, as he had many times, that Adrian needed to step up and take command of the case. Larry described him as laying on the couch, almost inert, as if knocked down by a bad wave and unable to get back up.

Finally, Larry felt he needed to get away from his son, not out of fear for his safety but out of frustration at his behavior. He ordered Adrian to leave the house. Adrian refused initially but then finally roused himself from the couch. Larry gave him $150, and Adrian walked off into the night to stay with a friend in Schenectady, New York. It was like the lawsuit had reached out across five counties and swallowed him whole.

What should have been an almost inevitable legal triumph now began to take on hints of a looming, cocked-up tragedy. Without new lawyers, the case would languish. How could it be repaired? How would Judge Sweet, a man not accustomed to putting up with BS, react? What lawyer would take a case like this more than two years down the road? Was it conceivable at that moment that Schoolcraft would simply fade away? It seemed that the case was heading toward becoming an orphan.

"This case is in the toilet," Larry said. "It's all just sickeningly tragic. That's why 95 percent of the time, they win. The only way you stand a chance is if you are disciplined, focused and persistent."

He talked about leaving town for good, moving to New Mexico or Arizona. "I'm going to pack up, take my dogs, go to the southwest and change my name," Larry said. "I have had it. I don't care what happens anymore. This has become laughable."

★

But that was just a moment, and things were maybe not so bad. Five days passed, and Larry still hadn't spoken to Adrian. But he did receive a call from someone who mentioned that a lawyer named Peter Gleason was interested in taking the case.

The conversation roamed across the landscape of the case. Gleason promised they would pursue a more aggressive strategy than Norinsberg had. He was shocked that no investigators have been hired. At the end of the meeting, Adrian had new lawyers. Plans were made for a strategy meeting in New York the following week.

Gleason was a bit of a character. He had served as both a police officer and a firefighter before practicing law. He had offered to put his lavish Tribeca loft up as bail collateral for an accused high-end prostitute madam, Anna Gristina. He once tried to buy Elvis Presley's house. The living room in his apartment was modeled on the Jungle Room at Graceland. He had been a real estate investor and had run for city council. He also produced a board game about the politics of 9/11—called "Ground Zero: It's Only a Game to the Politicians"—accusing Giuliani, Pataki, and others of using the terrorist attack for their own benefit. But if he was going to be a good advocate for Schoolcraft, that was enough.

A day later, Adrian and Larry made up. The fight was just a symptom of the massive strain that the case had produced. They met on November 23 with Gleason and his partner at the Diamond Mill Tavern in Saugerties, New York, and signed representation papers.

Norinsberg filed a document with Sweet's court removing himself as counsel, but he stubbornly left the SchoolcraftJustice.com website up for several weeks. For a while, he balked at turning over the files in the case until he was paid for his work, but he dropped that effort, too, Larry said.

On December 4, Queens District Attorney Richard Brown abruptly issued a statement that after a three-year comprehensive investigation, there was no criminal conduct on Halloween night when Schoolcraft was forced into the psychiatric ward by the police. The Schoolcrafts were shocked, mainly because they didn't even know Brown was conducting an investigation. They viewed it as yet another punch in the shoulder from city government and were suspicious of its timing.

"It smells of bias, obstruction of justice and a betrayal of the public trust," Larry said. "Once they took on the investigation, and failed to adequately investigate, that's obstruction of justice. District Attorneys can go to prison like anyone else.

"Why wasn't this presented to a grand jury or a special prosecutor?" Larry wondered. "If this had been presented to a grand jury, the citizens of Queens would have indicted. They would not let this stand. Brown would not let the citizens of Queens make the decision."

As so, as 2012 came to a close, a big question mark hung over the case, and it seemed like anything could happen. Judge Sweet's trial date was eight months away, set for September. There was more to come.

THE LIGHTNING ROD ON THE BUILDING

Someone in the know talking after hours about the Schoolcraft case once told me, "If you had walked into my office and told me this story, I would have said get the fuck out and find a good psychiatrist, and yet here we are." Indeed, a lot of people felt that way, and yes, here we are.

As the New Year began, things started to look just a little better for the Schoolcrafts. They were still struggling with money, and they had jettisoned yet another lawyer in Gleason, but they found a new lead lawyer in Nathaniel Smith and a second in former federal prosecutor John Lenoir. There was talk of lifting the gag order and seeking three years of back pay for Adrian—none of which came to pass by the end of April. But the lawyers did serve a subpeona on Queens District Attorney Richard Brown about his Schoolcraft investigation.

This move was, for the Schoolcrafts, a welcome sign that their new lawyers were going to be more aggressive—a strategy they felt, to put it charitably, had been lacking over the previous two years.

On the other hand, on April 8, the Schoolcrafts heard from NYPD Inspector Louis Luciani. After keeping Adrian's disciplinary case in limbo for three years, they wanted to go to trial. Luciani said the department would neither reinstate nor fire him.

"The department prefers not to take any employment action without a full hearing," Luciani wrote.

Meanwhile, lawyers for Jamaica Hospital moved to bar all case attorneys and the Schoolcrafts from speaking publicly about the case in any way, claiming Larry and Adrian and their lawyers want to try the case in the media.

The city Law Department, while denying the Schoolcraft allegations, repeatedly declined to discuss the case with me.

Adrian and Larry have endured a lot of indignities and a fair amount of harassment, suffered some embarrassments, and lived hand to mouth for what seemed like an endless period. They have been blown off, ignored, criticized, and disbelieved. They have been stretched very close to the breaking point. And yet, three and a half years later, they are still vertical.

According to Larry, at least, Adrian has emerged somewhat from his funk. On one particular day, Adrian texted his dad a picture of himself standing in a freight elevator next to a large pile of plastic-wrapped legal boxes—the case files as they were being moved from law office to law office. It is a testament to his character that he can still handle the slow, dripping paper cuts of a war of attrition like this one.

But there is a mountain of work left to be done. With Sweet's tentative trial date of September 2013 just months away, quite incredibly, not a single deposition has been taken in the 30 months since the complaint was initially filed. Just as shocking, no money has been spent on investigation—that is, interviewing the dozens of characters who make up this complicated storyline. And the attorneys have seen very little from the files of Jamaica Hospital.

The city's slow-it-down strategy has been more than effective. Indeed, even this far into the case, the city is still arguing for a schedule that would put a trial off for yet another year.

On the other side, after all the disclosures of the last three years, Commissioner Kelly's approval rating is as high as ever. A mayoral candidate, Christine Quinn, has already said she will keep him on if she is elected to replace Bloomberg. Kelly even seems to have his own TV show in Tom Selleck's portrayal of Police Commissioner Frank Reagan on *Blue Bloods*. "Don't worry about me, I've got pretty broad shoulders," Regan said in one episode. Paul Browne has his own doppelganger on the show too, in the wry and wise counselor Garrett Moore, played by Gregory Jbara.

On February 5, 2013, there was another signal of Kelly's stubborn front in the face of controversy. The department released a report that concluded there was no racial profiling in the stop and frisk campaign. The message was clear: Kelly wasn't going to back off on his defense of stop and frisk, despite the public criticism and the looming trial in the stop and frisk lawsuit.

As for some of the other characters in this story, most remain in one kind of limbo or another. Adhyl Polanco is no longer suspended with pay. He is now assigned to a VIPER unit in the city, where he spends stultifying days watching a video screen linked to public housing security cameras, his career on hold as his lawsuit plods through the courts. He, too, testified in the stop and frisk trial.

Robert Borrelli, the cop who stepped forward to report downgrading, remains assigned to the Bronx courts. He was out of work to recover from an operation for a while, and says he sometimes regrets coming forward and speaking to the media because of what happened to him after he did. It has been a difficult period for him, too.

Deputy Chief Marino remains in Staten Island, in a quieter command than he would probably like. And Mauriello lingers on as the executive officer of Bronx Transit, awaiting the end of a disciplinary process that seems never to end.

If you haven't noticed, there is a theme here. Each of these men has basically been put on ice, pending some outcome in the misty, uncertain future. Setting aside the individual allegations and taking them as a group, one could argue fairly compellingly that they are all collateral damage in the struggle over the effects of CompStat. And Kelly really has no incentive to put them back into the fray until he (perhaps) and Bloomberg leave office in January.

So said a retired detective: "They are going to stall this until Bloomberg leaves. He's out in January 2014. This is it for him."

This detective said nothing larger will happen until the electorate sees the accuracy of crime stats (and the fairness police tactics) as a major issue. "Look, they are fudging the numbers in the 8-1, 7-5, 7-3, 8-4, whatever, but it only changes when the people in the community demand to see the numbers, when they say we're going to vote around this, we want to see the true numbers."

At this point, well before the trial, Schoolcraft's legacy remains hard to foresee. As of this writing, he still has not received that Serpico moment— the big press conference outside City Hall, the big moment on the witness stand, that cathartic outcome, after which he can move on with his life.

In a complex story, Schoolcraft is a complex character. He is a bit of a cipher, a word that has two very different meanings. One meaning is a device that breaks a code, but it can also mean someone of no importance. Neither is completely true, but there is some truth to both. His work exposed a range of problems with CompStat, but he also disappeared upstate and in essence removed himself from the landscape.

Clearly the story suffered a bit after 2010. But perhaps the reaction to the Schoolcraft story was a sign of the times. Those big bold New York moments of the Knapp Commission, the Mollen Commission—those revelatory moments seem rarer these days. It's as if the public doesn't have the political will it once did to stand up to the big institutions. On the other hand, perhaps those Watergate moments never did really exist. Perhaps it was all miserable slogging through long wars of attrition, and only the movies exist to tie it all up in a neat drama.

Unfortunately, some in the media were unable to separate the man from his work. Indeed, Adrian is difficult, as is his father. But just because Schoolcraft was not the perfect source—few whistle-blowers are perfect, most in fact are fairly eccentric—that did not mean that he did not do a remarkable thing. In a bygone era, perhaps Schoolcraft would have gotten more of the respect that he earned. On the other hand, the media is like the ocean, and not even King Canute could stop the tide from rolling over the beach.

Most importantly, one can never lose sight of just how hard it is for one man to take on the most powerful police agency in the country and a city with such deep pockets. If one takes Schoolcraft at his word, he did not step forward for material gain. Thus, it did not make sense for him to then seek fame or glory or political status.

However, that is not to say he left no legacy no matter the outcome of his lawsuit. His tapes were a groundbreaking piece of history, and they influenced a whole series of debates. They gave unprecedented weight to allegations of quotas, crime stat manipulation, and civil rights violations. His tapes inspired other officers to come forward, too, and gave veracity to legal challenges against NYPD policies. Other officers have taped their commanders demanding quotas.

"He's gotta be up in the top two or three of the most influential NYPD whistleblowers of the past 50 years," said Darius Charney, a lawyer representing the plaintiffs in the stop and frisk class action lawsuit. "It's so rare for officers to come forward at all, and the depth of the corruption he exposed is pretty amazing. Just look at the viciousness with which the city has responded to him, and it's not only the police department."

Charney said one signal of how dangerous the city views Schoolcraft is how they went to war over letting the tapes into the case as evidence. "They really tried to keep them out," he said. "First, as hearsay, and then, they claimed they couldn't be authenticated. They demanded he come to court. The court ruled the deposition had to be supervised. So he had to sit there in the federal court-house in front of all these lawyers. They are obviously afraid of this stuff."

Frank Serpico, who exposed corruption in the NYPD 40 years ago, told me the story that he was once asked to give a speech at an awards ceremony for high-achieving police officers, known as the 10 Top Cops Award. After he spoke, each of the officers came up to him and whispered in his ear. What do you think they whispered, he asked me.

I don't know, I replied, that they liked the speech?

"No, no," he said. "What they whispered was, 'I gotta talk to you'."

He continued: "And that's the bottom line: the system has not changed. And that's why it's up to individuals to make the difference. That's why New Yorkers should be grateful to people like Adrian because these are the good cops who are out there looking out for our welfare. They are the safety valves who try to correct a rotten system. But look at what they did to him for it."

It was a hard road to force a tough man like Police Commissioner Raymond Kelly to do anything, but eventually Kelly had to take a series of actions to blunt the impact of the tapes and the ensuing fallout. In addition to the internal investigations, he had to reorganize the way sex crimes were investigated, he had to issue a series of orders to remind cops to follow the rules in taking crime reports, and he had to alter his stop and frisk strategy to some degree.

Although he did get away with never releasing his crime statistics panel report.

In March 2013, in the august chambers of the U.S. District Court, Schoolcraft's tapes were played in the stop and frisk class action trial, the rough voices of police bosses under CompStat pressure, echoing across the room, and resonating across the city. This was hard evidence that Adrian's efforts had not gone to waste.

The growing support for an independent inspector general for the police is another piece of evidence that his ordeal was not a waste. And these issues may well be fodder in the mayoral election, which will then lead to new approaches in the next administration.

Unfortunately for the Schoolcrafts, these steps are not enough. They still hold to the hope that one day the feds will come in and either seriously investigate the many issues raised in the tapes or appoint a monitor to oversee the NYPD. They still want someone held accountable.

"What I worry about for Adrian is that if that doesn't happen, or something similar doesn't happen, that down the road years after this is over, he won't be able to get past it," Larry said. ·

The arc of this story ends, for now, on one of those bitterly cold days in Johnstown, right when one has tired of the snow and just wants spring to arrive. From his little, cluttered house, Larry was talking about the whole thing in his garrulous way. "They've created this incredible system of indentured servitude," he said. "Adrian was different. He had no friends on the job, no history in the city, he didn't want to be a detective, he didn't want to work overtime, he didn't have the house, the mortgage, the wife and kids, so they didn't have the management tools that they use to pressure most of the other people.

"So you put Mauriello, the hard-charging CompStat cop, and Adrian, who has nothing to lose, in the right precinct and at the right time.... It was all already happening. Adrian just happened to be the lightning rod on top of the building. Put it all together: the quotas, Adrian fighting his evaluation, October 7 and QAD, which all went right to 1PP and City Hall, and, what if he takes that to someone in the newspapers. They knew Adrian wasn't going to pull over. He was leaving the apartment that night. They came there to get him. They came there to take control. There was no way they were going to leave him there alone."

There in Johnstown, amid all that has come before, Larry remained defiant on behalf of his son, who has been through so much. "Adrian doesn't want money, he doesn't want fame, he's been through the worst of it and is still standing, and he's ready to go through the rest of it. The city doesn't want this to go to court. It reminds me of the saying, the harder it gets and the worse it gets, the *more* I get."

INDEX